What It Means to Serve

From Airborne Ranger to Peace Corps Volunteer

by

Robert Donayre

DORRANCE PUBLISHING CO., INC.
PITTSBURGH, PENNSYLVANIA 15222

All Rights Reserved
Copyright © 2007 by Robert Donayre
No part of this book may be reproduced or transmitted
in any form or by any means, electronic or mechanical,
including photocopying, recording, or by any information
storage and retrieval system without permission in
writing from the publisher.

ISBN: 978-0-8059-7456-0
Library of Congress Control Number: 2006931614
Printed in the United States of America

First Printing

For more information or to order additional books, please contact:
Dorrance Publishing Co., Inc.
701 Smithfield Street
Third Floor
Pittsburgh, Pennsylvania 15222
U.S.A.
1-800-788-7654
www.dorrancebookstore.com

To my mother, Leslie A. Davis

Contents

Introduction: Induction into Federal Service

Why is it that Americans choose to work for the U.S. federal government under the guise of *public service?* For many, it would seem obvious: decent salary, great benefits, job security. (The term *non-competes*, meaning non-competitive, has been used by those in the *private sector* to classify government employees.) For other Americans, choosing to work for Uncle Sam is much more than just a way to pay the bills. It means *something.* Human nature works that way. Many of us have a longing to be a part of something grandiose, something that will make an impact and a difference in the world. Of course, this "natural" feeling often stems from, and runs in conjunction with, our own vanity and self-centeredness. "I want to make the world laugh, but I would like to earn millions of dollars in the process . . . I donated $100 to the Red Cross, and I feel great (or better) about myself! Everyone should do their duty by serving in the armed forces, while in the process receiving college money for the future." Even for self-proclaiming "anti-establishment" types, there is still a need and/or desire to belong to something, even if that something is a not-so-small gathering on the outer fringes of society. "*We* are revolting against the government."

For me, growing up in the 1980s, the image of public service seemed to be both noble and liberating—*public service is freedom,* an Orwellian oxymoron perhaps. But, like most American kids and teenagers, I was completely clueless about the vast and often nightmarish, tentacled maze that is the federal bureaucracy. My idea of service consisted solely of the armed forces. Having taken an interest in history at an early age, around twelve, and being a stereotypical boy, I was interested in reading books with pictures about the glories of the U.S. Military in past wars, mainly the Second World War. Although I probably had a fair share of teachers and relatives who were patriotic and had "done their duty," many of my own ideals about duty, honor, and service were inferred from some of those history books that most of my classmates found to be too boring and a waste of time. I thought it would have been awesome to parachute behind enemy lines into France or assault the beaches of Normandy on D-Day with the main brunt of the Allied invasion force. Of course, in *my* World War II record, I make it all the way to Paris, liberating the city as beautiful young Parisian ladies wish to express their gratitude (wink, wink). I do not die a horrible death from being burned alive in my tank or lose half of my face because of an exploding grenade's shrapnel fragments. But during my teens, although I was staunchly "anti-Communist," whatever that meant at the time, I never really believed there would be a successful parachute assault against the "Evil Empire" of the Soviet Union. Even I knew then, as probably most adults did, that the whole shooting match once begun would end in the flaming nuclear destruction of planet Earth.

It wasn't until my mid-twenties when I started to take notice of different avenues toward public service. Two courses I took at the University of California, Santa Barbara (UCSB), with Dr. Fred Logevall, focused on the history of U.S. foreign policy from 1776 to the present. We discussed some of the major figures who had served in the U.S. State Department, including George Kennan and James Byrnes (two that I can remember offhand right now), as well as those who served in the enemy's camp—Foreign Minister Molotov of the U.S.S.R. comes to mind. *These non-competes,* excluding Molotov (since there was technically no private sector in the Soviet Union), were businessmen wheeling and dealing on behalf of their respective nations. I thought that if I were to serve as a low-level diplomat somewhere, I could help contribute to the strengthening of diplomatic relations between the U.S. and other countries. But also of great importance, I thought it would be cool to chill in an embassy pool in some exotic land. I assumed embassies had such luxuries. I often thought about what geniuses men like Kennan must have been: Ivy League educated and highly influential career diplomats with a mastery of certain foreign languages. As a student at UCSB, I tried my hand at German. By the end of a year and a half study-abroad program in Germany, I could at best hold a basic conversation in German—my first serious attempt at foreign language learning. During high school in Imperial Beach (San Diego County), California, I wanted to study German. After all, the Allied forces of the Second World War did not parachute into Spain or Mexico. And the jump into France was done to push the Germans out. The former three countries' languages were my only choices. So I ended up cheating my way through a year and half of Spanish at Mar Vista High School. I failed the fourth and final semester.

As I progressed through a master of arts program in history at California State University, Sacramento, I became more interested in diplomatic history. Yet at the same time, as we all must do at one time or another, I had to think seriously about a post-university career. During my final year of study in Sacramento, I decided to enter a certified teacher-preparation program for future secondary school teachers, which I began while finishing the history graduate program. I then looked into becoming a teacher for the U.S. Department of Defense (DOD), where I would serve as a secondary school teacher at a U.S. military installation abroad. Once again, besides granting a feeling of *selfless* service, such a federal job possesses many great opportunities: decent pay, medical and dental coverage, and travel opportunities. The catch was that I had to complete at least thirty semester hours—about two semesters—of an accredited teacher-preparation program in order to qualify. *No problem*, I thought, since I was starting such a program in the fall of 2002 and would be ready to teach somewhere the following year. Well before I started the final semester of the history program and the first semester of the teacher-prep program, I did an initial on-line application with the Department of Defense. As you can see, I had a plan. And as you know, plans fall through, for good or bad. But since I try harboring no regrets, it's *all* for the good.

During the summer of 2002, with my graduate degree in history around the corner, the teacher-preparation program on the horizon, and my DOD application in the works, I was sitting in a broken-down recliner (getting worse by the sit) in West Sacramento, watching a documentary on basic cable, *The True Story of Black Hawk Down*—the film *Black Hawk Down* being a Hollywood theatrical production of the role of Airborne Rangers and Delta Force elites in the October 1993 military "campaign" in Mogadishu, Somalia. While watching this seemingly objective documentary that incorporated the viewpoints and opinions of both American troops and Somali fighters who squared off against one another, I couldn't help but reflect on my own experience of having served as an Airborne Ranger in Somalia, however meager that experience might have been. Although my three weeks of service in Somalia as an M-60 machine gunner attached to Alpha Company, 3rd Ranger Battalion, pales in comparison to those soldiers of Bravo Company, whom the movie was based on, it is still an important story and will be covered in full later on. As I watched the documentary, I experienced a heightened sensation of self-righteousness in my chest and abdomen, which happens periodically, driving me to go out into the world *again* somehow and make a positive contribution. And I had to look into the matter right then and there. I remembered that a friend of mine at the University of California, Davis, just across the bridge from the city of West Sacramento, had briefly looked into Peace Corps (PC) service as a viable job option at the end of an undergraduate program. I thought, *What the hell. I'll take a look at their website*, with the expectation that my previous ignorance regarding the Peace Corps would be confirmed: they hire Americans to plant trees in some forsaken desert or swampland in Africa or South America—not to say that such a task is ignoble or beneath me. But there I was about to graduate with a master's degree in history, and I swore after army service that I would never again work in any kind of manual labor sector. Though educators are some of the lowest paid people around the globe, it still boggles my mind that teachers get paid to tell others what they know, or what they think they know.

Once on the PC website, I was ecstatic to learn that the Peace Corps was operational, and had been for a while, in parts of what had once been the Soviet-dominated states of eastern Europe. What topped off my enthusiasm: with a master's degree, it would be possible to teach English and other subjects at a university. So the very night that I was inspired by the documentary, *The True Story of Black Hawk Down*, I got the ball rolling with my future Peace Corps service by doing an initial on-line application, stating my preference to work as a university teacher in an eastern European country. When I stressed eastern Europe, I meant Romania and Bulgaria, and possibly Slovakia, since these were countries I had heard of and was interested in. Little did I know that I would end up in the former Soviet Republic of Moldova—a place at the time I had no idea even existed.

Serving in Moldova, as I type this on my four-year-old Toshiba laptop, it's amazing to me how many of my fellow Peace Corps volunteers knew something concrete about PC long before deciding to join. A few of them knew "exactly" what PC did and where, and also knew other Americans who had served or were currently serving in the "Corps," as I sometimes refer to it. Before joining, I had never met anyone who had been in the Peace Corps, but I always thought of it as a prestigious governmental organization with a solid reputation. It was definitely *some - thing* though—a form of *public service* if you will—that I never saw myself doing. For friends and colleagues whom I met in both the army and the Peace Corps, these two organizations have traditionally been seen as extreme opposites. In one sense they are. In the army, I was trained to kill enemies in combat, and I carried an M-60 machine gun. In the PC, I am a trained teacher of English as a foreign language (TEFL), and I carry dry-erase markers to write on my homemade "chalk" boards. Army buddies of mine whom I had served with were initially shocked that I would go into the Peace Corps. I was hit with rhetorical questions like, "You're joining what!? What are you, queer?" The actual questions and comments, of course, were much cruder. Among fellow volunteers, who usually only find out that I was in the army from other volunteers or from asking me what I did after high school, there have been expressions of surprise and disbelief, "You jumped out of airplanes in the army!?" and "Doesn't the military have the opposite goal of the Peace Corps?" Yet these two organizations are "cut from the same cloth," so to speak—they are both intricate parts of the U.S. federal government, falling under the auspices of *public service.*

Some volunteers actually delude themselves into believing they are not government employees working on behalf of Uncle Sam. After all, the standard image of a PC volunteer, an image held over from the 1960s when the organization was created during Kennedy's administration, is a "long-haired, dope-smoking hippie" straight out of college who is out to "save the world." I have definitely met American volunteers who fit that description, but I also know clean-cut, experienced middle-aged volunteers who have worked for years in the throngs of the American business establishment, living the good "capitalist" life. In his Moldovan adventures, the British writer Tony Hawks makes the comment that for him, the jury is still out on whether or not the Peace Corps is a benevolent organization assisting underdeveloped regions of the world, or a tool for promoting American economic and political interests—a little of both, I would argue.[*] (I recently had the pleasure of meeting Mr. Hawks in the capital of Moldova—Chisinau—at a party for Queen Elizabeth's seventy-ninth birthday, where he autographed two separate Moldovan one-leu banknotes for me and some friends. The Queen was not there.)

But unlike when the U.S. Army steps into a foreign country, a sovereign country "occupied" by PC merely has to say that it no longer requires PC assistance and shortly thereafter, PC will no longer exist in that country. As President Lyndon Johnson commented on France's withdrawal from NATO during the 1960s, forcing

NATO to remove its headquarters from Paris, "When a man asks you to leave his house, you don't argue with him. You grab your hat and go." Or was it *coat?* And as a current volunteer with ten months to go before my two years of service are complete, I can quit at any time. I also volunteered to serve in the army, but quitting during those four years, as you will see, was strongly discouraged.

Acknowledgements

I wish to express my sincerest gratitude to all of the people who have had a positive impact on my life over the years, both during my stint of federal service and long before official service of any kind was a realistic contemplation in my mind. Even those individuals in this work whom I did not have the greatest encounters with are still an integral part of my life experiences, and I am appreciative of that. I always try to maintain the attitude: out of every negative situation comes something positive. And for those who are specifically referred to in this memoir, whether in a good light or not, a special thanks to you has been reserved in the written pages of this book where our paths have crossed.

Understanding the importance of education and the rigorous endeavors that educators go through, especially after having personally substitute-taught in American public schools, I must start with my teachers from the past, many whose names and faces I can still recall today. Please forgive me if I have misspelled your name. There is the Bayside Elementary crew: the smiling and encouraging Mrs. Meaker from kindergarten, where I remember having successfully circled the red fire truck when asked to do so; my first grade teacher of 1979—Charlie Brown (that's his name)—a tribute to African-American educators (there are far fewer blacks in education than whites, even today) and a standard-bearer for teachers in general. My mom to this day credits him with teaching me how to read and fostering my desire to continue reading; Mrs. Pryor from fourth grade, who first taught us about the societal contributions of Dr. Martin Luther King, Jr., and believed that I was ready for mathematical exponents at such an early age—I wasn't. The family friend and fifth-grade teacher of mine, Mrs. Teagle, who seriously listened to my complaints about the other students in my writing group not selecting my written "works" for posting on the chalkboard.

Let's not forget the history teachers, who go all the way back to sixth-grade social studies: my first "F" ever was on a world geography quiz in Mr. Elwell's sixth-grade class. I realized then that geography and history go hand in hand, though today I'm still not that great with maps. Plus, he told us that if nuclear war broke out between the United States and the Soviet Union during class time, we would be allowed to go home; eighth-grade U.S. History teacher at Mar Vista Middle School, Mr. Rause, who, allowing my motivation for the subject to tip the scales in my favor, even though I clearly hadn't done all of the work expected of me, gave me an "A-"; Mar Vista High School summer school teacher after the tenth grade, Mr. Broz, whom I took Modern U.S. History with just for fun and received an "A," subsequently retaking it again with Mr. Oniell in eleventh grade, when I could have petitioned not to take it again. I also received the highest grade in that class. Mr. Oniell was my mentor in high school, who sometimes let me hide out in his classroom instead of attending Trigonometry with Mrs. Thomas. When I tried to correct him in class, pointing to a quote stating that the British did fight for the Confederacy in the American Civil War, he didn't hold it against me. In fact, I know now why he was right and I was wrong.

In community college, there was Mr. Diaz (mentioned a couple of times in this book), who properly prepared us, those who cared enough, for bluebook written examinations at the university level, making my transition into academic life at UCSB a little less severe; history professors at UCSB, starting with Dr. Talbott, who encouraged me to keep working on my writing abilities in his seminar: "Keep writing like that and you'll get an A." It worked. And it's when I saw his name quoted in a book by the distinguished historian Robert O. Paxton that I realized what studying at a university means; Dr. Marcuse and Dr. Logevall (both mentioned in this book) wrote graduate school letters of recommendation for me.

At California State University, Sacramento (CSUS), my friend and mentor—Dr. Aaron Cohen—allowed me to work as his teaching assistant for a year and a half, where I learned more about world history and Powerpoint usage than I could have imagined. He, along with Dr. Patrick Ettinger, served as invaluable advisors in preparation for my exams. And Dr. Jeffrey Dym, with the two of them, served as a grader for my exams on Twentieth Century European and U.S. History, after which Dym said that he had to assume my answers were correct, seeing as how his specialty is in Asian affairs, with an emphasis on Japan. During the oral exam, I successfully fielded his question regarding a Cambodian perpetrator of genocide in the twentieth century—Pol Pot; Dr. Joan Moon, who taught us the skills necessary to teach history at the college level with her course, Teaching History in College, and who was also kind enough to allow me to housesit for her on a few occasions in the ritzier part of Sacramento—a nice break from my five roommates in West Sacramento; Dr. Karl von den Steinen, who encouraged (forced) me, and all the other students in his mandatory research class, to become the best writers and researchers possible. After I earned his only "Special Award of Merit" granted that semester for my writing achievements, during my last semester of the history program, I felt assured of my abilities to pursue a Ph.D. if I chose to do so. As he would say, "You get what you pay for."

From my five-year career in Pop Warner football (age 10-14), the Guevara brothers and company as my coaches on the Imperial Beach Cardinals: their pursuit of excellence on the field, mixed with hilarious and kind personalities off the field helped prepare me for the competitive and humor-filled aspects of life. "Who are we? CARDINALS!"

And last but certainly not least, there are my friends and family members, many of whom are referred to throughout this book: Paige Wilhelm; Xzabriel Marcellous Vanzant (now known as X.M. Lee or simply *Zabe* for short), the coolest name I've ever heard, who is my friend and former football companion from sixth grade to the present. He is the epitome of what it means to be a loyal friend; Christopher Bernard Hicks (mentioned in the book), the coolest black guy I know with the whitest-sounding middle name, who I have admired for his intelligence and leadership abilities since middle school; Paul Anthony Romero, who, like me, got off to a less than ideal start in life. He'll be an "ideal" lawyer soon. After chatting/debating with him about Karl Marx a couple of years ago when I was in graduate school, he said to me, "Man, who would have ever thought that we would know something?"; Paul's mom, Patricia, who has been a great friend to my mother and who rarely ever got tired of feeding me at her outstanding Sunday brunches whenever I would show up "unexpectedly"; Paul's brother David, who spent a lifetime achieving scholastic and athletic excellence, eventually doing what he wanted to do and not what others wanted or expected him to do; my next-door neighbor, mentor, and third father while growing up, Bill (William) Long; Jacqueline Dao (Frau Dao), Jennifer Ethier (Little Ethier), Jennifer Smith (Smitty), Ty Hartman, Cindy Hamfler, and Bon Agapin, who always maintained interest, whether real or feigned, in what I was doing since our study-abroad days in Germany. I tried to reciprocate; Maria Zur, whose love and desire for me made my Germany experience better than I could have possibly imagined; Hannah and Heinrich Matthias, my wonderful German host parents in Goettingen; the two Brits who made me proud of my own British ancestry because of their encouragement, friendship, and ambition—Steffan Jones and Alick Robertson; my history master of arts comrades—Mike Osman and Thaddeus (Thad) White—Mike giving me cause to look for the Marxist element in all things, whether or not I could find it, and Thad helping me see the ridiculousness in many things "historic"; the Hemlock Street crew of West Sacramento, with Steve Boykin presiding over the household, serving as owner, landlord, roommate, gardener, interior decorator and friend, along with Mark, Megan, Morgan, Misty, Jen, and Jeff; my army buddies from then until now—Richard Piltingsrud (Pilt), Peter Weldon, James Elliot (who reminded me that the M-60 is 23 pounds and not 13), Jeffrey King, Jim Scholl, Troy Godwin, and Christopher Cossman—all of whom showed me what real friendship and brotherhood are, or should be.

There is the latest in a series of Peace Corps friendships. You know who you are: my adopted aunt and uncle, Rosie and Patrick Burns; Ken and Danielle Klein; Marc and Chrissy Goldberg; Glendon Drew and Sarah Remus; Nick Steffens and Shireen Ghorbani; and a host of others; the wonderful Peace Corps administrators—both American and Moldovan—including Country Director Jeff Kelley-Clarke, former director David Reside, Assistant Country Directors Sherry Russell and Carol Gordenstein, TEFL Program Managers Nina Potoroaca and Lucia

Ciudnaia, Medical Officer Lica Soltan, Financial Administrator Margareta Osovschi; my Moldovan teaching colleagues and friends from Tiraspol State University, Natalia and Galina Rotari—Galina's guiding support helped make my stint at the university a saner one; Svetlana Frantova, who was less like a friend and colleague for two years and more like a favorite aunt; and of course, there is Julia de la Torre, my wonderful, loving girlfriend whom I had to go all the way to Moldova to meet. She is a phenomenal teacher who will go on to do many great things in education and in life. My stubborn resistance did not stop her from reading the working proofs for this memoir, after which she gave invaluable advice. She will be my chief editor from now on.

My extensive family, beginning with the Barker clan: Uncle Gene and Aunt Jeannette, who always came to cheer me on at my high school football games; cousins Mary and (Little) Gene, with his lovely wife Cheryl and their family; the Donayre bunch: Aunts Tammy, Maria, and Elizabeth (Lizzy), along with Lizzy's two daughters; Uncles Tommy, dearly departed Tony, and Mickey, with his lovely wife Melissa and their family; the Freeman gang: Aunts Rosemary and Ximena (Mena), along with my cousins Andy, Danny, Jimmy, Kimberly, Amber, and Lenny, and all of their extended families; Aunt Kimberly and Uncle Danny down in Texas with their kids; adopted members of the family Dean and Carol; all of my dead (and alive) cats, considered more like members of the family, especially Nugget and Tiger, who would greet me at my car door upon arrival from community college; the Haywood and Hogan crew of Northern California—no blood relation but family nonetheless: Jackie, Judy, Janet, Jamie, Danny, and Greg, along with their extended families; my grandparents: Rachel Donayre, Leo and Shirley Busboom, Richard (Shakes) and Lorraine Faverty. Grandpa Shakes used to review my assigned readings for college after I finished with them, along with the papers that I wrote. He was one of my biggest fans, yet died three days before I received my master's degree.

My immediate family: my sister Sandra Donayre, who I respect for her solid work ethic and determination to stay looking fabulous throughout the years; my wonderful father Leo Donayre, who got me started on this traveling bug; my step-father Bill Davis, who I truly came to appreciate as a second father and a loving husband to my mother; and of course, my mother—Leslie Davis—whom I have dedicated this book to. Her level-headed stability and loving praises over the years have constituted the anchor in my life that I so sorely need.

I am truly apologetic to those whom I have considered friends and/or family members at one time or another whose names I did not include in this list of acknowledgements.

Author's Note

I first got the idea for writing a book of personal memoirs when I was in community college, fresh from active duty service in the army. I still have the seven pages of that handwritten original attempt lying around somewhere. I told two of my best army buddies, Richard and Pete, what my plan was at the time. They were very encouraging, saying that some of *our* unbelievable stories would make for good reading. If nothing else, I thought that at least three persons, including myself, would read the finished product. In community college, I was a long way away from a master of arts in history; so were the needed writing skills that I had yet to acquire. Plus, I wanted to write a story that would be different from all the other army stories out there. The novel angle I was searching for proved to be elusive. I soon lost motivation for the project, believing that it would be painstaking work for little reward. And at the time, I wrote everything by hand and then transferred my scrawled writing onto a word processor—oh, the inhumanity! Putting the work on hold indefinitely, I continued carrying around the seven pages of my "memoirs," hoping that the inspiration to follow through with the project would one day hit me like a bolt of lighting.

With this finished product, eight years after the original attempt, I believe I have found my *novel angle*—army and Peace Corps service combined, compared, and contrasted. Plus, with Peace Corps experiences to include, I have much more to say. The fear of not having enough material was also another turnoff from going forward with the original project. Please note: when I came into the Peace Corps, the thought of writing any type of book was only conceived of as an almost impossible dream, although I did begin a Peace Corps personal "memoir" on the flight from New York to our transfer point in Istanbul, Turkey, before the battery on my computer expired. Lying there one night, about two weeks ago (fifteen months after that New York to Istanbul flight), the idea for writing about my adventures in federal service hit me. I was of course going to start next month or the one after that. Then I thought, *Why the hell can't I start now?* So I did, and I made calculations, "Ten more months of Peace Corps service—thirty pages a month times ten equals 300 pages." Fortunately, the process itself has been much more fun and uncalculated than I could have imagined. And I now have a better understanding of why some professors, who prefer writing over teaching, see the latter more as a "burden" getting in the way of their true passion. I always thought it would be the other way around, since professors must "publish or perish."

In order to drive the point home about my experiences in the Peace Corps, where appropriate and often in conjunction with side comments noted by the use of bracketed text like so [example], I have used old e-mails to friends and family in lieu of any reflective writing from the vantage point of the present. In this way, the reader can perhaps better understand my observations and experiences as they are happening. Plus, it's just more fun that way sometimes.

In an effort to maintain an acceptable level of anonymity for those involved in this non-fictional work, while at the same time adhering to truthfulness and literary authenticity, I have excluded, with the exception of my own name, the familial names of the key characters involved. In cases where I only have the family name to go on, I have modified and/or shortened the original name to an unidentifiable degree of its former self. Only in instances where I feel that the professional and/or public career of the individual warrants the use of the family name (Dr. *so and so* from such and such university, for example), have I used the person's real name.

*   Hawks, Tony. *Playing the Moldovans at Tennis*. New York: St. Martin's Griffin Edition, 2002.

Army Service Is Freedom

"I want to go Special Forces in Europe." These were the first words, besides "Hello, my name is . . ." that I uttered to my army recruiter—one Sergeant Arturo (Art)—during our initial telephone meeting. I was seventeen years old, a junior in high school, and I was living illegally at a friend's townhouse apartment down the street from my mother and stepfather's house. A few weeks prior, I ran away/moved out from my parents, citing "irreconcilable differences" on the hand-written note I left on the dining room table while they were out to dinner with some friends. But unlike the first time I ran away when I was sixteen, I left contact information. The friend of mine where I stayed—Chris—was a senior at our high school, and his father was out to sea on patrol with the U.S. Navy. My plan was to show my parents that I could "live on my own" and be a productive student at the same time. Plus in my "goodbye" letter, I stressed that by leaving, I hoped to strengthen the almost nonexistent relationship I had with my mother. Absence makes the heart grow fonder. Like many teens, I had severe emotional problems—so I thought—that could only be solved, or medicated, by releasing myself from the shackle of my parents' household. Well, Chris's pad became a regular drunken marijuana party of underage sexual liaisons. I had a great time but was back home with my parents after six weeks. Most of my grades were still crappy, except for the one in history of course. Also, I had studied for and taken the California Golden State Exam in history during my six-week sojourn, beating everyone in the school and scoring high honors in the process—noted by the golden seal on my diploma. But I had also gotten the ball rolling on my future service in the U.S. Army by placing that initial call to the local recruitment office.

I think the first time I seriously thought about army service was when I was a sophomore at age sixteen. Teachers and administrators were always stressing how important it was to do well from the ninth grade on, because colleges would look at your entire four-year high school record. "D'oh!," to borrow a Homerism from the Simpsons. My freshman academic performance would make it even harder to get into a community college.[1] I remember when a ninth-grade science teacher scared the hell out of me and probably a few others when he broke down the percentages of those of us who would basically succeed or fail in life. He said something like, "Only ten percent of you will enroll in college. Out of that percentage, only ten percent of you will earn a degree. And out of that percentage, only ten percent of you will earn good grades. And out of. . . ." When that fleeting thought of army service did cross my mind in tenth grade, I remember feeling elated. It's hard to explain, but once again, I felt that by choosing to go off somewhere—the army—I was doing *something* with my life. The idea of *something* was liberating and intoxicating, as you can see, but the *something* put into practice—the reality of army life—felt at times to be anything but liberating.

After I told Sergeant Arturo my preferred job assignment of being stationed in Europe with the Special Forces, as if I knew what the hell I was talking about, he responded, "Umm, okay. We'll talk about that later. First, why don't you come down to the office and you can take a written test that measures your knowledge and skills for specific jobs?" So that very night I took the ASVAB, which stands for Armed Services Vocational Aptitude Battery. I didn't even take the practice one for preparation purposes, as many future soldiers often did. I was happy finding out that I scored well overall on the ASVAB—an eighty-something percentile on the total score and some high marks in specific job-related areas. So as a junior in high school with one year of school left (today's newer and smarter army says that each recruit has to have a high school diploma or a GED), Sergeant Arturo took on the task of serving as my army recruiter. I entered the Delayed Entry Program (DEP) whereby new recruits can sign up for army service up to 365 days before their actual service start date. And since I was under age when I took the oath of office to "uphold and defend the constitution of the United States against all enemies, foreign and domestic," my mother and "real" father had to cosign the official paperwork. To this day, I still take a bit of pride in having joined the United States Army at age seventeen. My grandmother Lorraine had run away at age sixteen to become an army nurse during the Second World War, only to be discharged (honorably) after her underage status was discovered.

I have to admit, as my mom likes to remind me time and time again, part of my enthusiasm about joining the army at the time was a ploy aimed at getting my parents to let me move back home from the party pad down the street. Back then, I had a bit of long hair in the back—a *Joe Dirt*-esque mullet if you will—and I was told I had to cut it off before I could come home.[ii] Well, I did get a haircut, more like a trim, but I was backed by an army recruiter who could vouch for my decision to join the service. I think my mom was pretty skeptical about a proposed commitment on my part of any kind, as was probably most of the family. But many of them will tell me today, "Oh, we knew you would turn out okay." Right! Once my mom acquiesced in letting me come home and agreed to help ship me off to the army, my first entangled venture through the web of the federal bureaucracy began.

My time spent in the Delayed Entry Program was filled with many highs and lows, excitements and frustrations. I was actually excited when my recruiter asked me the standard question, "Are you or have you ever been a member of the Communist Party?" I was proud to say no. I didn't know then (1990), and I doubt he speculated either, that the Soviet Union was just months away from crumbling into oblivion. Though today, in 2004, I have Russian university students in Moldova who have expressed their desire to see a return to the Soviet era, back "when things were better," a few of us volunteers often joke. My girlfriend at the time, Paige, was not too happy when I told her that I was going into the service after high school. We stayed together during our senior year and were "high school sweethearts," but I often thought that maybe she was such a bitch to me because I would be leaving her in a year. Although I foolishly convinced myself that we could stay together while I served in the army, I was not foolish enough to ask for her hand in marriage. I could have broken up with her before graduating, but I was pretty whipped. Plus, I didn't really know what the army had in store for me. I did figure that there would be a long and harsh indoctrination into military life, probably without women around for a short while. As for other high school friends, then and after I completed my four years in the army, the whole idea of service in general, and me serving in particular, was a big joke. During my senior year, the First Gulf War against Iraq broke out, and one of my peers, by the name of Dustin, laughingly said, "Dude, you're going over there," meaning Iraq. Correctly speculating, I told him that the whole affair in the Gulf would be over in a matter of months (it was actually a lot less time than that), long before my start of service date. But, wanting to appear tough and trying to look as though I knew what I was getting myself into, I boastfully, yet honestly, said, "I'll go to Iraq."

When I first got back the results of my initial written examination for army service, Sergeant Arturo was more than happy to explain what type of jobs would best suit me. Before he could speak, I told him that I wanted to go into the infantry. After all, the Allied troops on the beaches of Normandy were infantrymen, and the 101st, jumping into France, was part of the famed airborne infantry. He logically explained to me that because I scored well in certain areas of the exam, I would be allowed to choose a certain specialized training program, making it possible to acquire important job skills for post-army life. I wouldn't hear any of it. "No. I want to be infantry." "All right," he said, "Then you want to be the best in the world. You want to be an Airborne Ranger."

Up to this point, I remembered having read briefly about Rangers fighting in Italy against the Nazi menace. I can still quote the caption from one of those *Time-Life* books, I think it was, that my parents gave to me, "On the Salerno-Palermo Road, after German atrocities, U. S. Army Rangers took no prisoners."[iii] So I agreed with my recruiter and chanted, "*I want to be an Airborne Ranger.*"

Along with answering questions about any Communist Party-affiliated status and selecting my preferred job assignment, I remember my recruiter presenting me with a list of choices that would signify why I wanted to serve in the army. But from this list, which included *travel, money, to serve my country*, and other reasons, I could only pick two, and they were to be written down into my permanent army records. I honestly picked *travel* and *to serve my country*, once again experiencing a feeling of elation that financial/material gain was not my priority for enlisting. But I also couldn't help but think that somewhere down the road, if I were to continue on with government service, the *money* answer might come back to haunt me or prevent me from getting a certain type of job. I often thought about those idiot marines who gave secretive information to female Soviet spies in exchange for sexual favors. Why didn't they just give them false information, or have their way with them and then turn them in? I guess you had to be there.

I was very fortunate to have the recruiter that I did. He kept me on the straight and narrow path during my senior year, and was honest when answering my questions and concerns. Later, while serving, I met other soldiers who hated their recruiters for having lied to them. During my second year of service, while on a training exercise in Scotland, Sergeant Arturo was there and purposely tracked me down because he knew that the Rangers were in town. By that time, he was stationed in Germany as a military policeman (MP), seeing as how that was his area of training; recruiting was only a temporary assignment that many army careerists have to do at one time or another. He had been flown to Scotland as part of a small contingent of army Customs' personnel to inspect our bags before we could head back to the States. While walking with pounds of equipment on my back, out of the blue I heard, "Hey soldier." I turned and was ecstatic to find that it was Sergeant Arturo. We chatted for a few minutes, and I gave him my contact information for the U.S. I never heard from him again. Upon telling some of my army buddies in Scotland that I ran into my recruiter, one of them asked, "Did you kick his ass?"

While working with my recruiter on my army contract, I had zero intention of ever going back to school after I received my high school diploma. I was a "C" average student at best, and academic studies had been such a tremendous chore. (After about two months of basic training in the sweltering summer heat of Fort Benning, Georgia, I thought to myself: *community college sounds pretty damn good right now.*) My options for an enlistment bonus were: up to $8,000 cash received upon entry into the army, or up to $25,000 for college after four years of service. The latter choice also required an initial payment of $100 per month on my part for the first year of service. Leaning toward the cash, I saw the down payment on a nice car in my immediate future. And with a car, of course, comes more *freedom.* So I said to Sergeant Arturo that I wanted the cash. He told me that since I would be entering a highly specialized, meaning costly, infantry-airborne training program—that of an Airborne Ranger—I could only get around $4,000 at the most. Then he rationally and calmly told me that I would be much better off taking the college money, because I would one day want to use it. I agreed. What is amazing to me about the U.S. Army College Fund and GI Bill, according to an article I read a couple of years ago, is that only forty percent of the soldiers who ever pay into it ($1200 per soldier who signs up for it) actually ever use it. Many of them stay in the service or get jobs when their enlistment is up. And sadly, those with concrete plans for a post-military education are sometimes killed during combat operations or in training accidents. I swore that upon being discharged, I would use every nickel of my army college fund. I did and then some. One beef that some of my fellow soldiers had with their recruiters was that they were promised both the army college fund and the GI Bill, but were only awarded the GI Bill, which is about half of the promised twenty-five grand.

With my Airborne Ranger army contract set, I merely needed to graduate from high school and stay out of trouble. Sadly, this was not a given. Plus, with a whole senior year to go, my emotions and anxieties were raging back and forth. Periodically, my recruiter would ask me if I was ready to go in. One time when he asked, I said no. During those waiting months, I often pondered over whether or not I was making the right choice by enlisting in the army. I thought that I could possibly become a local police officer instead—not exactly federal service but an important form of public service nonetheless. When I told Sergeant Arturo that I didn't want to go in anymore, he said something that to this day I still find remarkable, "Well, it's your life, and if you don't want to go in, I can get you out of your contract." *Amazing*, I thought. But because he said this, I realized that I *had* to go in. If this was a ploy on his part to *force* me to commit, he was definitely the maestro of recruiters. But I tend to think that he was just a good person and was not merely trying to fill his yearly quota of new recruits. When I told this story to a few fellow soldiers, one replied that his recruiter said there was no way in hell he could get out of his contract without breaking the law.

Living at home with my parents as a senior, I tended to walk around the house with the attitude, "I'm going in the army in a few months, so I can do whatever I want." It didn't help matters much when my "real" father told my mother just that. Both my mother and my stepfather, I'm sure, were glad to have me out of the house when I finally did leave for the army. I found out that after going in, they were staying out later than usual with friends and enjoying their newfound *liberation.* Good for them, I can say now and mean it. At school, I did the bare minimum to get by, and sometimes that wasn't enough. I remember my science teacher (not the one who broke down our collective success/failure percentages) telling me that if I wanted to go into the army, I still had to pass her class by doing the work. I wasn't a big fan of the hard sciences. I knew that my mother was afraid I wouldn't graduate on time, and this would postpone my army entry date, perhaps indefinitely. I also had a little run-in with the law.

A couple of weeks after my eighteenth birthday (February 1991), merely four months before my start of service date, I was caught shoplifting at a local convenience store. My girlfriend's birthday was coming up in May, so being the hopeless romantic that I was/am, I decided to swipe some candles worth about fifty cents each, to be placed around the room of a seedy hotel room down the street. As is the case with most petty theft shoplifting incidents, I had more than enough money to make the purchase. The whole scenario was humiliating but served as a valuable lesson—I never again stole another item (from a store). Until then, I often stole batteries and film from various convenience stores, wanting to photographically document my life in Imperial Beach, before heading out for army service. So when I was caught stealing candles, I was made to wait in the back room of the store until an officer from the local sheriff's department showed up. Then my picture was taken by the store manager, and I was banned forever from the J. J. Newberry's local market. As I sat there in the back, waiting for a policeman or policewoman to take me away, I looked up at the wall of mug-shots of those who had been branded with the status of "life ban." I saw one Polaroid in particular and said, laughingly, "Hey, that's Chuck," a friend from school. When I told him in front of some other friends that I had seen his picture at J. J. Newberry's, he somewhat embarrassingly acted confused and then changed the subject. What our peers thought of my incident didn't matter. I told everyone, except for my parents. But after I showed up for court with my recruiter, a friend of my father's who worked there called my dad and told him what had happened, so my father "coerced" me into telling my mother what I had done. During my "trial," I pled guilty, but my recruiter vouched for me, explaining to the judge that I was heading for a straight and narrow path in the army. Just as the judge was about to drop the case, the prosecutor said, "Well your Honor, I still think he should receive some sort of punishment." So I did, but I didn't have the $250, so I did about five weekends of community service, cutting weeds on the sides of freeways.

Well, I did graduate on time, in early June 1991, with nineteen days to spare before I left Imperial Beach, California, for Fort Benning, Georgia. I ate, drank, and had as much sex with my girlfriend Paige as possible. So my lifestyle never really changed in anticipation of military life. My mom asked me if I was going to do any kind of workout routine to prepare for the physical training (PT) of military service. *Why bother?* I thought, since army training would take care of my out-of-shapeness. But I did get a drastic haircut, not wanting to be ridiculed by drill sergeants by showing up with longer than normal hair. Paige cut off my mullet as a keepsake. I'm sure it's at the bottom of some landfill by now. At least I hope it is.

You're in the Army *Now*

I first realized that I was in the army the day before I left my home "port," as the sailors call it, of San Diego, California. It was early July 1991, and most of my buddies from school were enjoying the summer after graduation, getting ready to start some crappy nickel-and-dime job or begin the first of many semesters at Southwestern Community College. I was at the Military Entrance Processing Station (MEPS), where future recruits bound for any of the military branches depart, reaffirming through the signing of paperwork that I was committed to fulfilling four years and some odd months of army service. My recruiter, once again trying to steer me in a positive direction, had earlier suggested that I sign up for two or three years, and if I liked it, I could always reenlist. And of course I said, "No. I want four years," because anything less than a four-year commitment, in my eyes, was not hardcore enough. At MEPS, pencil-pushing officers from all of the branches were represented. As soon as my status of entry-level private was reconfirmed, there was an instant change of attitude on their part. "Here you go," I said to one of them, handing him my paperwork. "Here you go what?!" the officer snapped back. "Sir?" I answered/questioned timidly. Then I thought to myself, *Oh shit. What have I gotten myself into?*

I stayed in a decent hotel that night, courtesy of the United States government. (When I was accepted for Peace Corps service, I couldn't wait to get to the introductory staging area in Philadelphia, knowing that the feds would take care of our expenses from that point on.) The next day, some high school friends of mine, and my girlfriend, all drove to the airport together to see me off. I shed a few tears, a few of them forced, not wanting to appear insensitive that I was getting "the hell out of Dodge." One of my saddest thoughts as I said goodbye to this crew was, *I wonder which "friend" of mine will hit on my girlfriend first.* The plane travel from San Diego to Houston, and then on to Atlanta, Georgia, was uneventful and pretty emotionless, besides enjoying, as always, the thrill of flight. I did meet two or three other guys who were bound for Fort Benning, but never saw them again once we arrived. The loneliest journey I ever took in my life was that dead-silent bus ride in the pitch black of night, from Atlanta to our final destination of Fort Benning. I remember looking out the window, trying to make out shadowy shapes against the backdrop of a moonless sky, while thinking, *Where the hell am I?*

Our first few days of army service involved a rather busy indoctrination into military life, before heading "down range," which meant starting basic training with an assigned company. The lingo of this time might go something like, "Hey man, when are you heading down range? We're heading down range tomorrow." Early army indoctrination included getting our heads completely shaved, receiving our equipment and uniforms, performing some simple marching, or drilling as it is called, and of course getting yelled at along the way. We were even purposely coddled a bit, when one drill instructor (DI) talked to a big group of us, informing, "At least ten percent of you will receive Dear John letters during basic training." And every guy there (there were no women) shook his head, including me, in disbelief. What led me to cry my eyes out at one point wasn't that I received such a letter from my girlfriend, but that I hadn't received any letters! This was especially hurtful since some asshole in my training platoon kept bragging about receiving many letters from different girlfriends. Persons, both men and women, react differently to a non-responsive partner or ex. In the army, I had heard stories about soldiers and/or their partners taking extreme measures in such cases. Before I arrived at my "permanent" unit of Alpha Company, 3rd Ranger Battalion, a soldier there apparently killed himself with his own M-16 rifle over a woman. That's how the "no weapons in your room" rule supposedly became initiated.

Once down range, with our regular drill sergeants profanely screaming at us, we learned the basics of an infantryman's life. This included learning how to shoot rifles, throw hand grenades, march in formation, patrol in the "field," make our beds properly, and provide first-aid to fellow soldiers if need be. For this last task, we were presented with a real opportunity to demonstrate our recently acquired "expertise," and we all failed miserably. Shortly after receiving first-aid training, we went to the medical station to have one of many blood samples drawn for testing. After "giving" blood, our unit stood in formation at the position of *parade rest*, where both arms come behind the back and one hand is placed on top of the other over the small of the back. As we stood there, one private keeled over, falling flat on his face without moving his arms from the position of *parade rest*. So did we all remember our first aid training—assess the situation and act accordingly? Of course not. We all stood around looking at each other until a drill sergeant came over to make the situation all better. Well, this trainee turned out to be fine and probably just had a reaction to the blood test. To instill pride in our training outfit, we were made to chant about our "beloved" E (Echo) Company training unit. *Boom, ungow-ah', Echo's got the pow-ah'. We're lean and mean, dressed in green, and we're checking out this gnarly scene. Huh!* I speculated that the DI who made us learn this song, Drill Sergeant Crock, was from California, since the word *gnarly* was used. He wasn't.

Our training unit in Fort Benning was referred to by the acronym of OSUT (One Station Unit Training), combining the basic training that every soldier goes through, male and female, with a soldier's specified army task—in my case, infantry school. I was a terrible soldier for a long while, probably more so than many others, even after I completed training. But for some reason, I was able to stay in the shadows, which most trainees prefer to do, while others caught the brunt of the drill sergeants' wrath. My shaky theory is that they had a hard time pronouncing my last name of Donayre (dough-nar-ee), so I wasn't bothered as much. Also, there were a few new recruits in our group who thought they were hot shit because they had done some time in high school JROTC (Junior Reserve Officer Training Corps), thus starting service with a stripe or two on their collar, signifying that they were higher ranking privates. They were usually singled out by the DI's for leadership roles, and because of this, they usually commanded very little to no respect from their fellow trainees. It was also noted by me and others that some of these guys made for the worst soldiers, because they came into the army with preconceived and false notions about what military life was all about. Having gone camping in high school was probably not quite the same as an army "field problem" out in the jungles of Panama or the desert of 29 Palms, California. When I was stationed in South Korea during my last year of service, the scout platoon I was attached to on the DMZ (demilitarized zone) got a new private, fresh from infantry school, by the name of Marvin. He boasted about how many medals he had earned while in high school JROTC and about how he would be going on to a career in the special forces. During our first long road march (hike), he spent the whole time whining like a sniveling little child because of the pain he endured from *humping* (carrying) a field radio in his rucksack. So I asked him afterwards, already knowing the answer, "So Marvin, are you still gonna go special forces?" His reply: "Fuck that shit!"

Although I lagged behind other trainees in learning the craft of the infantryman, there was one thing that usually got me through the roughest of times—perseverance, or "intestinal fortitude," in Ranger terminology. For example, during the week that we learned how to shoot rifles, I was the last one off of the shooting range each day, because I simply could not get it down. On one day in particular, we were required to fire only three bullets, attempting to place them together in a tight shot group on the target. For the longest time, one of my three shots always landed wildly at a distance from the others. With perseverance, and a drill sergeant inflicting pain upon my eardrum, I actually did better than many of the "natural" shots when it came time to officially qualify with our rifles. The first time I qualified, I shot thirty out of forty targets, placing me at the level of *sharpshooter*.

My mother was right when she told me I should go into the service in some sort of shape besides pudgy. On my first recorded two-mile run time, I ran in just under sixteen minutes, ready to collapse. By the end of training I was running the two-mile test at around twelve-and-a-half minutes. And the fastest recorded time I've ever had, during my Ranger days, was eleven minutes, twenty-four seconds. I felt good about this, but I knew a sergeant ten years older than me who could run it in around ten minutes.

One of the most memorable experiences of training involved being shuffled through the CS *gas chamber*—a grossly misnamed apparatus, considering the historical and genocidal use of this term. CS gas (tear gas) is the type used, I believe, by police officers in riot control situations. In the chamber, for our training purposes, small groups of trainees would enter, wearing U.S. Army-issued protective gas masks while CS gas was pumped into the building. Drill sergeants were also in the chamber, making us remove our protective masks at some point while inside. Attempting to instill within us a sense of trust in our equipment was one reason for this type of training. Another reason, for some drill sergeants, was that it was funny to watch trainees run around the chamber squeamishly gasping for air. I think that sometime before my turn in the chamber, I had heard that when our masks are removed inside, the DI's would try and make us take deep breaths, except there is no "air" to breath. Once my group was inside, we received the order to take our masks off. So I did, right after I took a huge gulp of purified gas mask air and held my breath. Years of underwater swimming, courtesy of my swim instructors—grandmother Lorraine and her daughter, my mother Leslie—made lengthy breath-holding a relatively easy task. Then a DI egged us on, trying to make us inhale the gas inside the chamber. He got one trainee standing next to me to inhale what appeared to be quite a lot, subsequently making him writhe in pain and fear. The trainee sprinted for the locked door, trying like hell to get out, practically screaming in agony the whole time. Here I was, in the same predicament as my fellow recruit, and I felt sorry for him. When the DI taunted me to breathe, I faked like I was gasping for air, holding steady without actually inhaling the gas. But my eyes were open, and the gas produced a bit of pain and tears in them. The whole episode probably took no more than thirty seconds, after which we were released from the chamber. Later that day, we were put to a more severe test to see just how far we had progressed as future infantrymen for the United States Army. During an outdoor "block of instruction" about something that presently escapes me, a DI or two came up from behind us and ran through the assembled group of trainees, waving what appeared to be CS gas-spewing canisters at the tip of large pieces of wood. I am proud to say that I did what I was supposed to do: hold my rifle with my knees while hastily donning my protective gas mask. There were quite a few recruits who dropped their weapons and took off running—wrong answer. Those who had opted for the latter choice were expected to "have a little chat" with a drill sergeant before getting their rifles back.

As I said, my army contract stated that I was to become an Airborne Ranger. This was contingent upon completing not only basic training and infantry school, but also completing a three-week airborne (paratrooper) school followed by a two-and-a-half-week Ranger indoctrination program. Failure to complete any of the last two meant that I would be subject to worldwide assignment, meaning that I could be sent anywhere in the world, instead of being stationed at one of the three Ranger battalions inside the United States—two in Georgia and one in Washington State. Not being able to complete basic or infantry school meant a ticket back home for "failing to adapt to military life" unless there was a medical condition at fault. There were quite a few of us new recruits who were slotted to become

Rangers, but the odds were that only a small percentage of us would actually make it all the way—again with the percentages! One recruit in particular went AWOL (Absent With Out Leave) during basic training, meaning that he ran away from the service. It was rumored that he was caught at a local bowling alley just hanging out there, perhaps bowling. I remember when they brought him back, forcing him to live near us, but not among us, until he could be sent home for "failing to adapt to military life." I recall that before we went "down range," he boasted about how he was going to be a deadly warrior with the Army Rangers. Later, after our training actually started, he cried about not wanting to kill any living creature.

In the army, as in life, those who boast the loudest are often the ones who have something to hide—insecurities and ineptness are strong possibilities. During training, we had a few "substitute" Drill Sergeants—army reservists doing their annual two weeks of duty in the summer—work with us. Some of these guys were much older than our regular DI's, counting down their time until retirement. It was interesting to hear some of their stories from "when the army was much harder" twenty years ago. One of these DI's told us that the guys who talked the loudest were the first ones to run when the bullets started flying. And it was the quiet reserved types— the ones who weren't the best shots with a rifle in training—who won the medals in battle for "having gone above and beyond the call of duty." I tried to remember this, in case I was ever faced with the prospect of combat. And even if a soldier did everything perfectly in training and was the model of a modern warrior, his guarantee of survival was nowhere near etched in stone. A fellow trainee asked a DI once, "So, if we move perfectly from tree to tree (Infantry Movement Technique or IMT), we'll be all right?" The DI said, "Well, if your time is up. . . ."

One thing I hated about being a foot soldier—no matter how well trained one was, physically and/or mentally, was that there were too many things out of my control. Soldiers cannot prevent helicopters from crashing or shrapnel from flying in all directions or leaders from making terrible decisions. If you look at the death toll of Americans from the First Gulf War, a majority of those who died were killed from "friendly" fire incidents—*fratricide* (there's even a word for it because of its common occurrence). Not being shot up by your own troops should be a given. And with the attempt to stabilize the situation in Iraq today, I have read about too many soldiers who have died from accidents.

A recent historian (probably more than one), whose name I can't recall, characterized the U.S. Army as the great engine of "social equality," forcing Americans from all walks of life to integrate and work together for the communal good. Though I did not make long-lasting fraternal friendships until after I reached my first duty station, during my time in basic training, I befriended a few Americans from various corners of the nation. I also had my share of run-ins with members of the "community." One recruit in particular, Chadwick from Texas, was a bully, pure and simple. He often picked fights with other recruits in our platoon because he was psychotic. Either he was hated, or as is the case with bullies and murderous dictators, admired and respected out of fear. Once, he was the ringleader of a somewhat thuggish group of trainees who half-assedly overturned another trainee's bed mattress, with the trainee still on it, during the middle of the night. I remember this

11

because the bed was diagonally across from mine, and the incident woke me up. It reminded me, but obviously to a much lesser extent, of when Private Pyle was beaten by some fellow Marine Corps trainees with bars of soaps in the movie *Full Metal Jacket*.[iv] I always thought that if something like that happened to me, the angry rage ignited in me would temporarily quash any feelings of pain, allowing me to grab the closest person (hence the slowest, and probably the weakest out of the pack) to my bed and commence to beat him senseless, or until I was pulled off him.

The one time Chadwick really got in my face about something, and I stood up to him, he was on probation for "reasons unbecoming a soldier." Therefore it did not come to fisticuffs. We got into an argument in front of a few other recruits about something I can't remember (it's probably not worth remembering), and I told him aloud that nobody in the platoon *really* liked him. This did not sit well with him, and he threatened me, saying something like, "If I wasn't in trouble right now, I would. . . ." Throughout life, since I was a kid, I always felt reinvigorated as a person when standing up to some punk bully. And this time was no exception. Fortunately for me, this sort of strategy has worked in my favor, even if I was frightened, ended up fighting, or both. Granted, by no means am I a tough guy, nor do I like scrapping. I'd rather not even be around persons who *claim* to enjoy fighting. But in my family growing up, I was raised with the "don't let anyone push you around" mentality. My grandfather Shakes, a deceased naval veteran of the Cuban Missile Crisis and the Vietnam Conflict, used to say, "The worst thing that can happen is you get your ass kicked. At least you'll still have your pride." Well we've all seen violent news coverage in the past few years. Unfortunately, getting your ass kicked is not the worst thing that can happen anymore. After having stood my ground with Chadwick, he later told me, with what appeared to be sincerity, "Yeah, I think you'll make it [into the Rangers]." Later on, Drill Sergeant Crock was instrumental in having Chadwick thrown out of the army for "failing to adapt to military life"—good riddance! Crock said that he himself was verbally threatened by Chadwick with the words, "If I can't kick your ass, I'll get my father to."

Another run-in I had was with a McAllister from my home state of California— from up north, the city of Fresno I believe. He was a reservist or national guardsman like a few of the other recruits in our training outfit, where after infantry school he went back home to serve as a part-time "weekend warrior" for the military. For a long while, whenever he opened his mouth it was always to nag someone or bitch about something. One day, at the tail end of a long hot road march to some training area in the midday summer sun, the formation I was in started to cross over from one side of the road to where the other column of troops was. I started crossing over, copying what the guy in front of me was doing, who was following the person in front of him, and so on. I assumed that some order had been passed down from the front of the row I was in. And to my poor eardrums' contempt, McAllister was right behind me. He let out a whiny, "Why are you crossing over? No one told you to cross over." I snapped in my head, *Enough!* Then I turned around, looked him dead in the eye, and fearlessly said, "If we weren't in the army right now, I would beat the shit out of you!" Stunned, he whimpered,

"You don't have to get an attitude about it." We were on friendly terms from there on out.

As we progressed through training, the drill instructors gradually eased up on their micromanaged control over us, as long as we continued to prove ourselves. For most of us recruits, the hardest part about the training program was just being away from friends, relatives, and loved ones. The saddest episode for me involved talking to my girlfriend back home via pay phone, trying to patch things up with her while other trainees stood waiting in line during our limited phone-privilege time. I was futilely trying to get confirmation from her that she still loved me, when an operator broke in with one of those, "Please deposit twenty-five cents for the next ten minutes." It may have been five cents for two minutes. Regardless, I didn't have a dime! Then, in an open display of desperation, I yelled aloud, "Does anyone have a quarter (nickel)?" No one did. So in my state of sadness and acceptance, I told the phone operator that I didn't have the change, "but please tell my girlfriend that I love her." Then I hung up the phone. At our halfway point between basic and infantry school, we were given about a thirty-six-hour off-post pass known as Family Day, where friends and relatives would come to Fort Benning to see *their* recruit. As long as I lived in Georgia, my father Leo could and would zip on down from Pennsylvania whenever I had some free time. Working as a mechanic for an airline made this easily possible. On Family Day he picked me up, and we drove to visit my aunts Rosie and Ximena (Mena), his sisters, in Gadsden, Alabama. Between the two of them, I have six cousins from Alabama. In thirty-six hours, I had enough time to eat authentic Southern cooked food like biscuits and gravy ("Mmm, cholesterol," as Homer might say), drink a couple of beers, and watch a film or two. Oh yeah, and spend some quality time with my family as well. The saddest part about coming back from Family Day was seeing "kids" my age, eighteen years old, say goodbye to their fiancées or wives, a couple of whom had babies with them or on the way.

In preparation for the big day, graduation from infantry school, I needed to use the telephone to make arrangements with my father. Being the charmer that he is, he called my training unit headquarters and spoke with one of the meanest DI's there, a Drill Sergeant Velasquez from Puerto Rico. Velasquez used to throw those big and noisy metal trashcans around our training AO (Area of Operations) when he was angry. But he did admit once that it was often just for show and to keep the troops in line. After lashing out now and again, he said he would often go into the office and laugh it off. But as trainees, we of course took everything at face value. As he was not a native English speaker, and certainly not as coherent and adept as some of my students here in Moldova, it was often hard to understand what Velasquez was saying, even more so when he was mad. This made it especially difficult when he talked with recruits one on one, because if you exerted a look of frustration in trying to understand what he was saying, it just made him madder and madder. So this one particular time when my father called, Velasquez was "charmed" into letting me call my father back. This was especially important since all of the other recruits had lost their phone privileges for that day. Technically, the military works for the civilian citizenry. An angry parent calling up, demanding information about one thing or another, is probably the single greatest fear that military leaders are faced with—that and sending thousands of youths off to kill and/or be killed. At least I hope the latter is a real fearful concern.

On this occasion my father was anything but angry. It's better to do what parents request, within reason, before getting them upset. I went up to Velasquez and shakily said, "Uh, Drill Sergeant Velasquez. You, uh, said I could call my dad?" He shook his head in agreement. I was ecstatic after speaking to my father about our graduation plans of driving up to Atlanta, about two hours north of Fort Benning, to spend the weekend with friends of the family, one "friend" being a "southern belle" whom my dad was "courting." After finalizing the plans with him, I ran into the barracks and in a jovial state, jokingly shouted, "Aaatttention!" signifying that an officer had just walked in. I turned the corner to see my fellow recruits locked up at the position of *attention* (arms and hands fully extended and placed at their sides), as I broke out laughing. One of them said, "What are you doing [idiot]? Drill Sergeant Velasquez is in the office." A wave of fear washed over me. Velasquez came out of the office and asked, "Who said that?" I couldn't get out of this one. I snapped to *parade rest,* the position used when speaking to a noncommissioned officer or NCO (sergeant). "Uh, uh, I did, Drill Sergeant." He came up to me, saying, "What, do you want to be an officer or something?" "No, Drill Sergeant." He asked, "What, are you trying to be funny, making a joke?" I hesitated, then, "Yes, Drill Sergeant." A gradual smile formed on his face, and he ordered me, "Get the fuck out of here." And that was that, but it took me a minute or two to stop shaking. It's one thing to be in trouble, but it's another thing to get your whole platoon in hot water for being a clown. I didn't want the Private Pyle bar-soap treatment.

All in all, the basic training and infantry school combo lasted from mid-July to early October. One of the highlights of the whole training program took place on graduation day itself. For this event, all of the graduating trainees form up on a big parade field, in their Class A formal dress uniforms (or simply *Class A's*), with other infantry school units from around Fort Benning. There are multiple bandstands from where relatives, friends, and other loved ones can watch their future infantrymen of America march past. Well, almost all of the graduating trainees wore their dress uniforms that day. Myself and a few other select trainees, because we volunteered, were part of the "entertainment" that wowed the gathering throngs of civilians. While the *I Am the Infantry! Follow Me!* theme played loud and probably not so clear on the big speakers, informing the bandstands' patrons of the role the infantry has played throughout the nation's history, the "entertainment," dressed in various retro army infantry uniforms, dismounted from an army "fighting vehicle." It's probably not surprising to know that I was in the uniform of a U.S. soldier from the Second World War, "armed" with a Tommy machine gun. On the day we were selecting roles, I made it clear that I wanted this particular role. So one by one, as *Follow Me!* blared over loudspeakers, we lined up in front of the bandstands in chronological sequence by order of war appearance, beginning with the War for Independence from Great Britain. One thing I thought was hysterical, as Drill Sergeant Crock had planned: the role of the Civil War Confederate soldier was assigned to a dark-skinned New Yorker of Italian descent—a way of making amends or an offense to southernism? My father was on hand to snap plenty of photos of the day's happenings. Having changed into my dress uniform while the non-entertainment graduates were still lined on the parade field, he and I rolled out of Fort Benning toward Atlanta. As it had been recited that day, *I Am the Infantry,* I was now officially a small part of it, anyway.

Death from Above

"Why would you want to jump out of a perfectly good airplane?"—a question I have been asked before, during, and after my army service. A paratrooper, as I was to be for over two years with the Army Rangers, received an extra $110 a month on top of the regular base pay. This was known as *jump pay*. The money was a nice bonus, allowing for the consumption of more beer than I probably needed. But I was certainly not enticed into jumping out of planes merely to earn the approximate equivalent of what I currently pay for a furnished apartment in the Moldovan capital of Chisinau (pronounced Keesh-uh-now). Again, it goes back to wanting to be a part of something unique and grandiose, with the hope of making a positive contribution in the process. Anyone can take up skydiving as a sport. But not everyone can invade a foreign land by jumping out of an aircraft in flight, while simultaneously ensuring the continued existence of the American Republic. And, in line with my army contract, it was imperative that I first acquire airborne status before completing the other half of the Airborne Ranger equation.

I had orders to report for airborne school training within a week, I believe, after graduating from infantry school. For good or bad, the schools were literally "down the street" from each other. But Fort Benning is an enormous place, more like a large town. A better expression would be to say that they were on "opposite sides of town." This is important to know, since recruits in basic and infantry school are isolated from the rest of the post while they become accustomed to military life. Airborne school was located in the hustle and bustle of Fort Benning, surrounded by the niceties I had known before army training began, including fast-food joints and big supermarkets. Plus it was coed. Knowing this, I did not think it would be very tough, and it wasn't, compared with the training I had just completed. Although I am a feminist sympathizer at the least, believing that men and women should receive equal pay for equal work, and that women should be given the opportunity to compete in roles that have traditionally been occupied by men,

16

I am also a gender realist. As a whole, women are physically weaker than men, and airborne school, as I recall, did not have separate physical training (PT) requirements for the two genders. The school itself was a much-needed "vacation" between infantry training and my upcoming Ranger Indoctrination Program (RIP).

Airborne training was a total of three weeks, assuming that the trainees made it successfully past the first, second, and third weeks. Each of these weeks had a theme: week one was *ground week*, where we learned the basics of exiting from an aircraft without actually doing so; week two was *tower week*, where we learned how to properly land from a successful or a not-so-successful jump without actually parachuting from a plane; week three was *jump week*, where we had to complete five actual parachute jumps from military aircraft before graduating and receiving our *airborne wings*. Failure to complete any one of these weeks would result in either being dropped from airborne school altogether or being recycled until the particular week could successfully be completed. For example, if I failed *tower week* for some reason with the Bravo (B) Company training unit, I would have the option of quitting or being recycled to Charlie (C) Company, picking up from that training unit's start of *tower week*. As long as an airborne school student was motivated and stayed relatively healthy, he or she could be recycled many times over. There was probably a limit to the amount of individual recycles. I fortunately never had the dilemma of choosing between recycled status and flat-out quitting, having made it straight through the three weeks of training with the same company. If a student quit, that student would either be sent back to his or her regular military unit (soldiers from different branches of the military often attended airborne school) or would receive orders to report to a non-airborne duty station. I knew a soldier who, as early as basic training, modeled his future maroon beret—the headgear worn by most infantry airborne units at the time—only to quit airborne school a few days into it.

During airborne school, I became accustomed to many facets of military life—both in and out of the army uniform—that had been unknown in my previous training situation. Not only was I around women on a regular basis for the first time since leaving home, I was now in an army school with persons of different ranks and various jobs within the military. In basic and infantry school, we were more or less all the same rank—peon (private). Now there were officers and non-commissioned officers from prior leadership roles in attendance as airborne students. One of my roommates was, I believe, a lance corporal with the other "Corps"—the United States Marine Corps. I recall him saying that he had trained out in San Diego at the Marine Corps Recruit Depot (MCRD). I myself have been asked at times, "Why didn't you go into the navy or marines, since you are from San Diego?" Being from San Diego is another reason why I chose a branch of service that would send me away from home, somewhere where my mommy and daddy didn't live. I knew guys from high school who became sailors and were stationed in San Diego, living with their parents or nearby. And I met fellow soldiers in Georgia who would drive home every weekend because they could. They might as well have joined the Boy Scouts as far as I was concerned. Plus, while growing up in southern California, plenty of negative stereotypes and crude jokes involving

17

Seabees and "Jar Heads" had been imbedded into my psyche. There was never a consideration of joining the Marine Corps, or its boss, the U.S. Navy. It was during airborne training when I first realized that we do indeed live in a small world. A sailor in attendance told me that he used to reside on Silverstrand Boulevard in my hometown of Imperial Beach.

The training of airborne school was like no other. *Ground week* involved being strapped into a body harness, which was sort of like a huge intricate bungee cord, and jumping out of a mock aircraft door forty feet high. On the ground, grading us on whether we exited the "aircraft" successfully (GO) or unsuccessfully (NO GO), was one of the many airborne instructors, known as black hats because of the special headgear (a black-looking baseball cap) that they wore. We were obliged to call each one "Sergeant Airborne." In turn, we were referred to simply as "Airborne." Our student ID number was stenciled on our helmets (K-Pots). While standing in the door of this training apparatus, before jumping, we were required to yell our ID numbers down below to Sergeant Airborne. When we were given the okay from him or her, we jumped, attempting to maintain the perfect form of someone who was actually parachuting out of an airplane. This meant keeping our eyes open while counting, "1000, 2000, 3000, 4000" (if the chute hasn't opened by this point then there might be matters of life and death to contend with), keeping our hands positioned over the reserve parachute in front of us, and then checking above, around, and below to ensure that everything was "normal"—falling from the sky at an average rate of speed. After each practice jump and the bungee slide across the training area that followed, we reported to Sergeant Airborne for a GO or NO GO. If we didn't have a certain number of *Go's* by the end of the week, we were recycled to a new airborne company, unless of course we decided to quit instead. After one practice jump, I received a *NO GO*. "Ah, weak!" I exclaimed aloud, like I might to a buddy back home. "Yes, you are weak," retorted Sergeant Airborne.

I also had my first crush on a soldier during *ground week*—a female 2nd Lieutenant, 2LT being the rank of an entry-level commissioned officer. I first lost respect for her as an officer when she was standing in line behind me at the forty-foot tower, literally crying because of difficulties in obtaining a *Go* on her "report card." One instructor, whom she technically outranked, attempted to comfort her. "What's wrong ma'am?" Whimpering, she explained her troubles, while I thought, *A woman or not, she is still an officer and should act accordingly.* She temporarily lost her outer cuteness one day when she started barking orders at me and some other lower-ranking soldiers about how we needed to hustle faster for some reason or another. "Yes ma'am," I would say, smiling, thinking the whole time, *Yeah, whatever.* She had a falling out with a few of the male marine students, including my roommate whom I mentioned earlier, followed by an actual falling out of one of our mandatory group running exercises that we did first thing in the morning.

When running with a large group, from platoon size (around thirty to forty soldiers divided into four squads) on up to a larger company-size unit of multiple platoons, it is common for one member of each platoon to *call cadence* for his or her

18

respective platoon. Cadence is a way to keep the troops marching, or running, in step with each other, as well as provide entertainment and keep one's mind off any experienced physical pain. Usually the cadence caller will say or sing a line, and the rest of the platoon will repeat the line one time, running or marching along the way. For example, "*Left . . . left . . . left, right, left,*" is repeated by the other soldiers, as the left foot hits the ground on *left* and the right foot hits between each *left* and on the word *right*. It takes some getting used to. Calling cadence is something I liked doing, and later on in my Airborne Ranger unit, I was one of the few privates who volunteered to do it on a regular basis. But we rarely went on "fun" platoon-size runs or larger, focusing instead on strength and speed conditioning of squad-size workouts. One of my favorite cadences: *Me and Superman got into a fight. I hit him in the head with some kryptonite. I hit him so hard that he went insane, now I'm doin' Lois Lane.* Anyway, certain marines got into hot water with this 2LT because of the use of profanity and/or obscenities in their cadences, which she found offensive. I believe she went to a black hat and filed a complaint, after which these marines were prohibited from using profane/obscene language during group-run activities. They literally had the last laugh when she fell out of a run, meaning that she couldn't keep up and bailed out. When most soldiers fall out of a run, they at least continue to run at their own pace. She just stopped running altogether. In airborne school, failure to maintain a nine-minute-mile run time (plus or minus fifteen seconds per mile), which is much slower than other military running standards, was grounds for expulsion or recycle. She was summarily recycled. Later on down the road, after I completed airborne school, I saw her at a local military supermarket, known as a PX (Post Exchange). She utilized crutches for a broken leg. And she was still a *leg* for not having completed airborne school.

It was at the end of *ground week* when I made my first venture into the city of Columbus, just outside of Fort Benning. I had 700 and some odd dollars in my bank account. This was serious cash, seeing as though just four months prior I was depending on my parents and my father for $10 here and $40 there. Plus, any money I had in the pre-army days went toward the beer-consuming sexual escapades that my girlfriend and I often held at a local motel. Here I was now, a certified army infantryman—fit (so I thought), girlfriendless, with money to burn. So where did I go on my first free weekend? To a strip club of course. And one of the main roads running right through Columbus, Victory Drive (also known as VD drive), was full of them. They ranged from dumpy little holes in the wall where the "exotic dancers" were anything but exotic or dancers, to exclusive nightspots frequented by well-to-do business gadabouts. Though I've made appearances at a few strip joints back in my day, I can honestly say that they were not something that I was into, unlike other soldiers whom I've known. I knew guys that would go to strip clubs almost every weekend and spend nearly a whole paycheck on inflated drink prices and g-string dollar-bill stuffings, only to come home empty-handed. My philosophy, "If I can't touch it (or myself), then I don't want to look at it." But I also know of soldiers who married strippers/dancers, often because of an unexpected pregnancy—pretty standard. Though love may be in the air, or in bed, soldiers make for appetizing meal tickets. Once, in my Ranger past, I did hook up for a "night-cap" with a waitress/dancer from one of the lower-end establishments. And right after that, she—my friends and I referred to her as ET because of some resembling features to the movie star—wanted my friend Pete, who wisely (this instance), declined. But then our mutual friend, Thomas, went after her a few days later on his motorcycle. As an airborne school student at a strip club for the first time in Georgia (I went to a couple down in Tijuana, Mexico, when I was in high school), I asked a young lady who worked there, "How about $40?" not so subtly hinting that I was interested in more than just dancing and superficial conversation. Her reply, "You better add another zero to that." Touché. I took a cab back to the barracks, alone, and passed out in a drunken stupor.

Going to airborne training every day (Monday to Friday) was a bit like going to a comedy club. Well, at least it was like that in my company, I was to find out later. The airborne staff, or black hats, would put on hilarious presentations (skits) about how to properly leap from an aircraft or land from a jump before having us go forward with the training ourselves. Besides this entertainment value, eating at Burger King regularly (mmm, Whopper), and actually jumping from airplanes, the rest of airborne school after *ground week* was pretty uneventful. At the end of *tower week*, after having "mastered" the art of the PLF (perfect landing fault)—ending a jump by landing on the balls of your feet, knees bent slightly, both arms bent at the elbows and protecting your face, and doing somewhat of a combat roll upon impact with the ground—we were hoisted to the top of a 250-foot tower, parachute and all, and released. The point of this exercise was to see if we had indeed learned the art of the PLF. But for some reason we were not required to receive a GO in this instance in order to advance to *jump week*. This was good, because I got yelled at for not properly landing. "Why didn't you do a proper PLF, hah, Airborne, why?" I got up from my improper landing, didn't say a word to this instructor, and ran out of the training area. Around the base of the towers (there were three or four), soft dirt blanketed the ground, making it almost impossible to get hurt, even if you didn't land "correctly." Real drop zones (DZ's) are much harder, often producing sprained angles or worse. In the film *Independence Day* with Will Smith, there is a scene where he parachutes from his aircraft after a run-in with an alien vessel, landing with a painful thud.[V] Yeah, it's kind of like that.

During the final week of airborne school, *jump week*, we performed five airborne jumps of various standards. A couple of jumps were with a C-130 prop-propelled plane and the others were from a C-141 jet-powered aircraft—the latter being the preferred choice of the airborne ranger units. As well, on some jumps we had to wear "combat gear," meaning a lightly packed rucksack with a side carrying case for our weapon/firearm. In airborne school, we used "rubber duckies"—rubber-made toy M-16 rifles—instead of real weapons. And our "combat" loads were a pittance of what I had to actually carry in my days of training for combat with the Army Rangers. I can't remember what my very first jump was like, but I do remember specific jumps since then. Regardless, every jump, whether it's the third or the fifty-third, is an adrenaline rush like no other. And part of the excitement and exhilaration starts long before you actually exit the aircraft. In accordance with standard airborne procedures, while sitting there lined against the wall of the aircraft as the plane makes its way toward the drop zone (DZ), you get the word from the *jump-master* (he or she, having successfully completed jumpmaster school, is supposed to make sure the jump itself goes smoothly), "Ten minutes," as you repeat it down the line and flash the hand gesture for ten minutes, loudly letting each other know how much time before reaching the DZ. Then, I believe, "Stand up," is again repeated down the line. This is followed by, "Hook up," at which point you hook the end of your chute, the hook, to the static line running above you down the length of the plane. Next comes, "One minute," followed by, "Thirty seconds." During this whole preparation time, I would usually focus on the little light next to the open door of the aircraft. When you see it turn from red to green, you know it's time to go. "Go, go, go," as streams of paratroopers jump from the airplane, counting, "1000, 2000, 3000, 4000," in anticipation of the chute opening. If it doesn't, try the reserve. Once in the air, the whole scenario lasts what seems like a fast thirty seconds.

In airborne school, after a successful jump, we hopped on buses that took us back to our barracks. How I longed for those buses when I was in Ranger battalion, where a jump was usually followed by a long trek through the pitch-black night of the woods and the start of some five-day outdoor training exercise. During *jump week*, one black hat told a group of us, "Come back and see me when you have a sixth jump." At that time, there was money to burn and soldiers would spend taxpayers' money by attending airborne school just for kicks, never planning on jumping after that. "Five-jump chumps," we called them.

Graduation day from airborne school came at the end of October 1991, on Halloween as I recall. Again, my father made his way down to Fort Benning, Georgia, for the festivities. This time, I was out in the ranks with all of the other trainees, wearing our BDU's (battle dress uniform)—the camouflaged everyday work uniform. During the ceremony, there were a few dignitaries and high-ranking officers in attendance, a couple who gave keynote remarks, welcoming a new generation of airborne soldiers. I remember that one student among the graduating trainees, as announced during the ceremony, was the son of "such and such colonel" or someone of higher rank and importance. Not so coincidentally, this student received the distinction of being named honor graduate. Though this trainee may have been a good student, or even a great one, this confirmed my belief that the military is a highly nepotistic organization. This is not to say that the children of high-ranking somebodies are not expected to perform well. But I remember it being odd back in basic training when the drill instructors told us to list the names and ranks of any relatives we might have had who were currently serving in the military. More poignantly, I remember them inquiring about high-ranking relatives of ours. I didn't have any, low or high, except for my sister Sandy, who was enlisted in the army reserves. It was a special moment for me, and probably more so for my father, when he came down from the stands after the ceremony, along with other guests in attendance, and pinned on my airborne wings. The tradition is that you are supposed to have your "blood wings" pinned on by having someone, usually a fellow soldier, pound the two metal-tipped backings of the wings into your chest. Just a couple of years ago, some marines were caught on film hazing some other soldiers in this manner, taking this "tradition" to the extreme. I told my father that he had to hit the wings into my chest. He lightly tapped them, not wanting to hurt me, as no father should want to do to his kid. But I would get my share of "hazing" as an Airborne Ranger upon being promoted from a lowly private third class (pay grade of E-1) to a private second class (E-2). With infantry school complete and newly acquired airborne wings upon my chest, I was now qualified to administer, as the airborne motto stated, "Death from above."

RIP

It was in **RIP** (Ranger Indoctrination Program) where I would get my sixth and even seventh jump, thus dodging the "five-jump chump" status, as well as get a glimpse of what being a ranger was all about. Before going off to serve, I asked my recruiter if Ranger training would be tough. In his honest style, he said that my body would be dragging with exhaustion much of the time. Though this was often the case later on, I did not find **RIP** to be overly challenging, except for the mental letdown of being recycled. **RIP** was basically a two-and-a-half week "smoke session," where the Ranger instructors pushed us mentally and physically to extreme limits, often to a point where quitting seemed like a viably acceptable option. Usually, as long as a soldier did not quit the program, he would graduate from **RIP**. The real extremes didn't begin until after becoming an Airborne Ranger.

I believe it was graduation day from airborne school when we had to check into our **RIP** barracks, with training starting the upcoming Monday. **RIP** representatives, but not actual instructors with the program, came to greet and march us to our new homes—this time, literally just down the street. Our "welcoming" into **RIP** was done in a public setting, allowing the guests who came to watch us get our airborne wings to witness our first encounter with Ranger training. I think that because we had family (my father) and friends there, they went a little easier on us than normal. This was not out of sympathy for us necessarily, but to cover their own asses in the face of a parent who might get upset about how his or her son was being treated. My biggest fear then, and moments thereafter, was being humiliated and degraded in front of civilians, and not just my father. It is one thing for your superiors to treat you like a private among other soldiers, and it's another to be treated like garbage among civilians who might view your situation as if they were watching a circus act. At least, that's how I felt they would see it. Either that or they would hold pity for you in their hearts and minds. But which is worse: being pitied or being seen as a clown? Upon checking in at the RIP barracks and being assigned rooms, we were cut loose for the weekend.

RIP began in early November, and by this time, Georgia was cooling off quite a bit. Although the state gets nowhere near the freezing temperature of some of the Yankee states of the north, the ground does tend to freeze over at points during the winter. After having trained in cold and wet weather, most notably in South Korea, I'll take hot and dry, even humid, any day. Even now when it rains, eight years since my army service ended, I still think to myself and sometimes aloud, "Well, at least I'm not sleeping in it tonight," when so many persons were, are, and will be.

On the first day of RIP, we took the Army PT test, which was broken into three components—push-ups (PU), sit-ups (SU), and the two-mile run. The first two categories were timed separately, measuring how many of each we could do in two minutes. The run, as I explained earlier, was at our own pace and we were given points based on our performance time. The same for the push-ups and sit-ups—you were rewarded a number of points for however many you could do within the allotted time. The most points you could technically score on a PT test was 300, and I believe that 210 was the army standard for infantrymen; 240 was the standard for Rangers, but was considered a very weak score among fellow Rangers. I never scored all that well in push-ups and sit-ups as far as Ranger standards were concerned, my highest total score being 270—100 points on the run and 85 points each for PU and SU. But I could hold my own on long road marches as few others could, which usually helped keep me out of trouble with my Ranger superiors—temporarily anyway. I passed this first PT test in RIP, even doing the required number of pull-ups that were tacked onto the test as an extra measure of strength. I was riding high during this first week of training, especially after finding out that all of the requirements we were obliged to accomplish during RIP (PT test, 5-mile run, 8 to 12-mile road march, combat water survival test or CWST, and possibly others) seemed to be fairly simplistic for a fit airborne Infantryman such as myself. And hell, I already completed the PT test. So I thought.

During the second week of RIP, I was exhausted with a cold/flu. As is the case with the changing of the seasons, like many persons, I get sick. But this was no four-day standard cold. Making it worse, I had to redo part of my PT test in such a state. After receiving a "block of instruction" on some issue of Rangerness, I was called out of the bleachers with some other trainees. We were informed that our pull-ups on the PT test had not been recorded and we had to do them again, right then and there at a nearby pull-up bar. I panicked, knowing that I couldn't do the four pull-ups, or whatever the required amount was. Thus not only did I fail the ranger code of readily displaying "intestinal fortitude," I failed my first attempt at RIP and was at once assigned to holdover status, where I was to be recycled to the next RIP training class.

During my time as a holdover (about two weeks), waiting for the next RIP class to begin, I was laid up in the "sick ward" with about ten other soldiers suffering from the same illness. I remember taking some kind of slumber-inducing medication to help me sleep, only to be called to formation for some reason with all of

24

the other holdovers. I stood there in my PT uniform (light gray sweat pants and a light gray zip-up sweat shirt with the word *ARMY* sprawled across the front), ready to pass out because of the effects of the consumed medicine. While a holdover, I dreaded the prospect of starting RIP again and felt as if my efforts the first time had been in vain. Working hard for something and then not having that *something* come to fruition is an excruciating thought. I contemplated quitting, but I would have preferred getting kicked out before giving up. I heard from my grandfather Shakes that my mother had asked him if he thought I would quit. His comment to me, "Hell, I'm proud of what you've done already. It doesn't matter what you do [now]." Needless to say, I didn't quit.

The next RIP training class I was to be a part of started the day after the long Thanksgiving weekend. We were not assured by the holdover cadre that we would be cut loose for the holiday, unless of course we had a schmoozer for a father. And again, my father placed a call and talked to one of the higher-ranking sergeants in charge. So I was free to head up to Gadsden, Alabama, with my father, to visit my two aunts and many cousins for the holiday festivities, which they nicely do every year—still. This was one of three Thanksgivings I would spend there during my tenure at Fort Benning. The other two times, I brought some fellow Ranger buddies along, and they were thoroughly impressed with the good vittles and hospitality. From Fort Benning, Gadsden was only about a three-and-a-half-hour drive by car. By Greyhound bus, it was much longer. A couple of times I took the bus in either direction, to or from. On these particular occasions, my father could not drive me back to Fort Benning. Some interesting characters often ride the bus, to say the least. And this trip, being my initiation into the American trademark that is Greyhound, was no exception.

On my way back to Fort Benning, I met a young Alabamian gal, and we chatted it up a bit. I was attracted to her, mostly because I had not had the intimate company of a woman in a long while. I gave her quite the spiel about my California liberal wisdom and "open-mindedness" regarding different races. She dug it. And though she said her boyfriend, or mother, might be meeting her upon arrival, I didn't care. We were all over each other, keeping it just under an "R" rating for the most part on the almost-empty bus journey to Montgomery, where we both changed buses and headed off in separate directions. I've always detested the actions of a person who would willingly cheat on a loved-one or spouse, but I had zero qualms about hitting on someone else's girlfriend or wife, as long as I wasn't friends with the guy. And for the first couple of years of service, I had a really negative image of women as a whole. I heard too many stories, some of which I had seen for myself, about wives or girlfriends of servicemen out at dance clubs and bars, having a grand old time with other men, while lavishly spending their husband's and/or boyfriend's paycheck. Plus, I felt as if I had been able to take a critical look back at what I now saw as a subservient relationship with my high school "sweetheart," with the conclusion, "never again!" Perhaps a bit sadistic, I would often leave a visual bite mark or ten (multiple hickies) on such an unfaithful woman's neck, when provided the opportunity, hoping that her "significant other" would discover who she really is. I never took into account that possibly the guy was at fault in the relationship, and that she might be trying to find a way out of the situation. I didn't watch Oprah at the time, and where were you then, Dr. Phil? Not that I watch them now. Anyway, I did the same to my Greyhound companion, who was all of fifteen years old, leaving a purple streak from one ear to the other. I was a teenager as well—eighteen, to be exact.

I arrived back at the RIP barracks after the long holiday weekend, fat, not so happy, and definitely not looking forward to starting a new RIP cycle. Nonetheless, I started and made it through this time. Along with doing the PT test and other physical challenges, as future Rangers, it was imperative that we learn Ranger history. An old roommate of mine—Chuck—from my days at the University of California, Santa Barbara, would later quote, "When you get your bachelor's degree, you think you know everything. When you get your master's degree, you realize you know nothing. When you get your Ph.D., you realize that no one else knows anything either." Well, with a high school diploma marked with a golden seal, proving that I had achieved high honors on the California Golden State Exam for history, I thought myself to be a genius, in history anyway.

In the service, I enjoyed reading a few historical works, at my own leisure. But I hated the mandatory learning of Ranger history imposed upon us by our higher-ups, though I did retain a few tidbits of knowledge regarding that history after constantly being bombarded with trivial information. One reason I prefer working with students at the university level—the choice to learn is up to each student. Supposedly, the Ranger motto of "Rangers lead the way" was christened during the Second World War on the beaches of Normandy, when a non-Ranger officer pointed to the French cliffs of *pointe du hoc*, turned to the Rangers assembled and said, "Rangers, lead the way." It's an image straight from a Hollywood movie, and that's how our superiors wanted us to see it, not that they didn't believe the "magic" themselves. In fact, Tom Hanks' character and the troops he commands in *Saving Private Ryan* are Army Rangers who land on Normandy.[VI] What irked me later on were Rangers who claimed to be the inheritors of the same standards and traditions of those who fought and died liberating Western Europe from Nazism's clutch, viewing their own measly actions of training for combat as being of equal importance. That's like equating General Schwarzkoff's actions in Iraq with those of Patton or Eisenhower in Europe, which some in the media attempted to do. As well, there were Rangers who had jumped into the third-rate countries of Panama and Grenada—not exactly Hitler's fortress—earning *combat jump wings* in the process. Part of Ranger history also included an understanding of the black beret's coveted features, including the shielded icon in front with all of its symbols and how they came to be. At the time, Airborne Rangers were the only ones in the army authorized to wear the unique black beret. Now that the entire army wears them, I believe that they have switched to the less than appealing coffee/mocha-colored beret.

Part of being an Airborne Ranger, more important than knowing Ranger history, was the ability to recite the six stanzas of the *Ranger Creed* on cue. Each stanza, or line of the creed, began with a letter from the word RANGER (hence six letters, six stanzas). At one time I did know them all by heart. I had to. I would not have made it for two years in a Ranger battalion without having known them. But I do remember that the E, the fifth stanza, was the longest, beginning with, "Energetically will I meet the enemies of my country. I shall. . . ." The third stanza referred to the Ranger ethic of never leaving a fallen comrade behind in combat, no matter if he was dead or alive. Later on, after army service, my friend Richard from the Ranger days made a very good point. He said something like, "If I fell [dead] in combat and my being carried afterward were to slow down the unit's mission, I would rather be left behind." If Rangers truly wanted to live up to the standards of the Second World War, they would opt for burying their comrades where they fell or in a nearby military cemetery, as they did in Europe, of course, after the battle had been won.

It was at the end of the first or second week of RIP when each one of us trainees had to officially report to a sergeant from the cadre, where it was determined whether or not we were to be reprimanded to *Saturday school*. Such a "school" involved remedial training for those of us who were not up to par, so to speak. There was no way in hell I was giving up a Saturday to do PT, wall-locker inspections (where we stored our gear), or a host of other "jump through the hoop" activities. I waited in line for my turn to address one of the sergeants, when I overheard some private during his session getting chewed out for not having a pen on his person. We were required to carry a pen and a small notebook at all times. Today's newer and smarter soldier is always ready to learn. This pen-less private was given Saturday school, while being screamed at by the sergeant. He was then summarily made to *low crawl* (part of the infantry movement technique—where a soldier gets as flat as possible on the ground and moves by crawling along) out of the room. A few other privates and I heard and saw this go down, so we quickly made sure that we had pens handy. My turn was coming up, as my heart started beating faster. I finally went into the room where one of the meaner sergeants sat. Wearing my no-bullshit face, I positioned myself at *parade rest*. He then started, "Recite the fifth stanza of the *Ranger Creed*." Not missing a beat, I belted it as loud and as clear as I could, "Energetically will I meet the enemies of my country!" while staring straight ahead the whole time. I think I actually startled this sergeant a bit. At least I like to think so. He kept looking around the room and at another sergeant, as if to express, "This guy's not f'ing around." I was summarily free to enjoy Saturday in its entirety.

The last few days of RIP involved a "field problem," where we went out into the woods around Fort Benning and did some infantry training—practice raids on "enemies," ambushes, and things of that sort. We started it off with an airborne insertion into the pitch-black night, making this my first jump outside of airborne school. This jump was particularly memorable for the safety factor involved. Upon exiting the aircraft and counting four thousand, I immediately noticed that my chute was tangled with that of another RIP trainee. We were little more than two arm-lengths apart, speaking, and panicking, in a dialogue the whole way down. I remember him, alongside his prayers to the Lord, asking me, "Should we pull our reserves?" "How fast are we falling?" I shakily answered back, while looking around the sky, trying to compare the falling rate of other parachutists. It was really dark though, absent of the moon's illumination that I would truly come to appreciate in the future. I could barely make out some shapes of other parachutes. While we were trying to decide what to do, I looked down, "Oh shit, the ground," as we hit at what seemed to be a normal level of impact. I was shaking pretty bad as I hurriedly put my chute into its carrying bag. For training purposes, we usually had to turn our chutes into a collection point after each jump. But our chutes were so intertwined that we had to pack what we could into each bag, and then walk together to the collection point. It was so dark out that we could not even see each other's faces, and I hadn't known this trainee prior to this occasion. So we exchanged names, shook hands, and then went off to our separate rallying destinations. After completing our time in the field, a trainee came up to me in front of our barracks in broad daylight. He asked, "Are you Donayre?" even though my nametag clearly identified that I was. Upon my "yes" reply, he said, "I'm *so and so* from the jump the other night." "Nice to meet you," I responded, smiling and shaking his hand, once again. The Ranger Indoctrination Program was complete.

Cherry Ranger

A community college professor of mine, Arturo Diaz, once explained the irony of the United States of America, and for that matter, all Republican forms of government past, present, and future, "It takes an authoritarian organization—the military—to defend a democracy," or the superstructure, as the dead Karl Marx would call it. Professor Diaz, who is also a veteran of the armed forces, clarified, "If an officer [or a sergeant] tells a private to pick up a piece of trash, the private won't question 'why?'" In the authoritarian suborganization known as Ranger battalion, there were three levels of soldiering—falling by the wayside (because of a lack of soldiering), conforming to become an ideal follower (the perfect soldier), and becoming an authoritarian (a leader with command over other soldiers). As a Ranger, I was stuck at level one for the first nine months, eventually progressing to level two with lapses now and again back to the first level, and then brief, but unwanted flirtations with level three.

My graduation from RIP, in mid-December 1991, was unceremonious. But I can't recall for certain, so it must not have been something to write about. After RIP, all of us *cherry*, meaning inexperienced and new, Airborne Rangers departed for one of the three Ranger battalions that fell under the umbrella of the 75th Ranger Regiment, headquartered at Fort Benning, Georgia. We were asked early on in RIP which ranger battalion we would prefer to be stationed at; there was 1st Ranger Battalion, or simply 1st Bat, out of Savannah, Georgia, on the east coast; 2nd Bat was located up at Fort Lewis, Washington State, near Seattle; and then there was my future home of 3rd Bat, literally right next door to the RIP compound. I knew guys from California who requested to be up in 2nd Bat out of Washington, making their duty station a little bit closer to home. Partly because I was lazy and didn't want to trek my gear across the country, I requested to stay in Fort Benning. Plus I knew that it rained quite a bit up in Washington, and I already had family relatively close by in Alabama. Besides, the journey from Fort

Lewis to San Diego was no short hike, probably sixteen to twenty hours by car. So I got my wish. Upon completing the Ranger Indoctrination Program and receiving the coveted black beret, I headed off to 3/75 (3rd Ranger Battalion of the 75th Ranger Regiment) next door.

Someone from 3rd Bat Headquarters (HQ Company) came over to the RIP barracks and escorted those of us who were bound for 3rd Bat. I remember all of the trainees standing inside HQ, a bit scared about the unknown, and locked up at the position of *parade rest.* We were told that if we knew anyone who was already in one of the three "rifle" companies—Alpha, Bravo, or Charlie—we could request to be assigned to that particular unit. I had friends from RIP who were determined to stick together and request C (Charlie) Company, since we all knew prior *ripies* (soldiers in RIP) who were already working there. I never agreed to this. I remained a bit skeptical, viewing this attempt to "ease" our way into Ranger life as a ploy to entrap us somehow, which would be held against us later. I could hear it, "So, you are buddies with so and so. We'll see about that." As well, I thought maybe it would just be better, meaning easier, to go some place where I would be unknown—sort of a fresh and untarnished beginning. I've found that since then, in life, it is often more rewarding and exciting to start anew and build up, trying at times no doubt, while adding on to prior experiences in the process. So I stood there in the area of cherries without current Ranger friends, where I was randomly assigned to Alpha Company. To be exact, I was attached to Weapons Squad, 2nd Platoon, Alpha Company, where I would work for the next twenty-six months.

I was initially upset, with periodic bouts of anxiety and depression, about being assigned to a weapons squad—those who used the crew-served M-60 (automatic) machine guns that provided seventy-five percent of a platoon's fire power. The term *crew-served* is what first turned me off about being assigned to a weapons squad. In my illusions of grandeur about what it means to serve in the army, I pictured myself as an "independent" rifleman—nothing more, nothing less—charging the enemy with a fixed bayonet and a couple of grenades on my belt, just in case. Playing football in high school, running down the field on the special teams unit (kickoff), I would imagine what it must have been like charging the German-entrenched pillboxes of Normandy on D-day. Here I was now, in a peacetime situation, relegated to the lowly position of ammunition (ammo) bearer/assistant gunner to one of the three M-60 gun teams of weapons squad.

The gunner, who is first in charge as the gun team leader (the authoritarian), carries and operates the twenty-three-pound gun, making sure that his assistant gunner (AG) and/or ammunition bearer (AB) helps maintain the operation and perfection of the gun. As the gun is being fired, the assistant helps identify targets "down range," feeds the gun its ammunition, and changes the barrel of the gun if something should go wrong with the primary barrel. I've heard that because the assistant has more responsibilities, on the surface, this position in the Marine Corps is held by the gun team leader, while the gunner is actually second in charge. This makes sense, but as in life, it's usually the person not in charge who does the *grunt* work. And then there is the third in command—the ammo bearer. The name says it all.

He carries belts of ammo for the gun, taking over the gun's firing operations should both the gunner and the assistant fall in combat or in training. But usually, weapons squad did not have enough soldiers for the luxury of having three-man gun teams. For each team, there was usually only the gunner and his assistant gunner, who carried the tripod and assembly pieces for mounting the gun, the spare gun barrel, his own weapon (a rifle and/or a 9 millimeter pistol for a sidearm—the gunner also carried the latter), and much of the ammunition. If a gunner was an asshole, under the facade of trying to toughen up his assistant, he would make the AG carry all of the ammo, minus the rounds attached to the gun itself. During the brief episodes when I was a gunner in Ranger Bat, and later on while serving in South Korea, I would usually split the ammo load down the middle with my assistant. Each 100-round belt of ammo weighed roughly 6.5 pounds. And of course, carrying rounds of ammo for the *Sixty*, as the M-60 was referred to, was in addition to the other 50, 60, 70 pounds of gear in your rucksack that you were already struggling with. I remember having a pack so heavy that I could not physically lift it with my arms and place it on my back. I had to sit down, lean back against it, placing one arm through the left strap and the other through the right, and then roll over to my front and push myself up to my knees, gradually standing up. I was pretty stubborn about asking for help with my gear. The less help received, the less debt accumulated. I think one reason I currently have arthritic-type pains that periodically "attack" my back is from carrying all of that weight back then. Shortly after arriving at 3rd Bat, an ex-squad leader of weapons squad, one Sergeant Sam, laughingly remarked, "Being in weapons squad, you'll have arthritis by the time you're twenty."

I arrived at 3rd Bat in the middle of December 1991, just in time to be inundated with war stories about the Ranger victory in Panama from two years prior, back when I was a sophomore in high school. I heard about the adrenaline rush of Rangers standing in the plane, ready to parachute into combat, reciting the *Ranger Creed*—the 5th Stanza in particular—as rounds from the enemy below strafed the aircraft. But I also heard about a PFC (private first class with a pay-grade of E-3) who had been killed during the operations. Supposedly, he was a *door jumper* (the first one to exit the aircraft) and was hit while standing in the door ready to go. In a drunken haze, one of my superiors told me that this PFC would have been, by now, a specialist (SPC, E-4), also known as a Speck 4. This is the purgatorial rank between private and sergeant. What do you say to those who have been in combat? Nothing, especially if you are a newbie cherry. Just stand back, show respect, and feign interest—real or false.

As a new soldier, you can't help but think, *I wonder what I would have done in the same situation. Would I have lived up to the Ranger code of excellence in the face of death?* But after a while, one gets tired of hearing, "I was there, and you weren't!" And then of course, many Rangers air-landed in Panama after the drop zone was already clear of hostile threats. Such was the case of a sergeant I knew in Korea, who parachuted into Panama with the 82nd Airborne, after the Rangers initially secured the area. He wore a "combat" patch on his right soldier, signifying that he had been to "war" with the 82nd. He often gave me hell for having been a Ranger, and for wearing my 3/75 Ranger scroll on my uniform. Officially authorized by the army, I proudly wore this scroll/patch for having served in Somalia with the Rangers, despite seeing limited to no action. As I would boastfully chant when calling cadence in Korea: *Up from the DMZ* [demilitarized zone] *down below, comes an airborne scout with a combat scroll.* In Korea, for the first six months of my thirteen-month tour, I was in the only American scout platoon that conducted "combat" patrols—technically the two Koreas are still at war with each other—along North Korea's border with the South, qualifying me to wear some other type of medal and/or patch. But in Korea, as many of us soldiers knew, if shit hit the fan, the scouts I was with would have been mere speed bumps, barely slowing the advance of the Korean "People's" Army (KPA) of Kim Il Sung, and now son Kim Jong-Il, up in the North, until units like the Rangers could make their way over to the peninsula and reinforce our futile efforts to stave off a North Korean invasion. We would win eventually, but my fellow scouts and I would have been annihilated in the process.

There was a lot of barracks time and less field time than when I first got to battalion. After all, 3rd Bat was about to go on its *block leave*, meaning that its turn to take vacation among all three Ranger battalions was coming up. During the summer and winter, each battalion had a designated fifteen-day block in which to take leave. If you were a Ranger and you refused to take leave when your unit did, that meant you would have to wait until the next *block leave* was available—five to six months later—to go on vacation. When one Ranger battalion was on leave, the others remained on a heightened-alert status, in case of a worldwide need of quick deployment. On this RRF (ranger ready force) status, the barracks guard on duty had to be able to get hold of every soldier in case of an alert or practice alert. A phone number would have to be left at the front desk of where you would be, and we couldn't be more than an hour's drive away from Fort Benning. Many guys carried beepers. Cell phones weren't available on a mass and affordable scale then. Some soldiers actually got kicked out of battalion because a practice alert was put into effect, and they were up in Atlanta or somewhere outside of the authorized vicinity.

As I mentioned earlier, I had a few friends, cherries like myself, who were attached to Charlie Company a couple of barracks down from mine. Being a new guy in weapons squad, I really didn't care to hang out with other members of it when we were off duty. Besides, I didn't feel right about drinking beers with persons who spent their time yelling at me or making me do push-ups and flutter kicks (lying on your back, hands overlapping and placed underneath you in the small of your back, while moving your legs back and forth, up and down, one after the other, no more than six inches off the ground while trying not to rest them on the ground) in exorbitant amounts. Besides, I have never been the type of person to make friends by asking, "Will you be my friend?" Friendships should evolve and not be forced. So I had preexisting and developed friendships from RIP, which lasted until I eventually became friends with persons from my own squad and platoon. Anyway, during our RRF alert status, one day I wrote on the front desk board that I was at Charlie Company, where I ended up hanging out the whole weekend. I remember coming back to Alpha Company on a Sunday afternoon—the time when we were expected to make our two-person rooms spotless for the start of the workweek. Simon, my AG (I was the ammo bearer), who eventually became my gunner, wasn't too happy that I took off for the weekend and didn't leave a valid contact number. "But I wrote Charlie Company on the board," I pleaded in my defense. Perturbed, he yelled a bit, making me do remedial PT exercises.

Private Simon, later to become Sergeant Simon, was unlike any other soldier I had met in Ranger battalion. He was actually a couple of months younger than me but had remained my superior the entire time I was in battalion, arriving there just two months before I had. It is common for a soldier, not in my case, to catch another in rank and even pass up a superior. Even if I wanted to, it would have been hard as hell to ever match him in rank. I think he holds the Ranger peace-time record for fastest promotion to the rank of Sergeant (E-5). At times I envied him for his motivation and dedication to being a great soldier, and at other times I despised him for the same reasons. When I got to weapons squad, he was still pretty much a cherry, although he had proven himself on a few occasions. His most recent PT test score was 299 out of 300. My first one in battalion was an appalling 250-something. Plus, he was always striving to learn new techniques of Ranger operations, studying his Ranger handbook during his off time and taking notes in the process. I thought, *Jeez, live a little*. About a year later when we were both twenty years old, he gave my roommate—his ammo bearer—Jim (twenty-one years old), shit for caring more about "going down to Panama City [Florida] and chasing women" than bettering his work performance within weapons squad. I thought it was kind of sad on one hand, *what are you doing if you aren't chasing women at the age of twenty, twenty-one?* But on the other hand, I saw Simon's point. What if we get called into combat tomorrow and Jim, or any other cherry, is not properly prepared? Needless to say, Simon was one of the few privates who actually *commanded* respect from some of the sergeants in the platoon. Well that's what it seemed like anyway. At times, when he wasn't trying to be my superior, we were on friendly terms, especially after I had passed many cherry hurdles. I was "accused" one time by Jim of trying to be like Simon. One reason being, because I went out and bought the same type of knife that he used—a *Spyderco*. It was a very good knife, with jagged and sharp edges for easy cutting, and a few Rangers had similar ones like it. Jim hated Simon, probably to this day, based on one "smoke session" that Simon administered upon Jim.

When Jim arrived at battalion, about a year after I did, he was briefly the ammo bearer of our three-man gun team, with Simon serving as the gunner. We barely spent any proper time training Jim on the M-60. It was partly my fault. I should have taken more of an initiative to do so, but bottom line—the gunner is ultimately responsible. One day Jim, in preparation for completing the required tasks to receive an expert infantry badge (EIB), or "Everybody In [Ranger] Battalion," could not even perform some basic tasks with the M-60. This made our gun team look bad, and in turn, made our gunner, Simon, take "corrective measures" to bring Jim "up to speed" on the gun. He had him doing gun drills, like disassembling and reassembling it, over and over, while screaming at him the whole time. Jim, in a pool of sweat and with shot nerves, did learn some basics of the gun that day, but came to hold eternal contempt for Simon in the process. One reason I never cared about becoming a sergeant in the army is that I prefer not to yell at privates, which I did on a couple of occasions. It's just not something I ever wanted to get used to. I'm not sure which involves more yelling though, being a leader in Ranger battalion, or being a substitute teacher in the civilian world— I flirted with both jobs briefly. The latter definitely pays better and is less dangerous, but profanity cannot be used to get a point across to the kids. Jim helped me realize that I am a teacher and not a leader when he said, "You are more of a teacher than a leader." He meant this as a compliment. My style for welcoming new privates was not to break them down (even though *I* was "broken down") but to welcome them around the platoon as if they were new neighbors who just moved into the building. But I also know that my way was not the correct one. It's necessary to be tough on new recruits who might be shipped off to kill or be killed at any point. There are plenty of ambitious soldiers willing to play this toughening-up role. I was not needed for it. As I said, I wanted to be an *independent rifleman*—no more, no less.

The leader of weapons squad—the *squad leader*—was Sergeant Shilling. He was one of the ugliest and meanest persons whom I first encountered in the unit. This first characteristic was due mainly to the two black eyes he had supposedly received from someone or something after a night of severe intoxication. The story was that he blacked out, fell, and hit his head, causing his face around the eyes to look as though he had the shit beat out of him. His job as squad leader was to make sure the three gun teams were *squared away*—an army term meaning *good to go* or *up to standard*—and the three gunners reported directly to him. During my first encounter with Shilling, he came barging into my room and made me do flutter kicks alongside him until I could barely lift my legs anymore. I was being "smoked" because I had left my wall-locker open, with its personal contents within stealing range, even though I had asked my roommate to keep an eye on it. He said something like, "Ranger, why are your legs touching the ground? You should be able to keep up with me." "But I can't keep up with you, Sergeant," I said, "You're the squad leader." Then he made a seemingly conciliatory statement as if to say, "Never quit; no matter who you are up against." After which, he had me do the *roman chair*, I think it was called, where you put your back against the wall and squat down with arms extended, as if you are indeed *the* chair. In a drenched sweat and with legs quivering, I was saved by the "bell." It was time for a company formation outside. It's a bit ironic that I got into trouble for not personally safeguarding my own effects, though this was actually just an excuse to make me sweat. A week or two later, Specialist Murray, known by some in the platoon as "the philosopher," gave me hell for standing guard over my own laundry in the *latrine* (army lingo for bathroom), where we had a washer and dryer. He said, "What, do you think we're thieves around here or something? Go chill out in your room until your laundry's done. Nobody's going to take your clothes." During my first six months in battalion, there was indeed a "barracks thief" going around stealing PT uniforms and other clothing out of the washers and/or dryers. I don't think he was ever caught.

A few days before we went on block leave, the entire battalion—Alpha, Bravo, Charlie, and HQ Companies—went on a "motivation" run around Fort Benning's airfield (about eight-nine miles), where military aircraft flew in and out of. On this particular run, Sergeant Shilling did his damndest to make me fall out, which was of course aimed at "building me up" in the process. I fell out of two runs during my entire twenty-six-month stint in Ranger battalion, and this was not one of them (not overly impressive since many guys never fall out of runs in twenty *years* of service). As we ran in platoon formation with the other four platoons of Alpha Company, comprising one company among the other three companies of 3rd Ranger Battalion, Shilling ran behind me in formation. I wore my running shoes rather loose, and as we ran, he stepped twice on the back of one, knocking it off both times. The first time he did this, I naively thought that maybe it was an accident. I had to fall out, for a brief moment, until someone from the passing platoons fetched my shoe and tossed it to me. I put the shoe back on and sprinted up to where my platoon was. Sergeant Shilling again ran behind me, and I felt him purposely trying to knock my shoe off once more, barely missing with each attempt. He finally succeeded, and I was livid. Two words came to mind, fuck it! When I got my shoe back a second time, I decided to take the other one off and run the eight-nine miles in nothing but white socks for "protective" footgear. With both shoes in hand, I sprinted again up to where my platoon was, so I thought. I accidentally ran past my platoon and found myself running in 1st Platoon's formation, just in front of 2nd's. An E-4 (Speck 4) at the time, glanced at me, looking up and down, curious to know why I was running with the wrong platoon and with my shoes tucked away in one arm. I said, very calmly, "A sergeant keeps stepping on my shoes and making them come off. So I'll just run without them." "You'll mess up your feet running without shoes," he informed me. Then I excused myself and fell back to my platoon.

I continued to run, shoeless, but behind Shilling this time. He looked back at me, doing a quick double-take, wondering why the hell I was running without shoes. I nonchalanty said, "My shoe keeps coming off, Sergeant, so I'm just going to run without them." If anything happened to my feet, Shilling's ass would be the one in a sling with the *platoon sergeant*—his boss. He ordered me to put my shoes back on and stay behind him for the remainder of the run. Then he turned to a recently promoted Speck 4, Alexander (Alex), saying, "[The] fucker's motivated today." That episode, along with completing the run itself, when other cherries and some "old timers" fell out, earned me a little bit of respect from Sergeant Shilling and my fellow squad members. Alex, who up to that point I thought was an overambitious ass, said, "You're a pretty good runner, Donayre." I was just glad to be left alone for the rest of the day. My roommate, not as fortunate, had fallen out of the run. Although he was in a different squad, Shilling asked him, in a tone of disgust, "Are you just going to quit in combat also?" Then he left the room, saying, "Nice job, Donayre." My roommate and I had arrived in Ranger battalion at the same time. He was a small guy, barely clearing five feet. My second, and last, tobacco dip was from his can. The night we arrived in battalion, we spent the whole night cleaning our room and preparing it for inspection. I wanted the temporary buzz from tobacco, becoming nauseated afterwards. He quit Ranger battalion only a month or two in. He and another disgruntled cherry, upon their termination from battalion, had their sewn-on airborne wings ripped from their uniforms in a humiliating scene in front of the entire Alpha Company.

Our block leave was scheduled for December 30 to January 15, meaning that I had to spend my first Christmas ever away from home. It was definitely a low point as far as Christmases are concerned. Though I could not be with my family in San Diego, I had the day off from work. I ended up hanging out at the person-less bowling alley (probably the same one where that AWOL trainee from Basic went) with a couple of friends from Charlie Company. I wasn't really into bowling and didn't do it that day either. But it was one of the few places open for us soldiers stuck in Fort Benning. Between eating "tasty" bowling-alley burgers and playing video games, being a kid of the Pac-Man generation and all, I called home and told my family that I would see them in a few days.

What a change, both physical and psychological, a person can go through in just five months. There I was, back in San Diego for the first time since getting on that flight to Atlanta, via Houston, with a ranger *high and tight* for a haircut (completely shaved around the sides with no more than an inch on top, where the bald sides fade in to the hairline). The holiday season or two before this one, my mother bribed me with a few dollars into getting a haircut, so I would look presentable. This time, a friend's dad, a clean-cut navy guy, actually said more than two words to me now that I was a military man and not a long-haired bum anymore. The one-eighty he took with me was incredible. Before, it was difficult for him to muster up a "Hello Robert." Now it was (big smile), "Hey, how ya doin?" shaking my hand and asking me interested questions about life—military life.

As far as military life went, while on this first block leave, I really didn't want to go back to it, but I never entertained realistic thoughts (only fantasies), of just not showing up to my unit. Although I would have faced some sort of legal action from the army for being AWOL, I would have been ostracized from my family and shunned by much of society—probably the most detrimental situation for a person's livelihood. My grandmother Lorraine had said to me before I committed to army service, "The worst thing you can do [in life] is be a bad soldier." What makes for a worse soldier than one who doesn't report for duty? But it wasn't the army itself that I didn't want to go back to, it was the Airborne Ranger life that I had gotten myself into. I had only been in it for about two weeks before going on leave. The "life," I knew, was going to begin once I reported for duty at the end of vacation and began a new training cycle. I often thought at that point, and since then, *I should have listened to my recruiter and got one of those cush-jobs in the service, like working with computers or something.* Nonetheless, I was proud that I had even made it through RIP and was part of an elite fighting team. I must have worn my black Ranger PT sweatshirt, with the Ranger unit scroll of 3rd Battalion, 75th Ranger Regiment stitched on, all over town and even into Mexico, where I almost wore it to jail.

Going out partying with some friends from high school, we began the night on the U.S. side of the border, drinking beers in a moving car, while Mike drove. It was his car. The next thing we knew, a San Diego police car was behind us, flashing for us to pull over. Mike did, as the rest of us scrambled to hide the beers—

impossible, unless we willingly poured out our open containers of beer. We weren't willing. So the two cops had us line up facing their car, with arms and hands outstretched, while a K-9 in the back seat waited for the word to attack. As they checked out Mike's car, one of the officers joyfully tried to make us scared, saying that if we made any sudden moves, the dog would pounce on us. We didn't move. After their searching the vehicle, obviously finding bottles of alcohol, opened and unopened, we were told to go somewhere—meaning park the car—and drink the beers. "No problem, officers. Have a great night." In general, I think that the police then were a little looser with the drinking laws than they are now. After that little run-in with "San Diego's Finest," later on in the evening, we had a little run-in with Tijuana's not so finest. After hanging out at a few clubs and bars there, the five of us headed for the Mexican parking garage where the car was stored. A couple of us, myself included, decided to relieve ourselves of urine right there in some random corner of the garage. Of course, a member of the *Federali*—Mexico's federal police force—spotted us and proceeded to make an arrest. Notorious for corruption, it was either $40 apiece ($200 total) or three nights in jail for the lot of us. It turns out that we only had $40 between us, but we fortunately had one fluent Spanish speaker among the group who successfully explained our dilemma to the officer. We paid $40 total and were on our way, except that we now didn't have any money to get the car out of the garage. So we went back to a club where one guy borrowed a couple of dollars from some gal he knew. Then we headed back across the border (only four miles from my house). I should have been more thankful that everything turned out okay, but now I didn't have any money to get a *carne asada* burrito (a spectacular entrée native to Mexico, and now a well-known item to most of California and the southwestern United States) that I had been craving since the beer started flowing.

My mom and I had been on great terms while I was in Georgia, but now that I was back home, things seemed to revert back to "normal." I was eighteen, and of course I wanted to hang out with all of my "friends" from the old days. I only had two weeks of leave. She would have liked me to stay home more and spend quality time with the family. She even told my sister, by the time my leave was finished, that she was ready for me to go back. From that point on up until now, with every subsequent leave and/or vacation in San Diego, I've spent more and more quality time with my mother. This is partly because there is less of a "need" to get drunk with a bunch of half-assed "friends" from the old days, and partly because of a genuine friendship that my mom and I have developed. In fact, she's now the person back home I look forward to seeing the most. We went through our "knock-down drag-out" bullshit quarrels together when she was raising me, while my father got to be the good guy, leisurely swinging by on holidays and weekends to play his part-time role. My mom and I are now the beneficiaries of her hard work that I wouldn't wish upon any parent. And my poor stepfather, who I love dearly as a father *now*, chose to marry a woman with two kids—my sister and me. When my mom took me to the airport at the end of my first army leave, she asked if I needed any money for the trip back. I did—$20 to be exact—and she lent it to me, not ever expecting to get the money back. As soon as I got paid, I cut her a check and mailed it off. While the check was literally "in the mail" system, I opened a letter from her, which stated that I could go ahead and keep the twenty that I had borrowed. I smiled at this, glad that I had already sent her the money, and she was surprised to get it, responding with something like, "Wow, I guess you have grown up a bit."

One reason I had no money by the end of leave, besides paying on-the-spot fines to corrupt Mexican police officers, was because I had made the mistake of calling my ex-girlfriend. I was fine emotionally and psychologically before I saw her. I figured that since I felt "stable," it wouldn't hurt to give her a courtesy call at the least. So I did, and we met up. I foolishly tried to kiss her right away, and she wasn't having any of it. So what else was I to do? I had to lavishly spend money on her, instead of just accepting her immediate rejection and moving on. So I wasted time and money on us. I invited her to Disneyland for a day, with hotel included just down the street from the over priced theme park, and she accepted. On my E-1 private salary, this was a luxury trip. In our hotel, she was reluctant to engage in intimacy with me, saying that it would ruin her "reputation" of not sleeping with guys whom she was not in a relationship with. This was one of the few things I truly appreciated about her, since I took this attitude of hers to mean that she never cheated on me. I begged and pleaded with her—not one of my finer moments—while whispering sweet nothings in her ear, until she gave in to my pathetic attempts at coercion. I can say that I had a pleasurable experience for all of the thirty seconds that I lasted, and later in the middle of the night for about the same duration. (It had been a long while.) The next day, we had a not so unpleasant time in Mickey's park. Riding the train that circles Disneyland, she sitting next to me with her legs straddled over mine, it appeared as if we were together again—kissing and caressing each other ever so gently. I apologized for acting like an asshole the night before. Later, I bought her a pair of socks with Mickey's likeness on them, for probably $10.00, along with some other crappy merchandise. She said at the time, "Every man needs a woman to spend money on." While holding hands and "necking" every so often—less often than I would have liked—we eventually made our way back to San Diego, after stopping to see her father in Huntington Beach.

Back in San Diego, about two hours south of Anaheim, where Disneyland is located, I blew up at Paige on one occasion for some made-up reason. I was just pissed because she wasn't focusing all of her attention and affection on me. That same night, I even overheard a friend of mine remark to another friend, "He [meaning me] doesn't need her." I escorted Paige to her job—a modern-day Candy-Striper at a big department store—a day or two before I headed back to Georgia. I said goodbye and proudly did not try to kiss her. I shook her hand, and she smirked briefly, a bit surprised and confused by my newfound resiliency. Around Valentine's Day, six weeks later, I called her at work to see if she had received the flowers I had sent through a local florist. She unemotionally said that she had. I said goodbye, hung up the phone, and thought to myself, *Good riddance*. Six months later, riding high and living the crazy Airborne Ranger singles' life in Georgia, I tracked her down, via telephone, at some hotel deli job in San Diego. After exchanging the standard superficial niceties, I said, "Well, I just wanted to call and say that back then [high school], you were . . . you were a real bitch to me." Then

I laughed and hung up the phone. A couple of years later, I found out that my message had ruined her day and then some. My evil plan had worked!

Soup Sandwich

I first heard the Army term—*soup sandwich*—during basic training, when Drill Sergeant Velasquez explained its meaning. A soldier who is a *soup sandwich* is just like a real one—unworkable. Picture it. You take two slices of regular sandwich bread and try to fill them with soup in the middle. What happens? The "sandwich" completely falls apart. This metaphoric term was often applied to any soldier who performed less than what was expected of him. But it was usually shortened to just *soup*. During basic and infantry school, on various occasions, I received the distinction of being labeled as such, as was common for most new recruits at one time or another. Once, when it was my turn to work kitchen patrol (KP) duty, Drill Sergeant Crock got creative by calling me "soup boy" in front of a packed chow hall full of fellow trainees, who burst into laughter—not one of my fondest memories. A synonymous, yet cruder and harsher, term used was *shit bag*—preferred terminology in Ranger battalion. Directed at me, I would hear this on many occasions during my tenure as an Airborne Ranger, especially during the first six-nine months.

I arrived back in Fort Benning after block leave, moping over thoughts about what lie ahead. As I usually did at the end of leave, I arrived a day or two early, since I needed the extra time to prepare my room and wall-locker for inspection. Before departing for leave, all of our gear and personal belongings left behind had to be secured in our wall-lockers. The "fun" part was putting everything back in its place according to SOP (standard operating procedure). As the other Rangers began trickling in from other parts of the country in mid-January 1992, a 3rd Squad "veteran" private by the name of Peter (Pete) asked a few of us, cherries included, if we wanted a ride to get haircuts. A fresh Ranger high and tight was expected of us upon starting back to work. As I said before, I wasn't friends with anyone from my squad and/or platoon and didn't really care to know them. And I certainly didn't want or need any assistance in getting a haircut. So I declined Pete's offer, not wanting to pile into his red Nissan pickup truck with other Rangers who I didn't care to associate with. Little did I know then that Pete and I would become like brothers in a frat house, cruising in that beloved truck of his all over parts of Georgia, Florida, and Alabama, searching for easy women and hysterical laughter.

The new training cycle (January-June/July 1992) began with my promotion from an E-1 private to an E-2 private, which is the first stage of actually having any sort of rank on the uniform's collar—referred to as "mosquito wings" because of the shape of the rank's single stripe placed on each side of the uniform. This is when I received my "blood wings" that I was denied in airborne school, not that I was upset to have waited. Upon being promoted, about a fourth of the platoon (ten soldiers), lined up in front of me to pound each of the rank's metal-tipped backings (four in all) into my collarbone and surrounding area. Each of these fellow soldiers from 2nd Platoon pulled the metal stripes from the previous "wounds," placed them over new locations and pounded them with the bottom of their closed fists. My upper chest was black and blue for a couple of weeks. Another member of weapons squad, Thomas, who would later become like the big brother I never wanted, hit me so hard that I flew back a couple of feet in the platoon's hallway. He was a big tough guy, kind of like an ex-hockey hooligan from high school; on the surface, he was definitely the kind of person you would want on your side in a street brawl, but with a cool, laid-back personality, you'd also want him as a friend. And then there was Phillip, another weapons squad member I came to detest in Ranger battalion and thereafter. Phillip had me recite the 5th Stanza of the *Ranger Creed*—again with the 5th Stanza—while being "promoted" by fellow Rangers, because he and others thought it would be funny. So I did, and I didn't miss a beat that time either.

I don't have anything against shorter-than-average persons. I've known such persons whom I've considered better than average friends, and perhaps will so in the future. Phillip was definitely a "short person" in the sense that he tried to make up for his shortcomings in life, whether visible (he cleared around five feet) or mental, by making himself seem more important than he really was, while stepping on others in order to become more "important" in his career. I used to say, then and since, "He is the type of guy who often got his ass kicked in high school, and now that he has some rank on his collar. . . ." Phillip was also a private, albeit a higher-ranking one, when I arrived in battalion. And because I was more of a cherry than he was, I was expected to obey his commands, as if he himself were the squad leader. He was one of those superiors who would make a subordinate do remedial training, not necessarily to convey the intrinsic value to be learned, but to gain for himself recognition from higher-ups, or because he simply got a kick out of harassing newbies. Whenever a new cherry arrived in our platoon, Phillip would launch into his borrowed tirade from the film *Full Metal Jacket*, when the drill sergeant screams at Private Pyle, "Do you suck dick? Bullshit! I bet you can suck a golf ball through a garden hose."[vii] It was painful to hear over and over. First, it wasn't all that funny after a while, if it ever was. Second, I eventually concluded that Phillip was trying to deal with, or cover up, his own dilemmas of sexual identity.

In a way, I felt sorry for Phillip. I know that he had a tough time when he arrived in battalion and afterwards too, being humiliated in one form or another, time and time again. Because of his height, sergeants made him run around yelling, "You're a chicken and I'm a chicken hawk!" like that character in the old *Looney Tunes* cartoons.[viii] And one time when Phillip was having a rough time with me because I failed to follow instructions, he said, "I'm trying to treat you like a human being, like I wished I was treated when I got to battalion." Though he was in weapons squad for a majority of the time that I was there, and we butted heads on more than one occasion, we were never officially on the same gun team—"Thank God," I still tell myself to this day. And he may be glad to know that since leaving the army, I have had dreams (bordering on nightmares) now and then, where I am back in Ranger battalion with Phillip yelling at me, ordering me to do something or another. During one dream in particular, I remember kicking the shit out of him, as I and other subordinates of his really wanted to do many times over.

Along with my first promotion and getting to know some of the other fellows from weapons squad and 2nd Platoon, the new training cycle began with an "excursion" into Fort Benning's wooded area, accompanied by my first parachute jump as an Airborne Ranger, courtesy of the United States Air Force (USAF) who flew the planes for us. From the initial jump to the end of the training mission, I was a soup sandwich or a shit bag, if you will. For purposes of training, as if we were going into actual combat, we tended to treat most "field problems" as if they were *real world* missions—whether we conducted ambushes, raids, or played a supportive/defensive role for another unit. These exercises usually began with an airborne insertion, mostly by way of a USAF plane, but we sometimes parachuted out of army helicopters as well. Flying in choppers (helicopters), while sitting on the edge with legs dangling out in the wind, is one of the few things I miss about being in Ranger battalion. But, excluding the dangling part, I could do that as a civilian if I wanted. Before parachuting out of one type of aircraft or another, we of course spent a great deal of time getting our equipment and gear ready for the task at hand. Privates met with their team leaders to discuss the mission's objective, and the team leaders met with the squad leader, who met with the platoon sergeant and the platoon leader (a 1st Lieutenant), who met with the company's first sergeant and the commanding officer (CO, a captain), and so on, depending on the size of the mission and the number of soldiers involved. I remember being so tired during the planning phase of the first couple of training exercises; the greatest "relief" came when I could steal away for a minute to urinate.

For this first training mission that I took part in, we did a nighttime airborne insertion. It was less of a jump for me and more of a backwards flop out of the door. I was weighted down heavily, as was usual, with M-60 ammo, my own ammo, spare parts for the gun, and all of the other standard packing items—extra uniforms, an e-tool (a miniature shovel), water, food, etc. I felt as if I could barely muster up enough strength to walk to the door. During many jumps, it was soothing relief just to be able to get out of the door. The few seconds of drift downward from the sky was always a weightless break between standing in the plane with gear on (the chute and reserve added more pounds) and the long marches to be faced once hitting the ground. On this first jump in battalion, walking from the front of the aircraft to the rear, I staggered toward the right door, handed the jumpmaster my chute cord attached to the static line, at which time the plane seemed to have hit a bit of turbulence. Like a drunkard, I could not walk straight through the door. My right shoulder bumped into where the plane meets open-door, causing me to spin 180 degrees. I fell backwards out of the plane, making it possible to wave goodbye to the jumpmaster and the next paratrooper—an airborne school example of what not to do.

Once on the ground, it was time to link up with the rest of 2nd Platoon. I should have paid closer attention when being briefed on the mission's objective. That way I might have avoided getting lost. I assumed that on the ground, as was usual, I would run into someone from my unit with more "time in battalion," as we would say. Then I would just follow that person to the rallying point. I saw no one from my unit for quite awhile. But I used my compass to try and navigate toward the location I thought everyone would be at. I went the wrong way. (I found out much later, after a few tests in nighttime land navigation, that I am terrible at navigating. This is something that my sister Sandra and I have in common. She spent seven years in the army reserves, and still likes to tell people that she outranked me—truth be told.) After futilely searching for my platoon in the pitch black of night, I decided to take a break in a section of wooded area. This was a mistake. I sat down and placed a bag of M-60 (blank) ammo next to me. When I got up to head out, I left the bag there. Probably the worst thing that a Ranger can do is absentmindedly leave equipment behind in the field. I eventually linked up with my unit, but I'm not sure how. I think I ran into a soldier from a different platoon, who pointed me into the right direction. For the next training mission, Specialist Alex from my squad, whom I came to respect and think was pretty cool, made sure over and over that I knew where the linkup point was. "It's not that we don't trust you, Donayre, but. . . ."

Getting back to the bag of ammo left behind: When we got back to the barracks after the mission, a Specialist Maze, who was my gunner at the time (I was the ammo bearer), sternly said to me, "Turn in all of your ammo. If you have any on you when you come into the barracks, I'll smoke the shit out of you." There was a collection point outside the barracks where we had to turn in our unused ammo. I thought to myself, *It won't be a problem not having ammo on me, since I already lost a few hundred rounds.* I was much too afraid of the consequences to tell my gunner what had happened. But I thought that if that bag of ammo turned up at some point, it would be traced back to my unit, and ultimately back to me. Plus, it would be apparent within a couple of days that one of our prized ammo-carrying bags from the weapons squad box was missing. So I had to tell someone. I ended up telling my immediate "supervisor"—the assistant gunner—who everyone called Pilgrim for whatever reason. Perhaps that was it. Anyway, he said that I still needed to tell our gunner, and I did, fearful of the punishment about to be inflicted upon me. When I told Maze, he said, with no emotion, "Well, be more careful next time," and walked out of the room. *Wow, that's it,* I thought. That wasn't it, I soon found out. As in a college fraternity, though I've never been in one, the grapevine is in full effect in Ranger battalion. I naively thought that Pilgrim and Maze would have kept this situation within our gun team. I'm pretty sure that Phillip found out, though he never actually referred to what I had done, because he took it upon himself to have me do additional exhaustive and corrective training, making such references as, "You need to pull your head out of your ass. . . you can't be forgetting. . . ." He definitely had a point, but the fact that *he* was "reminding" me of what I was supposed to do in the future, instead of someone from my immediate chain of command (my own gun team), added to my contempt for this little man.

At this time in battalion, a Sergeant Zigzag was our squad leader. I believe that Sergeant Shilling had been given a sabbatical to attend a semester of college—something that used to be an option for careerist rangers—but he never came back to lead weapons squad. I didn't miss him. Zigzag was about five foot four and thin, but very fit. He could run like few others could. His two-mile run time was around ten minutes. On one of our squad PT tests, I figured that if I could try and keep up with him on the run, I would do more than okay. He left me, and the others, in the dust, but I did finish second among the squad—one of the few times that I beat Simon. I respected Zigzag to a great extent, and sort of looked up to him as a father figure. After all, I was turning nineteen soon—still a kid—and this man was ultimately responsible for my well-being out there in the field, whether in training or in combat. Plus, he was fair and encouraging when it came to his troops. Under his leadership, I had my two fallouts from squad runs while in battalion. I remember being sick to the point of defecating liquid blood, but I did not go on *sick call*—the army term for when a soldier shows up for the morning's formation and reports his or her intention to see a doctor. It never looked good for a new cherry to claim illness, whether real or imagined. So being in this state of illness, I was dehydrated to the point where I just couldn't keep up with the rest of the squad on two of our runs. Though Zigzag didn't try to find out what was wrong with me, he did give me encouraging support, "You're a stud. I've seen you carry the tripod [for the M-60]." And then there was Phillip, who just assumed that I was a shit bag and had begun to slack in my duties. I always took pride in the fact that I could run circles around Phillip and many others in the squad and platoon, when I wasn't sick of course.

Zigzag was not a homegrown Ranger, meaning that he had served in other army units before making his way over to battalion. He said that he wanted to serve in battalion to see if it was as hard as everyone claimed. "Is it?" I asked. "No," he assuredly responded. For me as well, though I was a cherry who hadn't really been anywhere else in the army, there were times when I was surprised how "easy" life in battalion seemed to be. I was astonished during one of my first field exercises when the chow hall actually brought us hot food out in the woods; it wasn't processed and plastic like the packaged MREs (meals ready to eat). Our time spent in the field was actually a lot less than other units, like the 82nd Airborne, I found out later, who stayed out on training missions much longer. While stationed in Korea, I explained it to a buddy of mine, Jeff, who was an ex-82nd paratrooper. "Rangers are part of a rapid reaction force, accomplishing missions in short

44

periods of time. Then units come in like the 82nd to relieve the Rangers and maintain defensive positions in place of them, for a few weeks at a time if need be."

As a Ranger, I don't ever remember being on one continuous outdoor training mission for more than four days. We might come back into the barracks after four days of training, refuel, and then head back out. I thought Ranger battalion would have been a continuous "smoke session," where I would literally not have been able to handle it. This was rarely the case, though my initial attitude as a cherry brought an excess amount of "smoke" upon me. My general attitude was that I'd get into trouble for something, no matter how *squared away* I was. So I didn't waste my time by putting forward 100 percent. As Bart said to Homer, "Read you loud and clear, dad—can't win, don't try."[ix] I usually got into trouble for minor infractions, such as failing to clean all of the mud off of my boots after a field problem or having dust in my wall-locker. Phillip liked to check for dust.

My first out-of-state Ranger training mission took place in late winter/early spring of 1992, in Fort Chaffey, Arkansas—not exactly a fulfillment of the travel opportunities I had hoped army service would provide. I was the assistant gunner on Simon's two-man gun team, and this trip to the JRTC (Joint Readiness Training Center) included our first live-fire exercise. I was soup. Before heading out on this particular mission, all of the gear that I was to carry to the firing line weighed in at around 100 pounds. This mission, like most, was at night. I was nervous as hell about doing such a training mission with live ammunition. As M-60 gun teams, our part of every mission usually involved setting up a support line, laying down suppressive fire on the target, while the three line squads from the platoon maneuvered across the objective. Members of weapons squad generally had the most weight to carry out in the field, but we got to "chill" on the support line while the line troops ran across the objective—a calling of mine that went unfulfilled. As a gun team, we had to be conscious of where our line troops were, especially when using live rounds, so as not to commit fratricide. Usually, someone from the line squad(s) would send up a colored flare, letting us know to shift or cease fire. On this particular live-fire exercise, I was yelled at on the way to the objective for following behind my gunner too closely—not a good start when using real ammunition.

Once on the support line, Simon began firing. Soon after, the gun "went down," meaning that it broke. I remember fumbling around, trying to change barrels and continuously keep the gun fed by linking rounds of ammo, while attempting to identify targets downrange in the pitch black of some wooded area in Arkansas. It was a real mess, with Simon yelling, trying to project his voice at me over the thunderous sounds of bullets being shot from all around. My eardrums were rattling and my nerves were racing, partly out of fear of not making any mistakes—too late. I nearly ran in front of other firing weapons, because I thought I heard the squad leader order us to move forward. Simon slapped me in the head, saying, "What the hell are you doing!?" Needless to say, I was glad when this debacle was over. I felt a smoke session coming on, but Simon seemed to genuinely believe that it was his fault as much as mine for the failure of the gun to operate at 100 percent. Later, after the mission, it was even determined that part of the gun—

the bolt (containing the firing pin mechanism)—had been damaged during the operation. Regardless, this didn't excuse my ineptness.

During another training exercise in Arkansas, Simon and I were "killed" off, meaning that we were designated casualties for training purposes (even the medics had to practice their craft) and had to go back to the rear with the gear until being sent for. We just hung out with some other "casualties," not making any real effort to go back into the field. The other bad thing you can do as a Ranger, besides leaving equipment in the field, is "get over," meaning to have a lax time while your fellow soldiers are out doing hardcore training. So when the platoon came back from the field, I got a lashing from higher-ranking soldiers, especially the platoon sergeant (the highest ranking non-commissioned officer in the platoon and the platoon leader's right-hand man), Sergeant Pickling: "Donayre, if you don't move your ass and help bring in some more cots, we'll use your bed to store weapons!"—something like that anyway.

My first real training cycle in battalion ended in June 1992, followed by our two-week summer block leave. Instead of heading home to San Diego, I went to visit my father in Pennsylvania, where he worked at the hub-site of a major airline. Although it was nice to spend Father's Day with him, I was relatively bored when he was at work. Even he acknowledged, "It would have been better for you to spend your vacation at *home* with your friends." When we weren't hanging out, I spent a lot of time watching TV and drinking a fridge full of beer. Early in the vacation, my eye had spotted a lovely young Pennsylvanian at an art store down the street, but I didn't have the gall to talk to her. And there was the girl at Subway Sandwiches—another opportunity lost. I also thought about my future role as an Airborne Ranger, whether one existed for me or not. We were always encouraged by superiors to do PT while on vacation. In Pennsylvania, I might have run once or twice, over a short distance. One thing I love about being a civilian: if I don't feel like running, I don't have to. Again, I was not looking forward to heading back to Fort Benning. But I was due for promotion to the rank of private first class (PFC), seeing as how I was approaching one year of completed service in the army.

Brothers among Soldiers

Lifelong friends—those outside of our immediate families whom we consider brothers or sisters—are few and far between for many persons. In our youth, we hope and plan, without the guidance of life experience, to stay in constant touch with our buddies and school chums. But as we move out into the world, for those of us who choose to do so, a harsh reality confronts us. As we change and evolve as persons, hopefully in positive directions, so too does our concept of the qualities that a "lifelong friend" should possess. Bottom line—If your friends aren't willing to change *with* you, you'll have to change *without* them, making new friends in the process. There are countless stories documenting fraternal bonds that have been forged during times of war, where *brothers in arms* have indeed become *brothers in life*. In the sororities and fraternities of universities throughout the United States, "familial" bonds often come about because of a shared social class among members or through a pledge's memorization of the index-card "facts" about his or her sponsor. As Airborne Rangers living in the same barracks day in and day out (kind of like a frat house), partying on the weekends together ("frat" brothers looking for easy sorority girls), and harshly training side by side for combat operations (*nothing* like college study groups), many of us acquired lifelong friends. And in the absence of warfare itself, I personally avoided the horror of seeing my brothers perish in front of me.

In the summer of 1992, before and shortly after block leave, there were many changes afoot at 2nd Platoon, Alpha Company, 3rd Ranger Battalion. For one, in an unceremonious event, I was promoted to PFC by the new squad leader of weapons squad—one Sergeant Matthew (Matt). Matt worked as the longest-serving weapons squad leader during my twenty-six months with the unit, eventually becoming the platoon sergeant. Although I felt at the time that he pushed my buttons on one too many occasions, he challenged me to live up to my full potential—not distinctly as an Airborne Ranger but as a soldier in the United States Army.

He was less of a father figure and more of an older brother or younger uncle, someone I might have called a friend. As well, I became the assistant gunner of Specialist Jonathan, whom I came to deeply respect for his "intestinal fortitude" and leadership style.

Jonathan was one of the most hardcore individuals I had ever met in the army. From the looks of him, one might think otherwise. He wasn't very big, pretty thin actually, with a height that might have cleared five foot nine. And he was a nice enough guy, not *usually* putting on an air of superiority about his position or experience—definitely not a Phillip. What made him hardcore was his total commitment to excellence as an M-60 machine gunner. He was a hell of a shot, and he could hump (carry) the gun as few others could. And he had speed, both on and off the road. He was fast at cleaning, disassembling, and reassembling the gun, and he was a marathon runner, able to run the two-mile test in less than ten minutes. Plus, he expected the members of his gun team to adapt to his standards as much as possible. He led mainly by example, encouraging subordinates to follow suit, screaming and yelling as little as possible in the process. As long as you did your job, he pretty much let you be. When I heard that he was now my gunner, I became terribly perplexed. My first reaction was, "Oh shit. Now battalion is really going to suck with 'maestro' in charge of me." But I was also spurred into action. I knew that I had to stop being a slacker in order to survive as his assistant. My attitude did a complete 180 overnight, putting my lackadaisical disposition in check for the time being. From Panama to Scotland and back to Fort Benning, we had the most squared-away gun team in the platoon, if not the whole company. On only one occasion as his AG did he drop me to do push-ups for corrective training purposes. I failed to get my uniform's rusty belt buckle replaced, after being told by Sergeant Matthew the day before. Not surprisingly, Phillip was the one who alerted Jonathan to my failure.

It was during this time of visible transition and being accepted (and acceptance on my part) as an integral part of Ranger battalion when I befriended a few of those *brothers among soldiers* whom I still call friends today—fourteen years later. I began to hang around with Peter (Pete)—the one with the red Nissan pickup truck—and Thomas (Tom or Tommy), both of whom I've mentioned earlier. Pete was in 3rd Squad of 2nd Platoon and had been in battalion about a year longer than me. Tommy was in my squad and had only been in about six months longer than me. They were both mutual friends before I came into the fold. Before I started hanging out with Pete, I used to cruise around with Tom on his motorcycle, kind of like the little brother tagging along. We would usually go to pool halls (he was a pretty decent shot at times) or seedy bars, looking to hook up with most any female who would say yes.

On one occasion, Tom and I met these two young ladies, friends of each other, and it was apparent, so I thought, that they wanted to get together at some point in the near future. One day they called our barracks and spoke with Tom and had made arrangements. After Tom told me the "good" news, I said with joy, "Awesome. Let's go meet up with them." Then he informed me, in front of others, that they only wanted to see him—ouch! That left me with a stinging pain of rejection for a short while, but I tried not to let it show. With Tom out frolicking with the two ladies, I moped around the barracks for a while. But that same afternoon, Pete asked if I wanted to head downtown. I did, accepting his invite. While out and about in his truck, he said, "Do you want to try and get into the Chickasaw?" which was a local dance club/bar. My being nineteen and under age, this required the use of a fake or borrowed ID. At the time, many places around Columbus, Georgia, were not sticklers for drinking laws. If you were a serviceperson with money to burn, then "come on in." But many places went through the motions of checking your ID, and some actually cared if you were under twenty-one. Pete was twenty-one, so I borrowed one of his IDs to try and get into this place for the first time. We all had the same hair "style"—a Ranger high and tight—so the use of another's ID is not that inconceivable. I went first into this club, while Pete waited outside for a bit. Then with me safely inside, he made his way in. The plan worked. This was to be the first of our many club-hopping nights at the Chickasaw and other establishments around town and in various states. Though Tom had his hands full on that particular occasion, he made up the other third of our *pact.*

Of course, as I alluded to earlier in this chapter, "pacts" change and get added to and taken from. Since leaving the army, I saw Tom once back in 1996 or 1997, when I was in community college. I haven't been in contact with him since then. I would say that he didn't survive the pact, but he would probably argue that the pact didn't survive him. Pete and I on the other hand have been in constant contact with each other over the years, and with other extended members of the pact, including having reunions every now and again.

The other member of the extended pact, whom I keep in contact with more than others, is Richard, or Rich for short. Richard, whom I mentioned at the beginning of this book, arrived in battalion about six months after I did, destined for army greatness. His father had been a high-ranking officer in army intelligence, and Rich went to high school in Norway, where I believe his father served and where his family is originally from. I was sort of envious of the places he had been—Europe—and I enjoyed asking him questions about his experiences in the Old World. He used to give Pete and me hell for hooking up with "anything" while he tried to keep up a long-distance relationship with a Norwegian beauty queen. One reason Pete, Rich, and I stayed in contact after army service, besides our connection to the Ranger "frat house," was because of our drive and motivation to study in college. Following a similar path and having common interests, it is easier to stay in close contact. While Pete earned a degree in information systems or something of that sort, and has a high-level job in Washington, D.C., Rich consolidated his coursework from various colleges and universities, earning a liberal arts degree. He also stayed in the service as a reservist, where he was deployed to Afghanistan, helping oust the Taliban regime and stabilize the situation.

See the World

As a kid, I was inundated with U.S. Naval recruiting commercials, claiming, "Join the navy, see the world." Or was it "Sea the world," word-playing on the fact that the navy navigates on open waterways? Regardless, I probably went to more places overseas in two years as an Airborne Ranger than the average sailor would during a lifetime of service. From the fall of 1992 through the spring of 1993, we conducted training missions that included ventures to Panama, Scotland, Puerto Rico, and South Korea, as well as my home state of California. This more than made up for the bad memories I had been harboring since the Arkansas debacle.

In late August 1992, the whole of 3rd Ranger Battalion geared up for three weeks of training at the Jungle Operations Training Center (JOTC) at Fort Sherman, Panama, located in the heart of Central America. In the meantime, I was back at Fort Benning with my newfound buddies, training on weekdays and living life to the fullest, when time permitted, at nights and on weekends, when we weren't out in the field. There was a local dive bar/club on the post of Fort Benning—The Hidden Door—that some of us frequented regularly. With no explanation required, it was referred to as the Hidden Whore. The place was within walking or inexpensive taxi fare distance, which was good for me, seeing as how I didn't own a vehicle and I couldn't always expect Pete to be around with his truck or Tommy with his motorcycle. For some reason, I can't remember why, I headed over there one night alone, which I didn't usually feel uncomfortable doing. On this one particular occasion, I was not drinking alcohol, only Coca-Cola. And this was one of the few places, at the time, where I didn't need an ID to purchase intoxicants, because they really didn't care. I probably had had a rough night the previous evening and was taking a break from drinking. While there alone, I caught the eye of some girl (a young married woman), I'll refer to her now as Roxie, whose female friend came over to where I was standing, encouraging me to go up and talk to Roxie. So I did, and we danced and talked. And of course I didn't care that she was married. But she did, initially. I figured that she was there hanging out because things weren't so smooth on the homestead, which turned out to be the case. Roxie and her friend ended up giving me a ride back to the barracks, and I was given the friend's number, just in case I wanted to hang out sometime. It would be unsafe to call Roxie at home, seeing as how she had a husband there, along with two kids. Soon after, I made a call to the friend's pad, where we arranged to meet up. As had been predetermined on the phone, I brought Tommy along for the friend.

Roxie and I "went out" a couple of times, and I intentionally made it seem that I cared about her, ensuring that we would "go out" some more. The night before heading to Panama, Tommy and I were over at the friend's house, and Roxie was paranoid, for good reason, that her husband would come over (from right next door). On one occasion before this, I had actually met the guy, as she introduced me as a friend of Tommy's, who just happened to be seeing Roxie's friend. As we were in the back room, trying to do our thing, with Tommy and the friend out in the living room, there was a loud rapping sound on the room's door, which led to the outside. She became panic-stricken, certain that it was her husband trying to scare us. I wasn't too concerned, since I had a tough ex-high school hockey star from Connecticut—Thomas—on my side in the next room. But this guy could have had a shotgun or some other kind of firearm. After all, this was the South. Nothing ever came of the incident, and I ended up seeing Roxie one more time after getting back from Panama. She was married, with two kids. I was single and free, and planned on staying that way. My lack of phone calls to her friend's house demonstrated my lack of interest in pursuing matters any further.

In early September, we headed for Panama aboard a nonstop chartered flight, which included in-flight movies and stewardesses (female flight attendants) bringing us hot meals. This was another example of how Ranger battalion was not as hard as I had pictured. I thought we would be in big, ugly, greenish-gray air force troop carrier planes the whole way, instead of riding in excessive comfort at taxpayers' expense. Well, if you're always giving someone the nickel-and-dime treatment, don't expect to get a dollar back. Besides, including the three weeks of intensive and exhaustive training in Panama, it was one of the most memorable places I had been to while serving in battalion, if not in life.

As an assistant on Jonathan's three-man gun team, I earned my mettle in Panama, along with the ammo-bearer, Clint. Clint was a relative newbie in battalion at this time, unlike me, who had a whopping nine months in. He was actually from the state of Georgia, and often went home on the weekends to visit his southern belle. His army contract was for a total of two years and seventeen weeks, which was unusual for those slotted for Ranger battalion. Once Uncle Sam trains you and spends money on you, he wants to keep you around as long as possible. I was extremely envious of Clint's contract at times, seeing as how he enlisted after me and would be discharged long before me. He became one of my better friends in the squad, and we hung out quite a bit. I talked to him once after I left the army. He went back to driving trucks (big rigs) in the Georgia and Florida regions, welcoming me to come visit him and "the missus" anytime. I haven't.

Though I hated—no overstatement here—traipsing around the dense and filthy jungles of Panama, some of my most rewarding experiences ever came from this episode of army life. It was one of those times when I was glad to have been a part of the experience, but don't ever want to do it again. This was my attitude anyway. During the first week of the three-week training period, we slept in makeshift barracks each night and would go out into the jungle each day for a few hours at a time. I remember that our *wake-up call* kept getting shorter and shorter as the week progressed. The first day it was something like 0530 hours (5:30 **AM**), then 0430 the next day, then 0330, 0230, 0130, and so on. It got to the point where I could only take a quick catnap before the wake-up call.

Staying out in the jungle—sleeping and working—for days on end was another thing completely. As a three-man gun team, once the platoon sergeant and platoon leader found an appropriate place for our platoon to set up a defensive perimeter for a night or more, each one of us took turns manning the gun during the evening, while the other two slept. On one occasion, we were set up next to a small concrete road bridge above a dried-up creek area. Jonathan thought it would be a good idea if we made our sleeping quarters under the bridge. This did keep the rain off us, and it did rain quite a bit in Panama, but I had trouble sleeping because crabs and other critters from the swampy jungle would run by and/or over me. It was bad enough that we had to keep a lookout for what I referred to as poison "black death" frogs. Before entering the jungle, we had classes, with visual aids, about the hazards of jungle life. Supposedly, the poisonous secretion of a particular native Panamanian frog is so deadly that if it enters a person's bloodstream, death will ensue in seven to nine seconds as the nervous system collapses.

For mobility purposes, I came to appreciate the denseness of the jungle during the daytime. Though many of the trees were laden with sharp thorns that made for painful encounters upon impact with clutching hands, unlike the somber trees of Fort Benning's wooded area, the excessive foliage sprouting from the trees provided vital cover from the sun's rays, helping to keep the enclosed jungle a bit cooler. Don't get me wrong. It was still hot as hell, and this was the tail-end of summer. But on one particular training raid, out in an open area with the sun beating down on us, not more than five minutes after all three gun teams of weapons squad were set up on an exposed support line, my entire body and uniform were drenched in sweat. I was only too happy to get back into the jungle.

The nighttime could easily lead to some twisted scenarios. For one, the jungle was so dense that moonlight, if there was any, could barely penetrate the exclusive jungle. It was recommended, even by our trainers and observers at JOTC, that we should not conduct Ranger night patrols. Of course, there is always someone who wants to be more hardcore than the rest. "Hey, do you remember that night patrol we did in Panama? We set the standard. Aw man, that was crazy." But most likely there is little to no choice involved. It usually comes down to a decision from above—"3rd Squad will conduct a night patrol at 2300 in the AO (area of operations) of . . ." and so on. In preparation for a nighttime training ambush, our platoon had to move down a hillside, no more than twenty yards away from the firing line. It took us probably forty-five minutes longer to set up than it would have in the woods of Georgia. I literally could not see my gunner in front of me, who was less than an arm's length away. Each soldier, baby-stepping like a duck in a row, placed his navigational compass, with its faint green glow, in a position that the man directly behind him might be able to focus on. This barely helped. Once on the ambush line, while waiting for the "enemy" to approach, I had to urinate ASAP. I quietly dug a hole below where my crotch was and relieved myself. Shortly thereafter, our platoon successfully conducted a JOTC ambush, "killing" make believe enemies in the process.

Getting extracted from a field problem, whether it be the woods of Georgia or the jungles of Panama, was always an exciting time for me and countless other soldiers. Not only was there relief about being done with a "mission," there was often a sense of satisfaction at having completed an objective. But it's one thing to be in a peacetime situation and laugh at the "hardcore" experiences from Panama, and another, so I've studied, to look back at a war-torn situation like Vietnam, reminiscing with buddies about other buddies who didn't make it out of the "shit." Not only was extraction a fun time, reinvigorating the troops who looked forward to some R&R (rest and relaxation), but the mode of extraction played an important role in the development of the individual psyche. Marching out of the field on foot was one way, and being airlifted out via helicopter was another way. I preferred the latter, but that wasn't always feasible or cost-effective.

In Panama, during one of our last training exercises, we had been marching through the jungles all day, over one hilltop, then another. Finally we made our way to the top of a big hill/small mountain, which served as our eventual helicopter extraction point. As we waited there for our turn to board the limited supply of Huey and/or Blackhawk flying machines—there weren't enough for all of us to board at once—I stood there in amazement, overwhelmed by the panoramic beauty of the landscape below. I could see the fresh greenness of intertwined jungles and river-filled valleys, propped up by a misty bluish-gray skyline. It was as if the exhaustive intensity of getting to this point had all been worth it. Far above us, an air force "gunship" circled around, firing on its practice target in a low-lying valley. The viewable impact of the rounds appeared to be so far away, mimicking the quiet popping sound of what an automatic BB gun might make up close. The open-door helicopter ride from this point back to the rear was a continuation of the wonderment I was experiencing, with the added sensation of an aircraft in flight, as we swooped down and through the jungles underneath. I smiled genuinely.

I was also happy spending quality R&R time with *brothers* in downtown Panama City, Panama. After all, venturing to foreign lands was a primary desire for joining the army. Unfortunately, we were usually denied the ample amount of time needed (for me) to freely explore the local area. Besides, we were there to train, not to hang out around town. But the main reason for the short leash was to keep us from getting into trouble. And no matter how short the leash, somebody always wanders a little too far away from home. Before being released on a twelve-hour Panama City pass, plus or minus a couple of hours, we received a safety briefing from the company's first sergeant. He basically told us which "houses of ill repute" were off limits. The only one I recall him mentioning was The Blue Goose (whose name in Spanish escapes me). I'm pretty sure I remember this specific one because it's the one I ended up at, along with Pete, Tommy, and a Specialist (E-4) Howdy from Pete's squad—3rd Squad.

Before our painting the town red, there was an announcement from Platoon Sergeant Pickling. In lieu of going to get smashed with fellow Ranger buddies (he didn't partake in the consumption of alcohol), he would conduct a remedial land navigation training exercise with those who were interested. Some newbies were strongly "encouraged" by their squad leaders to go land-naving with Pickling. My own squad leader, Matthew, said something to me like, "That would be a good way to prepare for an upcoming land navigation test." I laughed uneasily. But he left it up to me, and of course, I chose to head downtown. I was supported in this decision by my immediate supervisor, Specialist Jonathan, who was all about partying when he wasn't working so hard. The sad thing is, Jonathan got kicked out of battalion on two separate occasions, each being alcohol-related. Right before he became my gunner, he was reinstated to his rightful place in 3rd Bat after a six-month probationary period. Shortly after he left weapons squad to become a team leader in a different squad, he had another "incident," after which he was expelled from the "frat house" forever.

My buddy Rich, at this time, was a cherry, as was Jimmy, mutual buddies who arrived in battalion at the same time—both attached to 3rd Squad. They "volunteered" to stay behind and accompany Pickling on his land-nav quest. But I thought, as they thought, like most of us thought, *There will be more opportuni - ties for off-duty time before leaving Panama.* How wrong we were. Rich and I still talk about his land-nav days with "Yoda." (Pickling was referred to as such because of his likeness to the *Star Wars* character.[X] "Smoke you, I will," he was often mimicked saying.) One major difference between the army and Peace Corps: the army doesn't set aside serious time for cross-cultural sensitivity training, unless its policy has changed. And seeing how U.S. Army prison guards acted during the Iraqi prison scandal, I would say that it hasn't. But then one argument goes: If you get too close to the enemy, or potential enemies, you won't want to fight the enemy. Another from history: You cannot defeat your enemy until you know your enemy. There are probably thousands of sayings that contradict thousands of others.

I was partying in downtown Panama City with a few fellow Rangers, comparing the state of the city to that of Tijuana, Mexico—both poverty-stricken to an unbelievable degree. I remember being in one "normal" bar when someone said to me, "Hey Donayre, we're taking off." I followed, leaving this place behind. I jumped into a waiting cab outside, where Tommy, Pete, and Howdy were already situated. I asked, "Where are we going?" "To The Blue Goose," was the reply. I didn't flinch. The next thing I knew, we were at a relatively nice and roomy bar, with scantily clad women eyeing us. The owner/manager was friendly enough, welcoming us in English to buy drinks while encouraging us to make "friends" among the hired help. After a few beers, it was time to make friends. I vaguely remember playing pinball there at one point, chatting with a young Panamanian lady. Either she propositioned me or I solicited her, but regardless, we ended up in one of the back rooms, which were decked out with quaint (meaning nice and tacky all in the same) furniture. I was pretty buzzed at this point, trying to get to know this lady better (at the cost of thirty dollars per hour). She seemed reluctant to go the distance, just wanting to lie there together. I freaked out a bit, thinking that maybe this was some sort of scam operation. I left in a hurry and went and told the manager that nothing was happening, obviously disappointed. Moments later, she brought my watch to me that I had left in the room. I was surprised. *What honesty*, I thought. The manager reassured me, saying, "Okay, okay, I find you nice girl." I turned to face the lineup of about four or five Panamanian working women, selecting one beautiful and smiling one. I seriously tried to choose one who wouldn't be into it just for the money. I think I succeeded. As I went with her back to a room, the other Rangers I was with stayed in the bar area, contemplating what they should do. After all, they were the ones who brought me here. Earlier we had even run into the 1st squad leader from our platoon, who warned us that the Military Police (MP's) were on the way. Of course we didn't listen.

This second young lady I was with in the back room had a sweet disposition, giggling at my attempts to speak a few expressions in Spanish, "You are a beautiful woman. Do you want a kiss?" As well, I smiled when she tried to speak in broken English. She was very professional—no pun intended, making sure that I was properly cleaned with soap and warm water. Then she sat me on the bed, proceeding to put protection on me by using her soft mouth. In an intoxicated haze, I tried to go fast, reaching for her nether region below rather abrasively. She signaled for me to be gentle. I obeyed. Before long, we were in a fit of passion, heatedly embracing each other as if we *were* lovers, while I whispered sweet nothings in her ear—the same two Spanish expressions I had previously used. She was receptive and answered back. Then there was a terrible knock at the door. I jumped up. "Wh, wh, who's there?" I shakily asked. "Donayre? It's Specialist Howdy. We have to go. The MP's are here." That was an erection kill. I hastily started to put my clothes back on when she pulled me back to the bed to finish what we had started. I was quivering from the thought of being arrested and knew that my friends were waiting for me. I made an apologetic gesture toward her, smiled, and kissed her goodbye—forever. I ran out of the room into the lobby area, putting my shirt on as I bypassed two army soldiers with MP armbands on their uniforms. Waiting in a cab outside, again, were Pete and Tommy. Apparently they had been all too ready to leave me and let me fend for myself. But Specialist Howdy, being the senior-ranking person among this pack, lived up to his responsibility and to the 3rd Stanza of the *Ranger Creed*, "Never shall I leave a fallen comrade behind." I hadn't exactly fallen, but you get the picture. I should have been more thankful, which I was, that he didn't leave me to get arrested. But my mind kept reverting back to that sweet Panamanian woman who had dug me for the moment. The party didn't stop there.

As the sunset ushered in the evening, we headed back down to the area we were in earlier, before The Blue Goose had become a reality. My friends felt denied the opportunity to make friends among the locals that I had been afforded. So we went to some other establishment, not quite as nice as the Goose had been. I remember standing outside on some random street corner next to

Tommy, checking out passersby, as Pete and Howdy were making nice inside. One lady crossed our path, sort of glancing our way, when I crudely yelled out in Spanish, "Twenty!" (*Vente*). Then she waved for us to follow her. We did. She and I ended up dancing and kissing on the dance floor of some club. Before I realized it, the minutes had dwindled down to zero on our allotted pass time. And soon, we were back in Fort Benning, arriving at nighttime to extraordinary fanfare, as relatives, girlfriends, and/or wives welcomed their soldiers home from three weeks of training. I tried to imagine what it must be like to come home after six *months* of naval maneuvers. In a way it was kind of sad, knowing that I didn't have a loved one to welcome me back. Then on the other hand, I imagined that some of the wives and/or girlfriends lived it up with other men around town, liberally spending the paychecks of *their* hardworking soldiers. I was glad to bask in my aloneness with other Ranger pals.

It seemed as if we were back for no more than a week or two before heading out on another overseas deployment, this time to the United Kingdom and Northern Ireland—Scotland, to be exact. On this journey in early October 1992, there was to be no luxury-riding on a chartered airliner with stewardesses bringing us hot meals. This flight was with one of those big, ugly, greenish-gray air force carrier planes, nonstop from Fort Benning to somewhere over Scotland, where we parachuted out into the pitch black of night. As per the mission's plan, we were to link up at the company commander's location, upon impact with the ground. For training purposes only, Captain Turret wore a revolving orange strobe-light on top of his helmet, making it easier to find him in the dark. But for those who landed a half-mile to a mile away, spotting the light was still a task and getting there was even more tasking. Lucky for me, I miraculously landed a couple of yards away from the captain, as well as Jonathan, making for the quick assembling of our two-man gun team (Clint was now attached to another gunner) within minutes flat.

Scotland was much colder than Panama (an understatement) but a hell of a lot easier to traverse, except for the natural, but non-visible, potholes in the soil that I seemed to be magnetized to. "Leave it to Donayre to find the holes in the ground," Sergeant Pickling said. At one point, it was as though every few steps I took, one of my legs would sink down into the soil to about pelvis-deep. And with pounds of equipment on my person, it increasingly became a pain in the ass to pull myself out. One thing, the terrain we maneuvered on was a wide open plain, not counting the occasional patches of trees neatly placed like squares on a checkerboard, allowing one to see for miles. It was funny to me that we often walked through what appeared to be someone's backyard, opening and closing gates behind us, while chimneys of the farm-looking houses billowed smoke. I wondered if Her Majesty's government had put in a call to these people, asking them if it was all right to use their property for military purposes. Perhaps they were compensated, perhaps not.

We were in Scotland no more than a week, field marching and marching and marching. People often ask me, "So what did you do in Scotland?" "We walked throughout the countryside, but it was beautiful." I'm not sure, but I believe we even came across some remnants of Hadrian's Wall (the Roman Empire's defensive measure against "barbarian" invaders) on a few occasions. And on a few other occasions we crossed over barbed-wire fences, where I ripped my pants beyond a salvageable point. We also worked with contingents of the British army, as well as the Belgian army, who came across the channel to do some collaborative training with fellow Allies. On one of our walks, I noticed a Belgian soldier with his machine gun slumped over one shoulder, sort of how I've seen American soldiers carry the M-60 in films about Vietnam. Jokingly, I asked Sergeant Matthew if I could carry my weapon like that. "Yeah, right," he said, with a twinge of "only shit bags don't carry their weapons at the [firing position of] ready" in his voice.

There were only two things that I really wanted to do in Scotland; the first one of course was to go sight-seeing; the second was to earn my British jump wings, which required training with British parachute equipment and British aircraft. Both were denied me. During one full day, we spent many hours training with British jumpmasters, learning the differences of British parachutes and aircraft in comparison with our own—not enough difference in either case to warrant concern. I replied to one British instructor after a pre-jump inspection of my equipment, "Roger that"—a standard U.S. Army term of acknowledgement. He turned to his fellow soldier and asked, in a typical *Monty Python*-esque British accent, "Why does everyone keep calling me Roger?" Once on the British plane, we were to conduct an airborne drop in broad daylight, which in Britain often means darkened overcast skies. There were a few planes ready to unload many Rangers, but weather conditions were bad—winds kicking hard accompanied by drops of rain. I was at the stand-up point, ready to jump, along with those in front of and behind me. After a couple of flybys over the drop zone, the cancellation signal was given by the jumpmaster. As this happened, I looked out of the window and saw other paratroopers exiting their aircraft, streaming by in the cloudy sky. Apparently, they didn't get the same cancellation notice. Part of me was relieved, seeing as how that would be less work to do once on the ground. And we found out later, that a few jumpers were blown way off course, almost to the point of danger. A couple of them even suffered minor injuries (sprained ankles, broken limbs)—a standard occurrence regardless of the weather conditions. But we needed to jump in order to get the "coveted" British jump wings that I so desired. My dead British great-great-grandmother would be proud, but maybe not, seeing as how she had immigrated to the United States.

For those of us who hadn't jumped this instance, and there were a few, we were afforded one more opportunity to do so. On the very next day, we were shuttled to an airborne training area for a second attempt at meeting the British jump standard. Only this time, we were not to utilize a military plane. We were to jump from some type of hot-air balloon. The whole contraption looked like a ride at an amusement park. Waiting my turn, I watched as this big "balloon" would come to the ground, pick up a paratrooper or two, ascend back up high, and allow its passengers to safely parachute out. Once successfully completing this task, we would be British airborne qualified, allowing us to wear foreign/British jump wings on our formal dress uniform, and this qualification would go into our permanent army records. The former was a mark of pride and sense of achievement. The latter would help in future promotional possibilities. I only cared about the former. So

I waited for what seemed like hours, hoping to get my chance to jump. When it was nearly my turn to go, the remaining jumps were canceled for the day due to bad weather conditions—such is Great Britain. This subsequently meant that there would be no more jumps during this deployment to Scotland and therefore no receiving of jump wings for myself and other unfortunate soldiers. What made it worse was that there were cherries, with a lot less time in battalion than me, who had successfully obtained their British jump wings. One of these newbies was Troy from Alaska, who would later on become part of the "pact." For the meantime, I was bummed (sad and pissed off).

I headed back to our sleeping quarters (barracks) to find that if I hurried, meaning that if I packed my bags and equipment for that evening's departure, posthaste, I could venture out into the local town with the other troops for a fun-filled three- or four-hour pass—wahoo! Sergeant Matthew even yelled at me, something like, "Move your ass, Donayre, if you want to go into town." I was not up to moving my ass (I had a lot to do) for what I knew would be a teasing experience. We were originally supposed to have a whole day of *downtime*, meaning R&R, but some higher-up thought it would be best if we trained for an extra day. By training I mean marching out in the field, because we really hadn't done enough of that. I thought the whole thing was bullshit. I went and bought some local beer at the store, tossed back a couple, and leisurely packed my things. Tommy and Pete kindly stayed behind to hang out, tossing back a couple as well, which I was appreciative of but certainly didn't expect or necessarily want. If there is one thing that I hate, it is friends not having a good time on account of me. The word had also been put out by the company first sergeant, the same one who forbade us to go into certain Panamanian "houses of ill repute," that his Rangers had better not come back drunk. I think there was a one- or two-beer limit—yeah, right. Heading back, we flew nonstop from Scotland to Fort Benning, parachuting onto the drop zone during daylight hours.

On the Home Front

Back at home after the Panamanian and British extravaganzas, we had a few weeks' time before heading out on our next adventure, this time a domestic one. In between rigorously training for "combat" operations in my home state's backyard of 29 Palms, California, a few of my Ranger buddies and I conducted other types of operations just across the border into Alabama. One of our favorite places to go clubbing was on the University of Auburn campus. From Fort Benning, it was about a forty-five-minute drive, but one of the coolest things about it was that Alabama was officially an hour behind Georgia. So if we left Georgia at 9:00 P.M., we made it to Auburn by 8:45 Central Standard Time. This gave us ample partying and "trying to hook up" time. Being a typical college town, it was not difficult to do either. There was one place in particular that we (Tommy, Pete, and I) frequented—The Ultrabox. We would often be the first patrons to arrive, around 9:00 P.M., and the last ones to leave, around 2:00 A.M. I met a couple of young ladies there, as most of us did at one time or another, who were in the throes of academia. On one particular occasion before heading to California, I met a young woman by the name of Abbey. She was smart (in graduate school), beautiful, career-driven, sophisticated (I was nineteen, apparently her "younger" brother's age, and she was twenty-six, about my older sister's age), and definitely out of my infantry grunt league. But I gave it a shot anyway. So I called her from Fort Benning every now and again and we met at The Ultrabox a couple of times, sharing a kiss or two on the dance floor with beers in hand. She didn't drink from a bottle because "it isn't lady-like."

The morning of our departure for California, now with Tommy as the gunner of our two-man team, there was a yell for me from the reception desk of our barracks, "Donayre, there's a call for you." It was Abbey, wishing me luck in California, saying she would see me when I got back. I was ecstatic, in front of my fellow squad members no less. All that Sergeant Matthew could do was make fun of her name, "Abbey?!" as he chuckled. We headed out to California, no chartered flight this time either, jumping our way into the dark sky that hid the barren desert below. That's when the *soup* in my *sandwich* briefly returned. Knowing that Tommy and I were buddies, Sergeant Matthew put us on the same gun team no less, with Tommy in charge of course. Matthew said something like, "I want to see if you can work together," meaning that he wanted to see if we would work as a "proper" gun team, complete with a hierarchical leadership structure, and not as equal buddies. The first few days of our time in California were a disaster, with all signs pointing to, "No, we can't be buddies while working together." On the initial jump into the desert, with pride swelling about returning "home" to my beloved state in *this* manner, the wind was seriously kicking up a minor sand storm. Upon contact with the ground, I was dragged a few feet through mounds of dirt and bushes before I could successfully pull the parachute release cord on one side of my chute. After untangling myself, I used my all-purpose, all-tools-in-one, *Leatherman* device on the side of my belt to cut some other equipment that was caught up. I made the mistake of taking the *Leatherman* off of my belt, absentmindedly leaving it behind in the desert, while in a hurry to get to the unit's link-up point. I had even paid a bit extra for this tool, having my last name engraved on its surface.

During the next few days, we continuously walked in the blazing ninety-something-degree heat of the daytime, while sleeping in thirty-something-degree weather at night. Fellow soldiers, including Tommy, remarked, "California sucks." I actually felt bad, trying to convince them that the desert was not an actual representation of the Golden State, or at least it was only one part of it. The word had even come down from up top that we were to only march in the evening, when it was cooler, and rest during the day. The opposite happened because we were behind schedule and had to walk a lot in the burning sunshine. Even Platoon Sergeant Pickling was angry and upset, wanting to pass out like the lot of us—obviously a "new" directive from company level or higher.

At our first live-fire exercise, conducted in broad daylight, Tommy tried to lay down a base of fire with the M-60, while I helped man the gun as his assistant. It jammed. No problem. We did the standard "change barrel" drills that we had rehearsed over and over and over. Once the spare barrel was on the gun, Tommy fired the automatic weapon—*wa-pow*—only one shot went down range. He cocked it again and pulled the trigger, hoping to hear that *wha-p-p-p-p-pow* sound of the M-60 in action. But it didn't happen. Again, only one shot. He repeated the drill a few times before finally pulling the gun off the support line, once the exercise was finished, to see what had happened. Upon inspection, it became clear. The gas-piston, the part of the gun that keeps it rocking as it should, had been put in backwards. Being the assistant gunner, responsible for the maintenance and upkeep of the spare barrel (among other things), which we had to switch to on the firing line, all eyes were on me. I was mortified, as was Tommy and others from my squad and platoon. How could this have happened? I knew better than to put the piston in the barrel backwards. That was "M-60 machine gun 101." I had been in battalion now going on one year. Perhaps Sergeant Matthew was right. We couldn't be on the same gun team and remain buddies. I had slacked with my buddy Tommy as my gunner.

As I lay there in the hot desert, with arms extended to do remedial training, push-ups beyond end (Tommy to me in disgust, "Get the fuck down!"), I searched hard in my brain to find a logical reason, one that would save my ass, to what had transpired. Then, like hearing the distant thunder letting me know that the lighting was near, it struck me. As if I had traveled back in time to an episode before coming to California, I saw myself standing in the hallway of our barracks in Fort Benning, finishing up with our weapons cleaning for the day. I stood there, with Tommy next to me and Phillip sitting on the ground. Pete had come out of an adjacent room and asked if he could borrow the gun for a demonstration with his cronies from 3rd Squad. "No problem," Tommy said. While chatting with Tommy and me, Phillip toyed with the spare barrel, as if he was informally inspecting it for cleanliness and efficiency. This included unloosening the socket that holds the piston, taking it out, checking to see if it was clean or not, then putting it back in—*correctly*. I was then immediately transported back to 29 Palms, California, where I was currently doing push-ups. I shouted, "Phillip!" I began to swear up and down that it was Phillip who had put the piston in backwards, whether accidentally or intentionally. I was not taking the blame for this, but in fact I was to blame, because I had not re-inspected our gun team's equipment before heading out to California. I was livid and one hundred percent sure that it was Phillip who had sabotaged our gun team. As I often repeated since then, I would testify to this "before the U.S. Supreme Court." Eventually, Tommy also remembered seeing Phillip mess with the barrel at some point in the recent past. Perhaps he was merely placating my efforts to absolve myself. I was so pissed off that the issue was not pushed any further by the squad leader, Matt, or the platoon leader, who rightfully wondered why our gun went down (failed) in the mission. Though this was only a training exercise, the absence of our machine gun's effectiveness in combat would have seriously reduced the unit's amount of firepower, thus endangering the lives of each soldier.

This incident with Phillip was a culmination, and precedent, for our entire "relationship" in Ranger battalion. There were other moments. He asked me a couple of times, in private, to borrow some cleaning equipment, only to lash out at me in front of the squad when I asked him for a similar favor, saying something like, "You *all* need to start buying your own damn supplies." And then there was the time, many months after California, when he was no longer attached to weapons, but serving as a team leader in another squad. He was harboring thoughts about leaving the unit and felt conflicted. I was thinking the same way and told him so. Later on, he blurted out loud to other members of 2nd Platoon, in a demeanor that sought to humiliate me, "Donayre doesn't want to be here anymore." I hope for the sake of potential soldiers that he isn't an army recruiter. Perhaps he would make a great drill sergeant, since he is accustomed to trying to break soldiers down, often succeeding. But he would need some serious work in the other half of effective drill instructing—building soldiers up.

After this faulty-gun incident in California, Tommy and I began to progress as a gun team. During a bivouac exercise, where we set up desert camouflage netting for a brief "rest" during the daylight hours, we—meaning me—continuously shuttled back and forth to headquarters for supply needs, such as water and live ammo rounds for a future training mission. Tommy quickly became disillusioned with the amount of ammo we were being made to carry. More ammo equals a lot more weight in the rucksack, which means a lot more pain for the back. In order to fight the "bullshit," as he, and subsequently I, called it, we buried a couple hundred rounds (thirteen pounds at least) in the desert—another major "no no" in battalion, if not the army, and probably punishable under the Uniform Code of Military Justice (UCMJ). As a gunner, but probably more so as a friend, he tried looking out for me. It would have been me carrying the bulk of the additional rounds that we didn't need. And while we sat there in our makeshift positions, I was dead tired from walking through the desert with pounds and pounds of M-60 equipment. It showed. Tommy told me to *rack out* (get some sleep) for a bit. Soon after he said that it was time to move out again. This time, we were to conduct our final training mission of the deployment—a raid that we had rehearsed back at Fort Benning. And this time, Tommy and I set the standard for gun teams. As we lay there on the support line, in the early hours of a pre-dawn morning, our gun lit up the objective, faulty free, with the orange glow of interspersed tracer rounds on the 7.62 mm M-60 ammunition belt. While this happened, we could hear Phillip belting out orders to his assistant, "Link rounds!" They had not fired a single shot. As our gun exhausted its supply of ammo, we took a few from Phillip's team, seeing as how they weren't using any. And of course, his assistant was to blame for the whole debacle, as Phillip screamed at him for what seemed like three days, administering upon him an excessive amount of remedial and deconstructive training.

Once done with our field exercises, we marched back to the vacant Marine Corps barracks where we were staying. As we marched in the wee hours of the night, every single one of us in the unit focused on a literal beacon of light in the distance—something we still talk about today—that let us know where "home" was. As we walked towards it from miles away, it seemed to be backing away from us. This process of the mind toying with oneself was referred to as "the Jedi mind fuck." The closer we thought/hoped we were, the farther away we seemed to be. But we did eventually reach the light and our sand-filled sleeping quarters, full of soil from the desert, as we breathed in a mixture of air and dirt—not good for the lungs, I imagine.

The next day we found out that a fellow soldier from Bravo Company (the company that would go on to fight in Somalia) had been accidentally shot and killed during the previous night's live-fire exercise. Supposedly, he had run in front of a firing SAW (squad automatic weapon) and took a three-round burst in the leg. A ranger medic tried like hell to save his life, but to no avail. Tragically, there were training accidents every now and again in battalion that resulted in the deaths of soldiers. While I served, a battalion commander (lieutenant colonel) was killed in a helicopter crash along with some other troops. In another incident, a soldier from Charlie Company, we were told, was killed on the demolition range because he came out of his protective "cave" to witness the explosion he had set, only to take a mortal piece of shrapnel in the neck. We were able to use telephones in this Marine Corps training area, once out of the field, so I called my mother and grandmother in San Diego. They had already heard the news that a soldier had been killed and were just happy to be able to talk with me. They said that they wanted to drive out from San Diego to see me—bad idea—but since it was still a good six-hour drive from San Diego to 29 Palms, and it wasn't clear (it never is) how long I would be there, they decided not to. Plus, I wouldn't have wanted them to see me take orders from my higher-ups as if I were not a free man. Our time in California ended with an all-out barbecue feast, hosted and prepared by our Marine Corps brethren.

Back in Fort Benning after California (November 1992), with only a few weeks to go before block leave, my third with the unit, I geared up to spend my first Christmas in San Diego since joining the army. The previous year's block leave had started after Christmas. In the meantime, there was once again ample opportunity to cut loose across the Alabamian border at our favorite pick-up joint in Auburn—The Ultrabox. And I had Abbey on my mind. In classic Auburn fashion, Tommy, Pete, and I piled into Pete's red Nissan pick-up truck and headed west. It was a night that I would never forget.

Unfortunately for me, Abbey, being the responsible graduate student that she was, was busy with her studies and was unable to hang out that night. No problem. I could always make additional friends. As the night progressed, the three of us stayed at The Ultrabox, knocking back beers, cutting the rug, and checking out the local "talent." Pete at one point was actually engaged in an interview with a part of the talent. Tommy and I were drunk and becoming increasingly rambunctious. It was around midnight when we decided to let Pete be and look for an alternate party/bar in which to congregate. In a drunken stupor, we left The Ultrabox on foot and wandered down the street into various establishments—a doughnut shop for example—asking persons (college students) if they knew where any parties were. Parties meant women, especially drunken easy women. At one point I even called Abbey, just wanting to say hi, but waking her up in the process. As I rambled on incoherently from inside a telephone booth, Tommy banged on the booth with both hands from the outside, trying to be funny, while yelling loud obscenities, "She's a bitch. She's a bitch," though he had never met her. She could hear the noise and asked who that was. My reply, "It's just some college punk." That was the last time I ever talked to her, not that I didn't try to call her again when I was sober.

After failing miserably in our efforts to find new sources of entertainment, and after eating a doughnut or two, we headed back to The Ultrabox. But just before we went inside, a man who appeared to be of college-age approached us and asked, "Hey, are you guys in the military?" Acknowledging that we were, he asked if we wanted to go to a party. "Will there be any women there?" was our standard question of interest. He assured us that there would be, but we had to drive to the party because it was too far to walk. No problem. He had a car but said that he was in no condition to drive. I volunteered, in my appallingly drunken state, and he let me. With me driving, this guy in the passenger seat, and Tommy in the back, we made our way. But of course, everyone agreed, we needed to pick up some beers along the way. So we stopped at a gas station, grabbed a six-pack, and hit the road once more. While sipping on a Coors, I believe it was, I could barely keep the car in the driving lane, steering the vehicle up on the sidewalk once or twice. (In Moldova, it's legal and normal for motorists to drive on sidewalks, honking at pedestrians who get in their way.) While "driving," I asked, "So where's this party at?" "Oh," he said, "It's up at this hotel." I saw the hotel, named something like the "I Love Auburn Motel," as we turned into the parking lot.

While sitting there in the driver's seat and Tommy still in the back, this time I asked, "So where are the women?" His reply, "Oh, first I have to get a room and then they will come." Sure they will. I looked glaringly back at Tommy and he glared back at me. This guy then jumped out of his own car and walked into the lobby. That's when I floored it, flying around the hotel and back onto the street. As soon as I punched the gas, I saw this guy in the rearview mirror, running out of the motel after us. While heading back in the direction of The Ultrabox, I wasn't sure what to do. Should we drive this car back to Fort Benning? During my process of pondering, Tommy leaned over the front seat, holding up what seemed to be an expensive pair of sneakers in one hand, while trying to pull out the car's radio system with his other hand. I cheered him on as he shouted with glee. The next thing I saw in the rearview mirror was a police car quickly approaching from behind. I would have panicked, but the mass quantities of alcohol that I consumed earlier were working their inebriating wonders. Nonetheless, I vocally expressed my concern to Tommy, who just told me to relax.

As we turned left at an intersection, a police car with sirens blazing cornered us, forcing me to come to a complete stop. In seconds flat, policemen from all sides had their guns drawn on us, "Freeze!" I quickly put my hands up over the steering wheel. Tommy and I were then pulled out of the car, and *he* was made to lie face down on the ground while cuffs were slapped on his wrists. I was brought around to the trunk of the car, trying to explain our story, exactly as it had happened. The officers—two of them—looked in the trunk, making a comment about drugs/narcotics. I rambled something like, "Yeah, the guy said that he was doing drugs [cocaine?] earlier," which he had been bragging about. We were then arrested and taken down to the Auburn police station for booking and incarceration, so it seemed. Once at the precinct, Tommy and I sat on the same bench facing a room full of officers working at their desks, laughing at my drunken attempts to divulge what had happened with the "stolen" car. We were told that a detective would be by later to ask us for our individual stories. While waiting for the detective, I kept nodding off, nearly knocking over a lengthy stand-up ashtray in the process.

Once the detective arrived, we were "interrogated" individually, seeing if our stories matched up. They did. This guy tried to pick us up for whatever reason, sexual or otherwise, by luring us to a hotel under false pretenses, so we took off in his car after he stepped out. The detective then spoke with us at the same time, verifying that our stories did match up, while telling us that the guy with the car was a bit shaky on his own version of the evening's events: two guys ran out of the hotel, jumped into his [running] car, and then hit the road with it. He then called the police immediately. That's how they tracked us so quickly, which turned out to be a good thing. Perhaps if we hadn't been arrested as fast as we were, we might have done something more terribly stupid. And when the guy came to pick up his car at the station, he was uncooperative with the police, stating simply that he wanted his vehicle back. The detective was very surprised that Tommy and I hadn't been officially booked when we first arrived. He kept asking us, "Are you sure no one booked you or gave you a drug test?" In the course of the night, the charge against us went from *grand theft auto* to *unlawful use of vehicle* to *you're free to go*. I could just have easily been charged with underage drinking, a DUI, and driving without a license. Both Tommy and I (one whole gun team) would most likely have been thrown out of battalion if any of the charges had stuck. But they didn't, and we weren't. The detective took our photos for future reference and said that he would give us a call if there were any new developments regarding the automobile. Around 6:00 A.M., with the sun peeking over the Earth's horizon, Tommy and I were driven back to where it had all started—The Ultrabox. Pete was there in his truck, sleeping and waiting for us, like a good soldier and friend. Plus, an officer had alerted him a couple of hours earlier to the fact that his two friends were in custody. I think he had ended up hooking up with some gal after all, making his way back to the truck afterward.

M-60 Machine-Gunner

It was mid-winter (January) 1993, and we had just returned from another exciting block leave. I now had a year in battalion under my belt, and with it, I was expected to be more responsible in performing my soldierly duties. Sometimes I was, sometimes I wasn't. Jim L. (also known as L-Man), had arrived in December and was placed on my gun team. It was now Simon, me, and Jim, in that order; I still served as an assistant gunner. I remember when Jim first arrived in battalion, because it totally ruined my four-day weekend trip I was planning to take with fellow Rangers, probably to somewhere like Panama City, Florida, a favorite stomping ground of ours only four hours away by car. Don't get me wrong, I still went, but I stressed about this newbie the whole time. When a new arrival gets placed on a gun team, it is the responsibility of the gunner and/or assistant to make sure the new soldier is squared away—equipment in order and accounted for, documents signed, familiarization with the SOPs of the unit, etc. Also, it's customary to smoke the private and yell at him, making him do a countless amount of "exercises" while being deprived of sleep, as he cleans his room and other parts of the platoon's AO. I mentioned earlier that I never really cared much for the yelling part of being a higher-ranking ranger. Plus, I was still a private myself—private first class (PFC)—and under enough pressure and stress as it was. Why would I want to put someone else under the same strain? Though not a Christian per se, I firmly believe in the credo, "Do unto others. . . ."

In February, it was the birthdays of both Specialist Howdy (from The Blue Goose episode) and myself—the fourth and fifth of the month, respectively. On the fourth, Howdy, a few other Rangers, and I went out to one of the happening clubs around Columbus, Georgia—Al Who's. It was Howdy's twenty-first birthday and I was turning twenty the next day, so I of course had to borrow an ID card of some kind—a driver's license or standard-issued military ID. Every now and then (Fridays and/or Saturdays), Al Who's hosted "wet t-shirt nights," where not-so-random women in attendance would be selected to partake in the contest, center stage. Earlier in the evening, Howdy kept saying how the owner/manager of Al Who's was going to let him spray the contestants with water, since it was his birthday and all. I didn't really think much about it, with a "whatever" attitude. As a few of us were there at the club, drinking pitchers of beer around our table and eyeing the throngs of ladies in the area, a fellow Ranger from Texas, but not a Texas Ranger, kept egging me on to talk to this girl or that girl, saying that he would help me hook up. I've never been cool with this kind of badgering, telling him, in front of Sergeant Alex, "Dude, I can hook myself up." So I did. I wandered away from the table, as I often did, branching out on my own. I never cared for playing the "wingman" or any other sort of sidekick when it came to first encounters, not that this role hasn't helped. Shortly after making a solo move, I met a "sophisticated" lady (late thirties/mid-forties). Older women, and probably men, who hung out at dance clubs seemed to want more than just to have a ladies' night out with the gals. Within what seemed like minutes, she and I were sucking on each other's faces. Then I looked up at the center stage of the club and there was Howdy, spraying the contestants of the wet T-shirt competition with a water bottle. I cheered, not so much for the ladies, but for my friend Howdy. And I got this woman's number, but she never did return any of my future voice messages.

Around 2:00 A.M., it was closing time for the club, so my fellow Rangers and I went to Denny's, of course, which next to Shoney's or the Waffle House, was a favorite after-hours establishment. And at 2:00 A.M. on the fifth of February, it was now officially my birthday. I asked and received the free Denny's "birthday meal," complete with dessert, which used to be a theme of Denny's before its discontinuation. Howdy also received a free meal, making his retroactive. It was truly a birthday to remember, especially compared to the previous year's birthday, when I turned nineteen after my first five or six weeks in battalion. I got my birthday meal then too, but I was also with other newbies who were whining about being in battalion. They ended up quitting soon after.

In late winter/early spring, our entire battalion began training for the EIB (expert infantry badge). Well, those who didn't have it trained for it, and those who had it led the training. In order to receive an EIB, infantry soldiers must conduct a series of separate infantry-related tasks, each within an allotted period of time. The tasks include such things as "camouflaging" your face and uniform properly—according to army regulations, shooting at an expert level with an M-16 rifle, hitting specific targets with practice hand grenades, and demonstrating other infantry-oriented skills. The EIB was also known as "everyone in battalion," the standard being that everyone in battalion would get one sooner or later, earned or otherwise. Besides a pair of British/foreign airborne wings, the EIB was the other thing I wanted most while in battalion, and I made a concerted effort to get it, training like hell during the time leading up to the actual testing. I did receive my EIB, which proudly became part of my uniform, helped by the fact that Sergeant Matthew convinced the cadre at the hand grenades' station to allow me to throw one more grenade than was allotted for qualification. That extra toss landed me a "Go" at the grenade station and an "expert" infantry badge to boot. Well that, and we *all* packed extra rounds in our bullet-carrying magazines at the rifle range. Hence the descriptive *misnomer*, everybody in battalion.

While training for and conducting the EIB tests, I remember being disgruntled at one point with the whole infantry profession. I just simply did not want to do it anymore. I was tired of humping around dirty wooded areas and other parts of nature with pounds and pounds of M-60 machine gun equipment. Of course, I didn't really know how to tell my superiors what I was feeling. They rarely ever asked. But usually, we had monthly counseling sessions with either our team or squad leader, where they would cover our negative and positive points of Rangering. And still, they rarely ever asked how we felt. One time though, about four or five months before EIB testing, back around the time we were preparing to go to Scotland, Sergeant Matthew did ask me how I felt about being in battalion. He also asked me, "Don't you aspire to be a squad leader one day?" "Honestly, Sergeant?" I replied. "No. I don't." Then I told him that I had mixed feelings about being in battalion. I know that I was not alone among the troops in saying that it was a love-hate relationship. I even told Sergeant Matthew that there were times where I really didn't want to be there at all, but would never contemplate quitting, partly because I didn't want to be ridiculed by the other Rangers. He said something like, "What does it matter? At the most, you might run into one of *them* down the road at some random airport." Needless to say, I didn't quit then, going on to do EIB testing a few months later. And as I moped around about the prospects of a never-ending career as an M-60 pack mule, I got the "call" from Sergeant Matthew, "Donayre, you're now a gunner." *Wow!* I thought. *Me!?* Wanting to live up to the new responsibilities that had been bestowed upon me, I was completely reinvigorated about being in Ranger battalion. Here was a chance and a need to excel at the leadership position of an M-60 machine-gunner.

My first big deployment as a gunner came in the form of South Korea, where the entire 3rd Ranger Battalion, and possibly other parts of the 75th Ranger Regiment—1st and 2nd Battalions—jumped onto the Korean peninsula in broad daylight. The training mission itself—*Operation Team Spirit*—was comprised of four branches of the U.S. Armed Forces—army, navy, air force, marines. The magnitude of the operation even made it into the local San Diego paper, my mom having cut out the small article for a keepsake. It was also revealed that the North Korean Government was outraged over this US-led South Korean training mission, viewing it as a practice round for a possible future invasion of the "Hermit Kingdom" to the North, which it probably was. Korea, I thought, was ridiculously cold. We would march and sweat at night, only to have our sweat turn to ice water once we had stopped moving. I remember my feet being so numb and frozen that I used the heating packs for our food rations (MRE's) to warm them at night. This allowed me to steal away with what seemed like a few minutes of blissful sleep.

With Clint as my assistant, we did a more than decent job in the Republic of Korea, though at times, I was often overly excited about "chucking some brass" with my M-60. On one training mission, Clint and I had spotted some "enemy" personnel (Japanese allies who were helping with the training mission). When the SAW (squad automatic weapon, an individually operated mini-machine-gun) gunner from our unit tried to open fire next to me, only to let loose a one round *ku-chink*, Clint and I had to pick up the slack by opening up with the 60. In my overexcitement, I started firing the crew-served weapon as I would an M-16 rifle, placing my left hand on the front stock, instead of putting it toward the back of the M-60 and holding it steady in front of my chin. This would have been okay if we were on the move, but I was lying in the prone with the bipod legs from the M-60 fully extended. Nonetheless, we prevailed and got some "kills" in the process.

On another night mission, with only a couple of squads from the platoon (we didn't always use the whole platoon for missions) and a gun team attached to each squad, Clint and I lay there as we saw the enemy approaching. Two men were getting closer and closer, yet nobody was doing anything about it. So I decided, once I felt that they had gotten close enough, to fire off a couple of rounds at them. This turned out to be another Ranger moment of what not to do, since I apparently alerted the enemy to the fact that we possessed crew-served weapons. I thought I had done the right thing by taking the enemy out, because nobody else had done anything. Sergeant Matthew mildly scolded me once the mission was over, laughing it off after I told him my reasoning for opening up first. The rest of this mission included running full speed across an open rice paddy, firing intermittently at enemy targets and locations. Clint had a hard time keeping up (he was never the best runner of the squad), and Sergeant Matthew actually served as my assistant gunner at one point, linking and feeding the M-60 its supply of ammunition as I fired downrange, until Clint could catch up. We made it all the way to the base of this monstrous hill, where I, exhilarated, yelled to my squad leader, "Sergeant Matthew? Do you want us to take the hill, Sergeant?" feeling myself to be in some Vietnam War film. I was actually hoping he would say no, knowing that this hill's incline would be the end of me. We stood pat at the base of the hill until it was time to get extracted by a CH-47 troop-carrying chopper. But first, we made our way back to the area where I had first popped off a few rounds, where the helicopters were to land. When one of them came in for landing, the rear propeller nearly connected with the Earth, which could have caused a terrible scene of carnage—shattered metal slicing through human flesh; Sergeant Matthew preparing to yell, "Rotor strike!" while readying for the worst.

The rest of the time in South Korea during *Operation Team Spirit* was pretty uneventful, except for the R&R, which we had more of than in any other place that we had been to. I ended up going to a place called either Texas Street or Green Street, which was known exclusively for its rampant prostitution. I ended up with a lady who was not very friendly or accommodating, definitely not enjoying her job. I could have been alone and had a more pleasurable experience, saving a few dollars, and other worries, in the process. I was displeased with her to the point of ripping the cassette covers off of her stereo system when she was not in the room—not one of my classier or respectful moments. Korea all around left a bad taste in my mouth. I also thought that certain parts of the country—the towns—smelled like stale beer. I even said at one point, "I hope I never get stationed here." Exactly a year to the month after making this statement, I received orders to report for duty in South Korea, where I was to spend my final thirteen months of army service.

For my actions as an M-60 machine-gunner, and because I was still a private at the time, I received the Army Commendation Medal (ARCOM) for service in South Korea. Later, I heard Phillip remark, in reference to me, that it was bullshit for a soldier to receive a medal because he had done his job. Well, when you defend a capitalist system based on incentives, it's important to give the defenders a little incentive to keep on defending.

Later in the spring of 1993, we parachuted into the U.S. protectorate/possession/territory of Puerto Rico, where we trained for not more than forty-eight hours. With me serving as the gunner and L-Man as my assistant, the daytime jump was followed by some sort of public relations campaign. We were hounded by Marine Corps photographers, snapping away as we trained. One marine in particular, appearing to be a beautiful woman under her highly camouflaged garb, took pictures of Jim and me manning our M-60 defensive position. I didn't have the nerve to hit on her, wanting to say something like, "You can take my picture anytime." Though it was a brief excursion into Puerto Rico, I was amazed at how beautiful it was there, with palm trees swaying back and forth at the behest of a gentle wind, as the light offshore breeze kept the rays of the sun from getting too hot. Rampant poverty does exist there, though we personally were not exposed to it at the time, but we are rarely ever presented with this "other" side of Puerto Rico in the Continental news.

Black and Gold

When a new private arrives in Ranger battalion, he is expected at some point in his Ranger/army career to go to Ranger school and obtain the "black and gold" Ranger school tab (patch), which is then worn on the uniform for "life." Hence the expression, "Once a Ranger, always a Ranger." But, definitely owing to the fact that I never completed Ranger school, I preferred the expression, "Anyone can get a Ranger tab. But not everyone can be an Airborne Ranger." This sentiment of mine did have some merit. There were soldiers, and not just infantrymen, from various units around the army, who successfully completed four-plus grueling months of intensive Ranger school training, yet never went on to serve in an Airborne Ranger unit. To a much lesser degree, it was like the airborne school graduate who never went on to jump again.

As fresh privates arriving in Ranger battalion, we were constantly bombarded with notions that Ranger school represented the end-all be-all of our existence, personally and professionally. Until the Ranger tab was obtained through this highly acclaimed army leadership school, tab-less Rangers remained outcasts, waiting for their turn to enter this exclusive club composed of specialists, non-commissioned, and commissioned officers—anyone who was not a private. At any given moment during the workweek, sergeants often yelled out, "If you don't have a tab, hit the slab" or "get the fuck down," which of course was coded talk for "knock out pushups." This for me was often very annoying, since as a private, I was expected to drop whatever I was doing, such as weapons cleaning, and hit the ground. I imagine this to be another comparable characteristic with that of a frat house, where the pledge has to be all attentive to his sponsor/frat brother. From the first day that a private arrives in battalion to the day he departs for Ranger school, he is being prepped to graduate from Ranger school. Once the tab is received, he is then expected to come back to battalion and continue his service as an Airborne Ranger, working his way up the hierarchical command structure in the process.

And it was the recently returned Ranger school graduates who were usually the harshest on the battalion privates, proving they had what it took to be the future leaders. For others, inflicting pain and fear on a private was a reckoning for the way they themselves had been treated as privates. Either that or they were sadists. A few Rangers I knew even went on to serve in such elite special forces units as Delta Force. I was far from one of those individuals.

I mentioned much earlier in this book that I was never really ecstatic about being in battalion in the first place, except for some of the perks included—physical fitness, camaraderie, airborne status (pay), travel opportunities. And there was only one time, a brief one at that, during my Ranger service when I really wanted to get my tab and come back to serve as a true army leader. It was when the whole of Alpha Company was on top of the cement rooftop of our sleeping quarters in Mogadishu, Somalia. We were getting ready to go back to the States and the Company 1st Sergeant, Loony, told us how proud he was of the work we had done up to that point. This was an extremely rare moment—a once-in-a-lifetime occasion—since he was usually telling and showing us how f'ed up we were as a unit, forcing many good Rangers to quit under his watch. The rest of my time in battalion involved paying lip service to the appeal of going to Ranger school. "Donayre, sound off!" my gunner or squad leader would say to me. The response was, "Pre-Ranger!" (*pre* meaning not yet a Ranger), as loud as I could, often competing with other privates who were destined for the "black and gold." From the day I arrived in battalion until I left, twenty-six months later, I was never sure how long I would remain in the unit. I tried purposely to keep Ranger school far from my mind.

When a future Ranger school slot becomes available to the next platoon in line, it is usually the senior-ranking private from the platoon who gets the "call" for Ranger school. If it is the private's turn, he must first do a Ranger PT test, showing that he can meet the Ranger physical fitness testing standards, which were slightly higher than the regular army requirements. I mentioned much earlier that pushups and situps were never my forte, and my lack of obtaining the Ranger requirements in these areas on a couple of PT tests prevented me from entering Ranger school until a later date than normal. In fact, it was customary to be promoted from private first class to the rank of specialist once the tab is obtained. For my lateness in starting Ranger school and my subsequent failure to complete it, I remained a PFC for a much longer time than I should have. I used to joke that I was "the [senior-ranking] PFC of the Army."

I got the "call" again shortly after returning from Puerto Rico. This time I answered it, but not without a substantial amount of reluctance. I always dreaded PT tests and thought that they were a bullshit reflection of one's abilities, except for the two-mile run, of course, which I excelled at. I could carry a 23-pound M-60 machine gun 12 miles, but I couldn't do 82 push-ups in 2 minutes. (I read that the army PT test has been completely revamped in recent years, attempting to reflect more accurately an individual's varied strengths.) The night before this particular test, I was hanging out with Tommy, who by this time, had been kicked out of battalion for tab-less reasons, and was now basically serving as a clerk down the street at the local military police unit. We were at an army gym, working out with the various strength/toning machines and weights. Up to this point, I had usually rested the day before a PT test, since our muscles and joints, we had always been told, were supposed to be fully rested up. I figured that I wasn't going to pass the PT test for Ranger school entry anyway, so I might as well work out. I worked out like mad, with Tommy remarking, "You're going to fail every event of the PT test." Amazingly, I passed without a problem. I was on my way to Ranger school. First stop—pre-Ranger.

Pre-Ranger was the 75th Ranger Regiment's training program for future Ranger school students from all three Ranger battalions. It was a three-week "peek" inside what we would be doing in Ranger school, giving us somewhat of a leg up over the competition, seeing as how the actual Ranger school was comprised of soldiers from all around the army, as well as the other branches of the armed forces. Apparently though, other military units also have their own version of pre-Ranger training.

The pre-Ranger barracks were next door to 3rd Battalion, a literal jump over the fence, unlike for the other trainees heading in from the Georgian coast or flying in from Washington State. One major downer was that it conflicted with summer 1993's block leave schedule. While others were out getting liquored up with old buddies from high school, I was learning the perfection of knot-tying and land navigation, while being screamed at by the pre-Ranger cadre as if everything I had accomplished in battalion up to this point had been worthless. The very first week of pre-Ranger was a drag. Although battalion itself was hard enough work in and of itself, our downtime (weekends and evenings) was a lot of fun. There I was, locked in the barracks for a week, trying to plot some points on a map, as though I were back in basic training. I remember one afternoon in particular, as I stared out of my room's window, seeing my beloved Alpha Company building just over the brown enclosed fence. My mind kept wandering back to memorable party moments from Auburn, Alabama, wishing I was there with my Ranger buddies, "dancing" with this girl or that one. I even kept saying to other pre-Rangers I knew from 2nd Platoon, "So are we hitting up The Ultrabox this weekend?" only half-joking. Neither my heart nor my mind were yelling, "pre-Ranger!"

I did make it past that first week, and the subsequent second and third weeks. The overall training was not too severe. Pre-Ranger was sort of like an advanced version of RIP, including much more in-depth field training—planning combat operations like actual leaders in battalion. I felt lucky to avoid any major responsibilities like training as a platoon leader or platoon sergeant. But I did play the role of weapons squad leader on one occasion, absent-mindedly putting three gun team emplacements in a position where they were least effective. One of my fellow pre-Rangers called me on it, "What are you doing?!" I tried covering up the fact that I wasn't sure what I was doing, by saying something like, "Oh, I thought the enemy would be coming down this *other* road." He just stared at me, obviously thinking, *You f'ing idiot.* Either I didn't pay attention to the operations order and/or my part in it, or I hadn't really properly learned the weapon squad leader's job while in battalion—probably a combination of the two. The only thing I recall doing really well was serving as the designated "terrain model" designer, molding a tiny version of the target objective from dirt, sticks, and other easy-to-find material. When a platoon leader briefed the squad leaders on the mission's objectives, he always used a terrain model. Another pre-Ranger and I designed one complete with match fire, showing the enemy target being hit and in a blaze. A training instructor was highly impressed, saying that we would have gotten extra points for this model in Ranger school. That was a personal triumph for me, seeing as how I was never very artistically inclined. With no one raising an objection, I continued volunteering for this position, which also kept me from doing other less desirable jobs.

During my duties as "terrain model" designer, I got into an argument with an army chaplain, who was acting out the role of the platoon leader. (In Ranger school, no student wears rank on his uniform, so a private could tell an officer—both of them being students—to f' himself. A chaplain normally has a cross or crosses on the uniform in lieu of traditional rank.) If the terrain model is not ready by the time the platoon leader has to report the operations order to the pre-Ranger instructor, the whole plan, including the trainee in charge, will look like soup. With me being this chaplain's designer for the terrain model, I was extremely tired from all-night training. We all were. I only needed a few minutes to finish the model, and there was an hour or two before the instructor was coming by to hear the operations order, so I decided that I was going to take a nap. I told the chaplain, and he kept bugging me, "Are you sure it'll be ready? Are you sure?" I sort of snapped with the attitude, "Don't worry about it. Of course it will be ready. It's me, the terrain model guy," as I relished the fact that I was standing up to a "man of God." But I did recognize, and feel, the negative connotation associated with chastising a person who claims to be a servant of the Holy Father, having been taught and shown through the mass media that such persons have somewhat of a revered status in society.

Another key component of pre-Ranger training was the excessive amount of food that we were required to eat. This was done by the cadre to get us ready for the other extreme of Ranger school—a total lack of chow, where you were lucky at times (so I've heard) to eat one decent meal a day. A pre-Ranger sergeant even made some trainees eat a few little square packs of butter. One trainee, who had a bad day playing the platoon leader out in the field, made the mistake of saying, "I'm not hungry, sergeant." He was subsequently made to eat platefuls of leftover potatoes and eggs, turning green and ready to cry in the process. He could always quit, but quitting was never a viable option.

During the three-week pre-Ranger course, we were given two overnight weekend passes. The first one was a break from training and the second one was for us to get our gear ready for Ranger school. On the first break, I made a beeline for Auburn with Pete and a new friend from pre-Ranger, who worked as an army cook at one of the other Ranger battalions. Pete and I met these two young ladies, mutual friends, at The Ultrabox. The one I was interested in was from Kentucky or Tennessee, and was visiting her relative or friend in Alabama. Though my head was completely shaved—the standard cut in pre-Ranger—my self-esteem was running higher than usual. I noticed earlier in the day that I had acquired an abdominally ripped "six pack" (more like a forty-ounce) from my first week of pre-Ranger training. It lasted the whole night, being my first and last—ever! The four of us made our way back to the friend's place, while someone else used Pete's truck to give my cook friend a ride back to Fort Benning. The friend from Kentucky or Tennessee and I ended up having our way with each other, where I passed out in a drunken state after we (I) finished. The next morning included some of the same fun. Being the jerk that I was, I made references to breakfast just to see if she would make some. She cooked some eggs. Then I mentioned that it would be nice to get some cookies in the mail. When I went back to 3rd Battalion on the next break from pre-Ranger, there was a package full of chocolate chip cookies from her, with a letter stating that she had with me "the best sexual experience" of her life—quite the ego boost for a soldier who was all of twenty years old. I never wrote her back, just laughing it off with my Ranger buddies as I scarfed down the tasty morsels. One time I received a message that she had called the Alpha Company barracks, but I wasn't there when she phoned. She and her friend had even given Pete and me a ride back to Fort Benning the next day. I had gotten a few rides back to my barracks while at Fort Benning, occasionally having the driver drop me off down the street from my barracks, being at times ashamed that I had let my previous night's beer goggles get the better part of my abilities to judge with clarity.

There were four phases to Ranger school—darby phase at Fort Benning, mountain phase somewhere else in Georgia, desert phase in Texas, and jungle phase in Florida—though I'm not certain about the names and/or locations of the last two. If a Ranger student successfully made it through a phase, he advanced to the next one, earning his tab upon completing the fourth phase. Failure to complete any one phase resulted in a recycle, either back to the beginning of the phase that was not completed or back to square one—the beginning of Ranger school. And then there was of course the "right" to quit and be sent back to your unit. But as the message went for those privates departing from Ranger battalion for a shot at the "black and gold": "Don't come back without it." I never made it past the first *week* of Ranger school.

I began Ranger school with a couple of optimistic highs, easily passing the PT test, the five-mile run, and the combat water survival test obstacles. The PT test requirements were actually less than battalion's. For the five-mile run, if a runner fell back behind the unit formation to a certain point, he was seen as a fall-out and subsequently recycled or dismissed from Ranger school. For the CWST (composed of three stages: the fifteen-meter swim in complete battle dress uniform, the blindfold drop from the high-dive, and the underwater removal of personal combat equipment), I ran into my first weapons squad leader from 3rd Battalion, Sergeant Shilling, who was now serving as a member of the Ranger Training Brigade cadre or RTB for short. (RIP, pre-Ranger, and RTB were all notorious for staffing ex-Ranger battalion personnel who were either not cutting it as leaders in one of the three battalions or who were just not "hardcore" anymore or didn't want to be. I think Shilling fell somewhere into the latter category.) Shilling greeted me at one of the CWST stations, sternly remarking, "Don't come back [to battalion] without *it*." Then there was the land navigation hurdle to clear. One day during the first week, we were all given varied map-plotted points—numbered metal poles—to find in the surrounding wooded area, writing down the visible numbers of the specific points once they were found. I failed in this endeavor, along with a few others, to find the required amount of numbers in the given period of time. But we were given an opportunity, as was the Ranger school standard, to attempt passing this task on the following morning, while everyone else was eating hot food in the chow-hall. I wasn't too happy about this scenario at all and quickly lost interest in running around the woods trying to find random numbered poles in the middle of nowhere. So I took my time traipsing around the land-nav area, while I noticed other Ranger school students frantically running, literally, around trying to find their points so that they could advance to the next stage of Ranger school. For what? What's the point? Having failed to pass the land navigation requirements for Ranger school, I was recycled back to day one, which had only been four or five days beforehand.

Since I had to wait for another Ranger school class to officially start before I could begin again, I was sent back to pre-Ranger for remedial land navigation training, with some other pre-Rangers from battalion. During this remedial time, I met another private from 3rd Battalion, James, who was attached to Bravo Company. In one of our discussions, we talked prophetically about the possibility of our unit being deployed on a real-world mission, meaning combat operations, while we were stuck in Ranger school. We both agreed that would suck. The rule was: soldiers would not be pulled out of Ranger school if their regular units were deployed anywhere in the world. Sergeant Matthew once asked me, right before we were deployed to Somalia, "Donayre, which would you rather have, a CIB [combat infantry badge] or a Ranger tab?" Without a second's hesitation I replied, "Oh, a CIB, Sergeant." I think he asked me this to see whether he should send me (back) to Ranger school or allow me to go on deployment with the unit. For James, who went on to get his "black and gold," the prophecy came to fruition. While he was out trudging around in one Ranger school phase or another, in the relative safety of hunger and sleep deprivation, his Bravo Company was slugging it out with Somali warlords, gunmen and gunwomen, and any other weapon-toting individual overcome by the desire to pop off a few rounds at the "invading" Americans. I remember a specific scene after Somalia, when Alpha and Bravo Companies were back in Fort Benning. I looked out of my room's window toward the Bravo Company barracks, seeing James, with his fresh Ranger tab on his uniform, walking across the lawn to greet his fellow Bravo Company Rangers, while he seemed to smile with uncertainty and confusion. Should he be happy that he now had a tab, having done what all good Rangers should do? Or should he be upset that he didn't get to join his fellow troops in the murk of Mogadishu? On one hand, he might have killed or been killed in Somalia, or at the very least, he would have seen some of his buddies/comrades die there. And on the other hand, here he now was, with tab and all, expected to command authority and respect among his subordinates. How the hell do you tell a private, decked out with a combat infantry badge and a bronze star, to get down and do push-ups because he doesn't have a measly Ranger tab? You don't. I felt for James.

Back for my second shot at Ranger school, I found myself once again conducting land navigation in some wooded area of Fort Benning. And once again I found myself not really giving a shit about completing Ranger school. I started thinking about my future as a tabbed Ranger. With a Ranger tab, one was expected to come back to battalion for a minimum of what was rumored to be one year, serving in a "leadership" position of some kind. I wanted no part of this, especially with First Sergeant Loony overseeing Alpha Company's operations. He was the biggest asshole, to say the least, most of us agreed, keeping us on duty long after the other companies were finished for the day. If I had a family to spend time with, or was in a serious relationship, I would have been pissed off much more than I was. His reasoning for being so "hard"—"War is coming soon," which he would sometimes write on the dry-erase board located at the entrance of our barracks. In one of his tirades, he lashed out at the whole of Alpha Company for being ungrateful about his spending more time with us than his own family. It was pathetically sad, but true. He would often come into the barracks on the weekend, dressed in his starched work uniform, with spit-shined boots. A few of us were afraid to go downstairs, because he might put us to work or lambaste us for wearing the "wrong" type of civilian clothes. One weeknight around six or seven P.M., a few of us were raking the rocks out in front of Alpha Company, not being let off from work until this "task" was completed. Sergeant Matthew laughingly said to me at the time, "This won't last forever, D-Man," and he was talking about months, not minutes or hours. It was all so painfully ridiculous.

I found out fairly recently that Richard met up with Sergeant Matthew while serving in Afghanistan. They were happy to chat it up, Matthew now being a high-ranking non-commissioned officer—a sergeant major I believe. Matthew said that he had run into Loony a couple of years back, and Loony, in a drunken stupor, was crying and apologizing for the way he acted as Alpha Company's first sergeant back in the day. Apparently, Matthew told him off, pointing out that he had ruined some good soldiers' careers. I never let myself get to the point of having my army career ruined by this man or any other man.

While land-naving for the fourth time (my second repeat) in Ranger school, and making my way from point A to point B and so on, I was overcome by intense feelings of sexual desire in my groin, feeling a need to relieve myself before pressing on further. Utilizing a bit of Carmex lip protection for a much smoother ejaculatory experience, I pleasured myself in a secluded area of the woods. As is normal in a post-orgasmic haze, I felt a relaxing urge to sleep. So I did. I found a decent and soft part of the ground near some bushes, and I racked out for a half an hour or more. I woke up and realized that I was done with Ranger school. Failing to pass land navigation once again, I was summarily recycled, being placed on holdover status until the next Ranger school class began. But I wasn't to be a part of it.

While on Ranger school holdover status, we were expected to show up for periodic formations throughout the day, while conducting mediocre cleaning duties such as mowing the lawns around RTB. As long as we weren't assigned to any specific tasks, we were allowed to leave the compound but were expected to be back for each formation. One day I decided to head back to 3rd Battalion and gather up a few items to take back to Ranger school. I didn't have to endure the humiliation of my fellow Alpha Company Rangers, since they were out at Fort Bliss, Texas, training with the rest of 3rd Battalion. With the exception of a few soldiers left behind for various reasons, many of whom were getting ready to leave battalion for good, the barracks were like a ghost town—devoid of any activity. While there in my 2nd Platoon room, I took a nap. (The absence of training allowed me to catch up on my sleep.) When I awoke, I realized that I was running late for one of the RTB holdover formations and would never make it back on time, since Ranger school was all the way on the other side of Fort Benning. Part of me was concerned about the prospect of being in trouble and what might come of it—an AWOL charge against me. And part of me was relieved that I would probably be in trouble, reflecting on the benefits that would come of it—kicked out of Ranger school and summarily expelled from the "frat house" of 3rd Ranger Battalion. I decided to make the most (or the least depending on how you see it) of my predicament. I called up my buddy Tommy at the MP unit to see about partying it up like old times. I figured that I would eventually head back to RTB, but I would have a couple of days to myself at first. So I hung out with Tommy and an MP friend of his, drinking and carrying on like the old days.

One night, after coming back from some bar or another, I pulled the "military police battalion commander" designated parking sign out of the ground and took it to the room of Tommy's MP friend. Well, during the next day or so, the battalion commander was up in arms and threatened to do an inspection of every MP personnel's room and attempt to recover the sign, finding the culprits in the process. The MP friend was shaken, with good reason. The sign was "hidden" in his shower. So one night, Tommy and I, using Pete's truck while he was in Texas, drove down the street behind the MP barracks, stopping at the back window where the friend lived. Through his window, he ran with the sign and dropped it in the back of Pete's truck. Then we dumped it over by 3rd Battalion, next to an army dental clinic. During my time on AWOL status, I felt myself reaching an all-time low as a soldier. Though I was hanging out and having fun, I felt that I was in danger of officially being labeled as a bad soldier, something my grandmother Lorraine had warned me against. The MP friend even tried to talk me into going to Ohio with him for a couple of weeks, partying it up with him, his family, and friends, while he enjoyed his formally recognized vacation leave from the army. It sounded really tempting but I knew that would be the end of me. One night after treating Tommy, the MP friend, and myself to a case of Keystone Light, I decided to head back to RTB and face what was coming to me.

I arrived back at RTB and was asked from some of the other holdovers about where I had been. "I was hanging out at a friend's." Then they told me that someone—a high-ranking soldier in charge of the holdovers—was looking for me, since I had missed a couple of days' worth of formations. So at the next formation, when my name was called, I answered, "Here." I was then told to report to sergeant so and so's office. The encounter that I then faced was not nearly as bad as I had geared myself up for. The sergeant yelled at me a few times and demanded to know where I had been. I truthfully told him that I had stayed at a friend's, lying that I had cleaned some of my RTB-issued equipment there, allowing it to dry before heading back to the Ranger school compound. After scolding me some more and telling me that the information I provided him was going in an official report, which would then be sent to the command sergeant major of 3rd Ranger Battalion, he proceeded to sternly tell me and ask me at the same time, "When you get back to battalion you're going to quit Ranger. Aren't you? Aren't you?" Locked up at the position of parade rest, I convincingly shouted back, "Negative, Sergeant," while actually hoping that I would be kicked out of battalion. This would avoid the humiliation of being labeled as a quitter.

I arrived back at battalion after being kicked out of Ranger school indefinitely, overwhelmingly convinced that I would be separated from the unit for having failed, under disgraceful conditions, to obtain the "black and gold." It was August 1993, and my company, along with the others, was still training in Texas. I now considered myself part of the "infamous" Ops (Operations) Platoon of Alpha Company—waiting in limbo until being sent to a new unit, doing "special" tasks around battalion, which usually involved cleaning something. Overall though, being in Ops was cake compared to being in battalion. Ops personnel weren't expected to perform at battalion standard in anything, and there was much more downtime to go around. I even began to wear my regular army gray PT uniform again, for the first time since RIP, instead of the elite all-black uniform with the 3rd Battalion insignia etched on the front. And since Alpha Company was on deployment there wasn't much of a need for Ops soldiers to do extra work around the barracks. I remember having a leisurely afternoon of playing video games on someone's Nintendo, I believe it was. This hopefulness I possessed of not having to face my fellow Alpha Company Rangers in the short run was an exercise in futility. With only a couple of days of service in Ops platoon under my belt, I was told by the sergeant in charge that my presence was demanded in Texas, where my unit was training. *Oh shit*, was all I could think, while not knowing what to think.

I arrived in Texas with my gear in hand, having flown from Fort Benning to Texas alongside Ranger school students headed for desert phase, ready to officially hear what I already knew—I was out of battalion. When I showed up to where 2nd Platoon was "camped" out for the duration of this deployment, I was relieved to hear that the troops were out training in the field. Why face something today when you can put it off until tomorrow? At some point I was ordered to help out in the chow tent, serving in-coming soldiers their choice of either *chili-mac* (a combination of chili and macaroni—one of my army favorites) or some other type of meat substance. As I served this food, gleeful that my unit was out in the field, in walked the entire 2nd Platoon. All eyes were on me, heads shaking with contempt. As members from my platoon stepped up to where I was dishing out the goods, I smirked uneasily, not sure about what to do or what to say, except for, "Chili-mac or the other?" Actually, chow-line soldiers usually just said what they wanted or pointed to which entrée they preferred. Platoon Sergeant Matthew finally appeared in front of me, displaying an unreadable smile on his face. "I'll take the chili-mac. No, the other. No, the chili-mac. How about some more?" I loaded him up, getting scolded by some chow-hall private for giving out too much chili-mac. My squad leader—now one bumbling Segeant Clayton—just shook his head in disgust.

Later after my chow-hall duties, I met up with Sergeant Matthew, who of course proceeded to lambaste me, saying something like, "What the hell do you mean you failed land navigation twice?" (It was actually four times.) Then I told him about the report done on me at Ranger school and how it had been sent to the 3rd Battalion command sergeant major. But for some reason, I have no idea why, it never made it to his desk. When we got back to Fort Benning, my higher-ups kept telling me that there was no "report" to be seen. In Texas, Matthew gave me the dreaded choice that I was hoping to avoid, "Do you want to stay in battalion or do you want to quit?" I couldn't quit. I answered, not so convincingly to my own ears, "I want to stay, Sergeant." It was then put to a vote among the four squad leaders of 2nd Platoon, whether to keep me or not. The vote was split down the middle, with Sergeant Matthew the deciding factor. I was allowed to stay in weapons squad, 2nd Platoon, Alpha Company, 3rd Ranger Battalion, 75th Ranger Regiment.

South of the Border

Now that I was back with the gang again, it was time to carry on like "normal," even though I knew that I would be on the shit list for a while to come. When Matthew informed me that I would be staying in the platoon, he spoke of punishment (more like a taxation for the pleasure of being allowed to continue on with 2nd Platoon), threatening to turn me into a "pack mule" carrying an unnecessary amount of excess weight to and from the objective. With a "bring it on attitude," I told him, "Okay, Sergeant." After all, I had been a weight-carrying mule now for over a year and a half. How would another training mission be any different? The morning after my little chat with Matthew, he came into the tent where I was sleeping (I hadn't yet moved my stuff over to 2nd Platoon's area), yelling, "Get your ass up, Donayre!" reminding me of how my mother used to wake me up for kindergarten. I threw on my black Ranger PT uniform and linked up with weapons squad, who greeted me with lukewarm reception. By this time, I believe, the squad was composed of me, L-Man, Simon, Mesh, Thomson, two cherries, and Sergeant Clayton. We went on a slow trot that morning, as was the case most mornings with Clayton in charge. Long gone were the days of running with Zigzag.

Clayton wasn't much of a runner, but he could road-march like few could. On one of our squad PT road marches back at Fort Benning, we were stepping out with so much speed that my shins were on fire. Clayton led the pack while I was right behind him. I focused on his rucksack while attempting to stay on his heels. I was reluctant to fall back and have another squad member pass me by. When I finally looked back, the next persons closest to me—Simon and L-Man—were at least fifteen meters behind. At that point we were finished with the march, Clayton boastfully remarking, "We weren't even going that fast." I was thinking, with shins screaming in burning agony, *You have to be freakin' kidding me*, while calmly agreeing with him, "Yeah, I know." But I was ecstatic at having beaten Simon at something (a rarity for me), which he took out on me later in the day by blatantly referring to other "deficiencies" in my soldiering abilities, trying to regain his authority over me by attempting to quash the fact that I had out-road-marched him.

After my first run with weapons squad in over two months (since June), I gathered up my gear and headed over to 2nd Platoon's tent, waiting to see what sort of training I was in store for in Texas. Soon after I showed up, so too did Richard with his new Ranger tab, while the members of the platoon greeted him with congratulatory gestures. I sat there on my cot, pretending to be happy for him as well, trying not to care one way or the other. My friend Richard, coming into battalion a few months after I did, now outranked me. He was a specialist, and I was still a private first class—PFC of the Army, to be exact. Apparently, according to Matthew, First Sergeant Loony originally thought that I was one of the Ranger school graduates who had been flown to Texas to link up with the unit. The order to those troops holding down the barracks in Fort Benning must have read, "Have Ranger school *graduates* pack their bags for Texas," with someone glancing over the key word.

It took me a while to readjust to training with my unit in Fort Bliss, Texas. Bottom line—I had my head up my ass. Not only had I been demoted to third in command of a gun team—ammo-bearer—I couldn't do that right. During one night mission, the tripod to the gun kicked my ass, and I was not able to open it up without making all kinds of noise. Then I dropped one of my gloves at some point, which Sergeant Alex found and returned to me. At the end of a mission, while turning in our blank ammunition, I completely forgot that I had been carrying practice rounds for a grenade launcher in one of the cargo-carrying pockets in my pants. Clayton, with a "friendly" reminder to me, "Donayre, are you still carrying those rounds?" "Oh, yeah, Sergeant." With a "What the fuck?!" he shook his head and smirked. I looked around, also shaking my head, thinking, *What the hell am I doing (back) here?* In our tent during a little downtime, I somehow found myself riffling through an army training manual, of all things, when Matthew walked past my cot. He turned to Clayton and, referring to me, asked, "What's he doing in here?" Clayton, "He's reading a manual, Sergeant." "I don't care," Matthew retorted, "I don't want him in here." I was made to go outside and pick up some trash around the area. Part of me was glad to be back among some of my buddies—Pete, L-Man—who hadn't distanced themselves from me despite my less than ideal status in the platoon. We bullshitted as if I had never gone off to Ranger school, or maybe because I had. Pete had been in battalion a year longer than me and still didn't have a tab, despite many attempts to get one.

My eventual reinstatement as a "full-fledged" member of 2nd Platoon had less to do with the shit list I was on being a short one and more to do with the list becoming overburdened with new add-ons. While in Texas, we were given a day's pass to head into the local town of El Paso. As with most R&R excursions, some persons got into trouble. Only this time, a major "scandal" broke, causing a massive purge of 3rd Battalion's ranks. Before departing for some free time, Sergeant Matthew pulled me aside, reflectively asking something to the effect, "Since you weren't here for all of the training, do you think you should be allowed to go on pass with the others?" Alluding to my "rights" as a member of the unit, I replied,

"Well Sergeant, I'm still a part of this platoon." He allowed me to go on pass with the others. As is customary before the troops are allowed to run wild through the streets, we were briefed by the 3rd Battalion commander about the do's and don'ts of R&R. One thing was clear—no drinking, though this may only have been a directive for Alpha Company, coming from First Sergeant Loony. Regardless, this was a clear-cut order that Pete, myself, and a few others gleefully disobeyed. I like to think that I've built up a pretty decent capacity for remembering obscure happenings over the years, something friends of mine tell me time and time again I have the ability to do. One thing that I am certain of, as I was then, is that the battalion commander never once, during his battalion-wide "safety and security" briefing, gave a direct order prohibiting us from crossing over into the Mexican border town of Juarez, which he later said he had. It's ridiculous to think that twenty to thirty Rangers from Alpha Company alone, some of them with vested careers as Airborne Rangers, would completely blow off this order from a lieutenant colonel if such an order had been given. Thus the scandal broke.

While on pass, I hung out with Pete around town. We linked up with an uncle of his living in the area, who was kind enough to be our guide. Pete and I even seriously considered going to Juarez at one point. But out of laziness more than anything, the appeal of heading south wasn't there. Plus we were both from border states—California and Arizona—and had been to Mexico many times before. There was no "need" to go. We did buy a couple of beers each and knocked them back at the uncle's house. At one point in the evening, we ended up at some "under 21" Latino/Latina club, being stared at, I could only imagine, for being two of the few gringos in the whole place. If we were accosted by a couple of *vatos*, I didn't think it would matter much if I told them that I was a quarter Mexican, my grandmother's parents on my dad's side having migrated north. To our delight, there were only good times to be had at this club. I danced with a beautiful young *señorita* who must have still been in high school. While I was kissing her, Pete tapped me on the shoulder, rudely letting me know that it was time to go. I wasn't too happy about that. I asked for and received this girl's address and phone number. For me, it was infatuation at first kiss. I even had ideas in my head about visiting her on an upcoming leave in the near future. I called her once and we had a stale conversation, not knowing what to talk about. I never called her again. While waiting for transportation to take us back to Fort Bliss, there was a battalion sergeant complaining, "I'm twenty-[something] years old and I can't even have a fucking beer." I was only twenty, but I understood his anguish.

The next day all hell broke loose. Those who had gone over to Juarez or who had been caught drinking were rounded up. In formation, they were "smoked," forced to stand there for hours at the position of parade rest, while not knowing what kind of formal charges, if any, would be brought against them. One of these soldiers was my old chum and assistant gunner, Clint, who was by this time serving in weapons platoon, Alpha Company, after having completed sniper school. He told me later that he had a blast in Mexico, when a young working lady there wanted to give "it" to him for free the second time around. It reminded me of my Panamanian adventure. But his Latina debauchery eventually got him kicked out of battalion, along with the other "shit bags." Perhaps I should have gone. Clint didn't care though. Far from being a lifer, he was a short-timer with an army contract for a grand total of two years and seventeen weeks. He spent his remaining military weeks monitoring the self-monitoring centralized security system apparatus for most of Fort Benning's building complexes. I hung out with him a few times at his new posting, eating combo meals from Burger King.

With a new scandal for the higher-ups to deal with (we had four or five border-jumpers just in our platoon), whatever I may or may not have done in the recent past became a moot point for the time being. When the Juarez story first came to light, Clayton shouted an accusatory question at me, "Were you drinking yesterday, Donayre?!" "No Sergeant," I assuredly lied, relieved that Mexico had broken my fall.

First Class Delta

While in Texas, another "incident" took place, this one surrounded by mystery and intrigue. Our sister/brother company—Bravo Company—got the call for real-world deployment, leading the rest of us to speculate about where it was heading and which company, if any, would follow. The troops from Bravo packed their bags and hurriedly left Texas, and the rest of battalion, behind. As rumors circulated, those of us in Alpha Company were told to be ready, since we were next up on the Ranger ready force list. Supposedly, the company next on the list depended on which company's commanding officer had seniority among all three line companies of 3rd Ranger Battalion. And since our Captain Silly was second in seniority, we would follow Bravo company if need be. As many of us pictured where it was that Bravo Company might be heading, training continued in Texas until it was time to head back to Fort Benning. Part of the "training" conducted by 3rd Squad, where Pete served as a SAW gunner, included running back from the chow-hall after consuming mass quantities of army vittles. The reasoning of their borderline nutty squad leader, Sergeant Willy, was, "What if you're shot in the abdomen and your guts are hanging out, and you need to get back to friendly lines?" Somebody (another private) later rightfully remarked out of Willy's earshot, "I'm not running anywhere if my guts are hanging out."

Shortly after being back at Fort Benning, I vaguely recall finding out that Bravo Company was on its way to Somalia, if not already there, for some reason or another. Before departing for the East African coastline, it had undergone intensive and secretive training to prepare for its real-world mission. Now that Bravo Company's training for Africa was complete, it was our turn to get ready, in case we had to carry the mantle. Our next stop: Fort Bragg, North Carolina.

In preparation for traveling to Fort Bragg, it was important to decide who would be going on deployment and who would be getting kicked out of battalion. The 3rd Bat HQ played a bullshit back and forth game of whether or not the

Juarez crew would be training for a potential role in Somalia. One minute they were in, the next they were out, dragging their bags downstairs and then back up. I wasn't sure what was happening, but one thing was certain, somebody much higher up—the battalion commander possibly—was trying to cover his ass for the debauched "order" that was given in Texas. The final verdict: they were all expelled from further training operations with 3rd Ranger Battalion. This meant that we lost three personnel from weapons squad alone. Not exactly clawing my way back up, I was now an assistant gunner on Simon's gun team once more.

Once arriving at Fort Bragg, we were quickly whisked away to the "secretive" Delta Force compound, surrounded by razor wire and surveillance cameras on all sides. It was there that we underwent training with the infamous "D Boys," referring to them as such because of their mythical status. But after reading in a U.S. media outlet, "Can the Rangers and the elite Delta Force get Aideed?" thinking back to Chuck Norris's starring role in a series of *Delta Force* movies, and the projection of the "D Boys" in *Black Hawk Down*, I realized that it was safe to talk about the myth that I was told to stay quiet about. Very little remains mysteriously secretive and/or off limits from the mass media's striking claws these days. Before coming into Peace Corps, I was a bit disgusted to see the U.S. Army's *Best Ranger* competition "go Hollywood," being shown on ESPN, of all places. But perhaps this is a public relations ploy by the army to enhance its image among the American citizenry.

It was at the "D" compound where I had some of the most memorable and rewarding training experiences of my entire army service. We, meaning the entire Alpha Company, were there for two-three weeks of intensive training in September of 1993. While there, we were briefed on what was "really" happening, or not happening, in Somalia. United Nations food supplies transported to the East African country were not reaching their intended destination—the Somali people—because they were being confiscated and hoarded by the self-proclaimed "General" Aideed and his thuggish supporters. The film's opening scene addresses this issue. The Ranger mission, should there be one, was to pull security around various "hot spots" of Mogadishu, not letting anyone in or out, while the partner Delta unit goes in to nab Aideed and/or any of his "lieutenants." Since we were to continue on with Delta's part of the mission if any or all of its members fell in combat, we were required to learn the role of the Delta elites. This involved rehearsing live-fire "urban warfare" exercises in a mock "D" compound town-dwelling. Usually in four- or five-man teams, we practiced room-clearing techniques, attempting to shoot enemy targets while not shooting weaponless civilian-identified placards.

Urban warfare, also known as "house to house fighting," was some of the most exciting and fulfilling training for me. Again, it took me back to visions of liberating one town/city after another in Western Europe, on the way to Hitler's Germany. Plus, it was just so exhilarating, being an integral part of a small team. As a kid, I also had romantic notions about kicking down the door of a seedy crack house in my career as a police S.W.A.T. team member. But instead, about ninety percent of Ranger training took place in the great outdoors—the woods, jungles,

86

marshlands, or deserts. We weren't meant to fight in materialistically developed areas of the world.

As for our main purpose of assisting Delta, we rehearsed time and time again *fast-roping* out of helicopters and securing key locations around the mock town, complete with acting townsfolk, reporters, and "hostile elements." Fast-roping allowed Black Hawk helicopter pilots to unload troops without actually touching down on the ground. Also shown in the film, while the chopper hovered a few meters above the Earth's surface, ropes connected to the inside would be thrown out by the other end, allowing soldiers to *fast-rope* down to the ground. This supposedly provided maximum speed of troop deployment while better safeguarding the lives of the deployed soldiers and pilot, as well as the material well-being of the helicopter. As Simon's assistant gunner, I was attached to 3rd Squad for the duration of the training, and probably would be in any future combat operations. I was ecstatic about being attached to 3rd Squad, not only because my buddies Pete and Richard were members (though this was probably the main reason), but also because Squad Leader Willy and Team Leader Dandy had the right "gung-ho" attitude I felt we would need in combat. I was just as ecstatic about not being in the squad where that evil little troll Phillip was a team leader. As long as you trained hard with 3rd Squad and held to a "let's do it" intensity, you were one of the teammates. And though Willy often tried to project himself as a "pull no punches," tough son of a bitch, he could just as easily be a friendly and understanding person. Phillip, on the other hand, might have been one of those leaders fragged in Vietnam by his own troops.

Not long before coming to Fort Bragg, our weapons squad, along with the other weapons squads from Ranger battalion, traded in the outmoded M-60 machine gun for the new M240 G—a bit heavier, but firing many more rounds per minute with minimal need to perform "gun down" (malfunction) drills. Where one could hear spurts of rounds being fired by the M-60, the 240 sounded more like a chainsaw, firing with limited to no lulls in between shots. During our first fast-rope training mission, with the 240 slung across his back, Simon fast-roped into an out-of-control wind, pushing him dangerously into a set of trees. In the process, he damaged his arm, getting it snagged on a tree limb. In a state of pain, he was unable or unwilling to take up security at our designated location. After tailing him out of the chopper, I grabbed the gun and assumed the duties of M240 Gunner. From there on out, for the rest of our time in the "D" compound, I served as the gunner attached to 3rd Squad, while Simon stayed back "in the rear with the gear," nursing his arm back to health. In just three months, I had been demoted from gunner to ammo-bearer over the Ranger school debacle, appointed to assistant gunner because of the Juarez fiasco, and took over as gunner because of another's injury while training for combat operations. This was not at all what I had in mind when I was sent back to battalion after failing to obtain "the black and gold." But I felt up to the challenge, or I would at least give it a shot anyway. As a gunner training with the mythically elite Delta Force, I felt as if I was doing something constructive, or destructive depending on how you read it, for one of the first times during my twenty-six months of service in Ranger battalion. It was a rare moment indeed. While training for what could very well be my death, I felt alive.

Upon taking on the task of gunner at Fort Bragg, I thought that perhaps I would be a one-man gun team, seeing as how we were already short-handed over the Juarez affair. I actually hoped for this, since I preferred working alone. And being a *lone Ranger*, if you will, would appear to be hardcore. At least I felt hardcore at the prospect of going it alone. As I told Willy, "I don't need an AG, Sergeant." He wasn't having any of it. A private from weapons platoon—responsible for such weapons as mortars—was placed on my team, whether he wanted to be or not. After *his* injury, he most likely would have preferred not. During a daytime training deployment into Delta's mock town, those of us in the chopper—3rd Squad and my gun team—were told to be on standby for an insertion either by fast-rope or air-landing. If the latter occurs, soldiers just hop off the aircraft once it touches the ground. We got the call, "No fast-rope." So I took off my protection-against-severe-rope-burning gloves and placed them inside of my shirt, signaling to my AG to do the same with his, seeing how his confused state made it clear to me that he didn't know of an alternative location to put them.

At some point during this training exercise, my AG hurt himself to the point of needing a cast on his foot-ankle-shin area. On top of that, he lost his gloves somewhere shortly after debarking from the helicopter. They must have slipped right through his shirt after it came untucked during the running around that followed. I thought that it was partly my fault, since I gave him the bright idea of putting them in his shirt. It worked for me. With his gloves missing and a broken limb to boot, he did not hear the end of it from 3rd Squad. While running to the chopper's extraction point, he limped to the point of nearly trotting at a leisurely pace. With his SAW in hand, Pete was the most vocal in lambasting my AG for slacking on the mission, pushing and pulling him along the way. Pete yelled something like, "What the hell are you going to do in combat if this happens?!" I was sort of like, "Whatever." Unknowingly, Pete made an enemy that day. From that time forward in battalion (even into civilian life from what I've heard), as long as that guy was the same rank as Pete, he had a beef with Pete whenever the two crossed paths. It was not a pretty sight. Other members of 3rd Squad also gave my temporary AG hell, including Willy, ridiculing him in front of each other. I just laughed uncomfortably, silently feeling sorry for this guy. This perhaps kept me off of his "must die" list later on down the road. After his short sojourn with 3rd Squad and my gun team, he went back to weapons squad, where he was of no effective use to them in his state of health. I told Willy shortly thereafter, "See, Sergeant. I told you I didn't need an AG." He smirked, mumbling something I didn't catch. But for my remaining time at the "D" compound, I was indeed the one-man gun team.

With the 240 G, compared to the M-60, it was feasible to operate without an assistant. It was not imperative for the 240's firing operation that someone feed rounds of ammo into it. For the M-60 though, if belts of ammo were not fed properly into the gun, it could easily jam up, making it inoperable. During a night training exercise at the Delta compound, I had the opportunity to test the M 240 G's single-operator capabilities. With the 240 slung across my back in one direction and a bag of blank rounds in the other direction, I fast-roped into the mock town with the other members of 3rd Squad. On this particular mission, there were many persons posing as either part of an angry mob or playing that of another role, such as journalist. Despite the "kill them all" image of the military, held by many, we were taught time and time again to make a concerted effort to avoid causing civilian (non-combatant) casualties as much as possible. With our Ranger "rules of engagement" (ROE) card in our wallets, the first step when dealing with a mob: Shout at it with a bullhorn, telling it to stand back. Second: If the mob becomes more unruly and continues to advance closer, fire warning shots overhead. Eventually, the last ROE stated that the Ranger should take all precautionary measures to ensure the safety of himself and his fellow Rangers. But when the shit hits the fan, it would probably be much more difficult to think back to, "Let's see. Am I now on step two or three?"

While we were in position in this Delta training town, the confrontational mob became more and more antagonistic. Pete lay prone not far from my left side, firing his SAW at a flash of light coming from a rooftop. (It was revealed later that the person he shot at was posing as a journalist.) Somehow, the mob was able to take control of one of the fast-ropes, wrapping it around a light post. We eventually proceeded to move out on foot until being extracted by helicopter. I backpedaled alongside Sergeant Dandy—a 3rd squad team leader—so as not to lose visibility with the crowd. As the mob continued approaching us, Sergeant Dandy commanded: "240, fire above their heads." I pulled the trigger and held it down, but only one round fired. Panic swept through my torso. I quickly recocked the gun and fired. Like a chainsaw feeding itself from the ammo-carrying bag strapped diagonally across my chest, the gun let off an awesome *"whhhaaaaa!"* I was exhilarated. At the end of this training mission, like the others, a debriefing session was conducted with all of those who were a part of it. We were scolded for having allowed the mob to scamper off with the fast-rope, humiliating us by publicly wrapping it around a light post. Pete wasn't criticized for shooting at the "reporter," but was told to pay closer attention in the future. We had a good laugh about it many times over. (But not comical is the fact, pointed out by Chris Hedges's *War Is a Force That Gives Us Meaning*, that a tragic amount of war correspondents are killed every so often while doing their jobs.)[xi]

Back in the rear at our living quarters after each mission, it was time to clean weapons. Simon, of all people, was a bit mad with me because I had fired the 240 G during that one particular night mission, and now it was time to clean it. Technically, though I was the gunner now, he was still in charge of me. He griped about having to help clean the gun, asking me why I had fired it. It should have been a no-brainer to him. "I was on a mission and Sergeant Dandy ordered me to fire it"—case closed. Part of me internally questioned the fact that here was my superior—a *broke dick*, to use the army term for an injured and out-of-commission soldier—whose commands I still had to abide by. I wasn't very resentful though. By now I had accepted that this was the way of things. Remaining sarcastic and a bit of a wiseass helped me do what I had to do. Whenever I would hear, "Give me a private!" for some bullshit work detail, I would "sound off" with a less than enthusiastic "ahhh!" while obviously feigning interest in volunteering for whatever. Besides, at this point of time in battalion, I should have left behind the status of private long ago. One time at the "D" compound, Simon scolded me in front of Sergeant Clayton because of my lackadaisical attitude toward "volunteerism." He said something like, "Donayre, no one likes it when you 'sound off' with your [less than enthusiastic] 'ahhh.'" I personally thought it was funny.

During that particular weapons-cleaning session, gunner Mesh found a firing pin to an M-16 rifle or a Car-15 (like an M-16, but smaller and easier to handle). Matthew noticed Mesh with it and took it off his hands, deciding to confront the entire platoon with the information the next day. Without the firing pin (the name of the part says it all), the weapon is completely useless. While in formation, Matthew held up the pin for all to see, telling each soldier to check his rifle, if he had one. Since I didn't have a rifle, I was relieved that it couldn't possibly be my weapon's firing pin. Down at the end of weapons squad, to my right, Sergeant Clayton let out a, "Ahh, shit!" *Unbelievable*, I thought. My squad leader forgot to put his firing pin back into his weapon after cleaning it. There's even a simple procedure to check and make sure the weapon works correctly after reassembling it. Sergeant Matthew nonchalantly walked over to Clayton, gave him the firing pin, and said, "Try and be more careful next time." I was floored. I knew that if a private had committed such an inconceivable "crime," he would have been smoked to the point of quitting battalion. I was sick of such double-standard bullshit. A sergeant once remarked that "there will always be double standards." That doesn't make them okay or mean that we have to accept them. Clayton, embarrassed more than anything else, got down on his own and knocked out a few pushups. This episode stayed with me for a long while (as you can tell by my writing about it). I even brought it up to Sergeant Matthew at one point, after we got back from Somalia. He said, "What was I supposed to do, smoke him?" I told him that a private in the same position would have never heard the end of it. Some sort of reprimand, financial or otherwise, was in order. Sergeant Clayton went to serve as a member of the RIP cadre soon after. The lost firing pin was not to be his last misplacement of vital army equipment.

Other Ranger mishaps occurred while I was at Fort Bragg. A soldier from another platoon lost his nine-millimeter sidearm while on training maneuvers. It basically came out of his holster at one point, probably not properly tied down, as all of our equipment was required to be. Captain Silly threw nothing short of a hissie fit, nearly crying as he lambasted us for wrecking Alpha Company's (meaning his) good reputation in the eyes of our Delta colleagues. The pistol was quickly found, but the damage had been done. I figured that in actual combat, losing one's pistol would be the least of our equipment concerns. One beef I had with some of the leaders in battalion was that they often tended to be overly anal-retentive. 2nd Platoon's leader at the time, one Lieutenant Grease, questioned my using another's weapon that I hadn't practiced with. "Are you zeroed to that weapon?" zeroed meaning that the front and rear aiming sights are adjusted to the assigned soldier's particular point of aim. If my weapon broke in combat, I wouldn't stop short of picking up an identical machine gun because I hadn't trained with that particular one. It was an absurd thought. In college, I wrote to a professor, one Dr. Harold Marcuse of the University of California at Santa Barbara, asking him rhetorically, "Why should a professor who specializes in African-American history necessarily be black?" His reply to me, "Wouldn't you rather have an officer in charge of you who has had combat experience?" I see his point now.

One other time, Phillip pointed out that an "anonymous" soldier was going around to persons' weapons, taking them off *safe* and placing them on *fire*. This is something leaders would at times do to new privates, checking later to see if the newbie was paying enough attention to his weapon. Phillip was so vociferous about it that it was logical, for me anyway, to mark him as a suspect.

While living and working at the Delta Force compound, it was obvious to me and others where the government's money went. The "D" Boys had the best chowhall and training facilities I had ever seen—swimming pools for water training (we practiced fast-roping into one of their pools), state of the art gyms, and some of the best army food I had ever eaten. Besides, these catered-to troops were the elite of the army, if not the entire armed forces—highly skilled with unquestionable discipline. They had to be given the best. Still, they would not slack because of it. Sergeant Pickling, by this time working at a desk job in 3rd Battalion HQ (Sergeant Matthew was now our platoon sergeant) once told us of his experience trying out for Delta Force. After his second attempt, he was told to not come back for a third. I had heard rumors and stories about what it took to become part of Delta, things like completing a twenty-something-mile land-navigation course in so many hours. That, among other things, ruled me out.

While there at the "D" Compound, I recognized one of the Delta troops as a former soldier from Ranger battalion. He had been a Ranger who successfully went on to be part of this elite fighting unit. Many Rangers try but only a few succeed. Serving in Alpha Company was a sergeant from another platoon who had done some time with Delta. I didn't know him all that well, but he was the nicest guy. He didn't look or act "the part." As that drill sergeant told me way back in basic training, "It's not the self-proclaiming gung-ho types who prevail in combat. It's the quiet, modest troops who set the example for heroism." I imagined that only in combat would one's true colors come to the fore. I figured that it was better to give one's life than to let fellow brothers/soldiers down. So goes an expression: "It is better to die as a hero than to live as a coward," easier said than done.

As far as the prospect of dying went, should members of 3rd Squad die in combat, the others pledged to get the names of those who died tattooed on their arms. Being an attachment to 3rd Squad, I was never formally asked to take part in this pledge, nor was I excluded from it, but I resolved myself to be a part of the death pact. Such a tattoo was the only thing I ever truly contemplated getting inked onto my body. Tattoos, as many know, are a common sight throughout the military. I have army buddies with various tattoos. Many of the tats are from different units they served with—*3rd Ranger Battalion* for example. I thought about getting one while I was in the service, but it would have to mean something truly of lifelong importance to me, not just some lame-ass skull and crossbones, or a Native-Indian marking about which I have no idea what it means. I figured that if any of my 3rd Squad compatriots fell in battle, honoring them in eternal ink would be something important. I never did get a tattoo.

Mogadishu, Somalia

We headed back to Fort Benning in early October 1993, not sure when, if ever, we would be putting the training received at the "D" Compound into effect. Since Ranger units were not meant to serve on long-term deployments, the plan was to relieve Bravo Company from its melancholic duties—thirty to forty-five days "in country"—on the east African coast. Then war broke out.

We must have been back in battalion no more than a couple of days when word came down about Ranger deaths in Somalia. Because we had lost two to three cherries from weapons squad over the Juarez affair [see chapter "South of the Border"], I found myself now helping L-Man clean our squad's designated *common area*—the platoon hallway. I perhaps could have "pulled rank" and trumpeted my time in battalion—22 months—making him do it alone, but it was usually a two-man job, and I didn't have the heart to be that much of an asshole. James was my roommate longer than anyone else in battalion. We became buddies as he became the latest addition to the "pact." He was notorious for doing fantastic impressions of his superiors, including Sergeant Matthew. Matthew's affinity for being mimicked (an exaggerated New Englander accent) ranged from toleration to contempt, depending on who was asking James for the impression. If First Sergeant Loony was asking, Matthew just begrudgingly smiled, smoking James in private "sessions" later on.

In one videotaped scene involving Jimmy from 3rd Squad (perfectly imitating Loony, with coffee cup in hand and using a *Sling Blade*-style voice) and L-Man playing the role of Captain Silly (an Asian-American), "Loony" called up "Silly" to take charge of Alpha Company, as official protocol states. On screen suddenly appears L-Man, in "Oriental" garb, and with hands clutched together under his chin in a not-so-politically-correct fashion, assuming command of the company. Those who watched, including myself, laughed hysterically. It was all in good fun. And knowing L-Man, he is far from an intolerant and prejudiced person—just the opposite. Matthew eventually saw the footage and asked him rhetorically, something like, "Do you think it's appropriate to mock your commanding officer?"

As was usually the case with L-Man and me, we were up to the wee hours of the night on Sunday and into the next day, cleaning our room and designated common area. Every Monday, the floors to our rooms were required to be freshly waxed. We noticed that Sergeant Matthew arrived at the platoon's HQ a little earlier than usual on this particular morning. That's when he asked me, while I shined the hallway, if I would rather have a Ranger tab or a CIB (combat infantry badge). As I stated earlier, the prospect of receiving the latter meant everything to me. The former meant nothing. Matthew's day started with probably the hardest of his leadership duties: donning his formal dress uniform and informing Ranger wives and family members that their husband/son/father would not be coming home, ever.

Alpha Company was quickly put on official alert, immediately knowing where it was heading and when: lift-off by plane from Lawson Army Airfield would happen in less than twenty-four hours. I remember being told that we could call home and tell our folks that we were going "somewhere," but we were prohibited from saying where. On the phone with my mother that night, sitting in the freshly waxed hallway (thanks to me and L-Man), I told my mom just that, "Yeah, we're going somewhere, but I can't say where." She asked, "Are you going to Bosnia?" I reassured her that no, I was not heading for Bosnia—not that I knew of anyway. But the thought of heading to "Europe" was more appealing.

Because of what was going down in Somalia, our plan of action changed dramatically. We would no longer be relieving the troops from Bravo Company but rather joining them. In what, we (at least the lower echelon of soldiers) had little idea. Instead of us gunners taking the new M 240 Gs with us, we were reissued the old M-60 machineguns instead. This may have had to do with the lack of enough 240s to go around. Though my gunner—Simon—had healed from his injury sustained at the "D" Compound, all of the troops under Weapons Squad Leader Clayton were to serve as one-man gun teams, each being assigned our own "crew-served" machine gun. But we didn't carry them with us on the way over to Somalia. They were all caged up in metal crates and sent over, while we stayed armed with rifles until arriving in Mogadishu. Standing next to the airfield's tarmac in Fort Benning, waiting for our transport, we all lined up to get one last medical shot before heading to Africa, right in an ass cheek. Because it was dark out, we had to drop our pants next to what appeared to be one of those massive signal/advertising beams of light, in order for the administering medic not to miss his shot.

Most of the flight itself from Fort Benning to Africa was pretty non-memorable. We had a brief stopover in Egypt, where we spent a few hours in what seemed to be a makeshift base for U.S. soldiers in transit to many different places. While there, we ate and drank a variety of "free" snacks from back home. When time allowed, a few of the troops curled up in parts of a sleeping area to cop some z's for a bit. At one point, I ventured outside of this "fort" during the daylight hours, consciously attempting to implant a memory of my stay in the land of the Pharaohs. I slowly turned in a 360-degree circle, panoramically viewing what lay in front of me. All I could see was sand, for miles and miles around. There were to be no tours of the Egyptian Pyramids on this trip. Our time there was a last-chance opportunity to prepare ourselves, physically and mentally, for the challenge ahead.

My mental preparation for Somalia was an unprecedented and unsurpassed psychological undertaking. Most of us expected to fight it out once arriving in Mogadishu. And since this was to be our "reality," so we believed, each one of us had to come to grips with the possibility that we would not be going home. I convinced myself that I would *not* be leaving Somalia and that there was a better-than-average chance of me dying there. For the most part, this was mental preparation at its best, or worst, for accepting death. It was a way for me to deal with the situation, making it easy (easier) to be in this predicament. If I worried about my own life and getting back home safe and sound, perhaps I would not risk "going above and beyond the call of duty" to save someone else's life, or at worst, I would make for a poor soldier during the ultimate test—combat operations. While psychologically readying myself for the inevitable, I convinced myself, without a single doubt, that there was a beautiful afterlife of some kind and that it was okay to die. Call it heaven or whatever, I *knew* that this place would be far more beautiful and pleasurable than anything I had experienced up to this point in life on Earth. Plus, even though I was only twenty years old, I couldn't complain. I had had a great life up until then, filled with wonderful experiences involving great friends and family. Three years later, after discussing life and death in a community college World Religions course, I told Professor Banks of this feeling that I once had. She said that once you get it, you never lose it. I can't say that I have lost the "belief," but I have never been as close to that same feeling as I was in Africa. Belief in a pleasant afterlife is a comfortable thought for many. And death without one just sounds so boring.

Approaching the city of Mogadishu in our Air Force transport plane, we were given the sign to lock and load, readying ourselves for an attack that any Somali hostiles might muster up. Once landing on an airfield, we hurried off the planes into the broad daylight. Instead of mortar rounds and RPG's (rocket-propelled grenades) pouring in on us from unviewable forces, there were other American soldiers visible and nearby, dressed casually (only the U.S. Army-issued brown T-shirt covering the torso) and leisurely going about their duties, such as maneuvering forklifts to move crates of cargo. Besides Rangers and Delta Force personnel in Somalia, there were plenty of other armed forces' units—combative and supportive—as well as other United Nations troops from various countries. The plane I arrived on contained only half of the Alpha company contingent. The other half arrived a couple of hours later. We quickly took our gear over to our sleeping "quarters," a concrete building that was said to have been an airport parking garage back when Somalia was up and running like "normal." We identified our cots for sleeping, lined in uniformed rows.

Soon after settling in, those of us present from Alpha Company encountered some troops from Bravo. They were still fully dressed in combat mode, drenched in sweat to the point of experiencing a sickly dehydration. A few of them expressed relief upon seeing us—fellow Rangers for backup. I heard one say, "Boy, are we glad to see you guys." I recognized two of them who I knew from the Ranger

Indoctrination Program two years prior. The first one I saw was ghostly-white, obviously shocked (a gross understatement) about what had transpired. His eyes looked right through us as he tried explaining what had happened. One reason I remembered him so clearly from RIP was because of a mutual friend we had in common. Plus, he had also been recycled before moving on to battalion. During his holdover status at RIP, he went home on leave, wearing his Class A dress uniform, complete with black Ranger beret and jump boots, as if he were in fact a RIP graduate. At the time, if a Ranger sergeant, or any other army leader for that matter, would have caught wind of this fraudulent act, he might have never been allowed to continue on with RIP, thus preventing him from becoming a Ranger. Here he was now, as I gazed upon him with wonderment and awe, an Airborne Ranger hardened by combat's realities. I thought back to the contemptible forgery of his uniform back in RIP. That episode seemed so laughable now.

The other soldier I saw was an acquaintance from battalion, whom I talked to every now and again during passing moments at the 3rd Battalion compound. At one time he was even seeing some airborne school gal I had hooked up with a couple of times. In Somalia, he was a machine gunner (possibly portrayed in *Black Hawk Down*). We chatted for a minute or two, as we had on numerous occasions in Fort Benning. But this time, I wasn't sure what to say or how to say it. I could only find a crude bluntness guiding my actions. "So how was it out there? Did you get any kills?" I don't remember the exact numbers he told me, but he nonchalantly responded with a "Yeah, about six or seven." And there was absolutely no doubt or questioning on my part. How could there be? He had been in the thick of it, along with the others. The only way he could have not killed anybody is if he had missed (highly unlikely with a machine gun at point-blank range) or if his weapon had jammed. I (and undoubtedly more so he), couldn't quite grasp the reality of it. Here we were, having a friendly conversation about some persons he just killed.

That same day, there was a memorial service for those Rangers and Delta Force personnel killed in the streets of Mogadishu. Representing the presence of these soldiers and the duty that they had done, their boots were uniformly positioned in a row, rifles erected upright behind the footwear, and helmets placed squarely over the butt-stock of each weapon. Though these soldiers had stood only hours ago where I now stood, a surrealistic wave swept over me, and probably others, who hadn't been "in the shit." I was emotionless. I tried to appear sympathetic, like everyone else. Yet in my heart, I did not feel a deep sense of mourning for these men I had never known. But I wanted to, thinking that it was the right thing to feel. As Sergeant Matthew once said, "I do not feel bad for the dead soldiers. It's the people they've left behind—wives, children, parents, friends—who I feel sorry for." They must go on with a terrible void in their lives.

During that first day of Alpha Company's arrival in Somalia, we were quickly informed that a ceasefire had been called between the two sides—the U.S. Military and Aideed's fighters. So for the meantime, we would not be going "out there." But we were also told that the enemy was holding a Black Hawk pilot—Michael Durant—hostage. An ultimatum was sent to Aideed: release Durant in X-number of days, or we are coming back in, this time with fresh reinforcements. As I look back now on why we were there, it is apparent that we provided a show of strength to deter any future aggressive acts on the part of Aideed's soldiers. This is Psychological Warfare 101. Show the enemy that it is grossly outnumbered and they might buckle. But if enemies of the U.S. have a death wish, as we are currently seeing in parts of the world, or an unrelenting and unified goal (Vietnam for example), added numbers simply present a greater challenge and may even give an enemy a newfound motivation to continue its resiliency.

While sleeping on my cot that first night in our cement-fortified abandoned airport-garage complex, I was awaked by Simon, who yelled something about an explosion. I sat up in a dazed half-sleep, donned my K-pot helmet like the others, and waited for further word. Truthfully, I was annoyed. I had been in a deep slumber, and the "explosion," I thought, must not have been that concerning since I didn't hear it. It turns out, we learned the next day, that a Somali had randomly launched an RPG into an adjacent part of our compound, near where Bravo Company was quartered. Two or three soldiers, probably on their way to urinate in the latrine, were killed. A memorial service for them followed.

With the ceasefire in effect and Durant in enemy hands, our original mission, the one we had spent a good chunk of time training for in Fort Bragg, changed course. Our primary goal *now*, we were informed, was to secure the release of Durant through force, should the ultimatum to Aideed be rejected. By this time, what had gone down in Somalia had been blasted over the airwaves into every TV set in America. Only spouses of Rangers were initially notified where their husbands were. I thought this was a bit unfair, to say the least. This meant that married Rangers were the first ones to receive mail from the States. And seeing as how we were only there for three weeks, once my family knew where I was, it was too late for me to receive any mail. My father at one point had to call 3rd Battalion HQ, demanding to know, "Where is my son?! Is he in Somalia?" Someone finally told him with reluctance, "Yes, Mr. Donayre, your son is in Somalia." L-Man married his girlfriend of six weeks before coming to Somalia, despite our unfiltered warnings (mine being the loudest) not to do so. After receiving a package, he gloated about having a wife because of Pete's and my earlier objection to his marriage. "See guys. If you have a wife, you'll get packages too." I glanced at Pete and gritted my teeth, angrily lacking any words with which to respond. If I knew then what I know now, I could have said, "Well, you'll be divorced in a couple of years, and your child will be another broken-home statistic." Such an end result was exactly why we had warned him against a foolishly short courtship.

Training to go in and get Durant involved simulating setting up roadblocks with Ranger special operations vehicles (RSOV's), while Delta simulated going in and getting him out, via Black Hawk. I was assigned to the back of one vehicle with my M-60, while a sergeant manned a fifty-caliber machine gun or a Mark-19 grenade launcher above. We drove around an extended training area, designated a "safe area" free of hostile elements, trying to perfect our maneuvers. Lieutenant Grease was in my vehicle, manning the front passenger seat. During one of these daytime training exercises, I hopped out of the vehicle and manned my designated position. When the call was given for extraction, I looked back, waiting for the signal to pick up. I never received it. The vehicle I was assigned to took off without everyone (me) in it. I was glad it was only a simulation. Then Grease acted as if it were my fault—partly perhaps. "Donayre, when you see us moving out, you need to pick up and go." So I was supposed to keep an eye forward on any and all enemy positions while constantly looking behind me to see if extraction was happening? It didn't make a lot of sense.

One night we also did a Black Hawk flyover of certain "hot" areas of Mogadishu, showing the Somalis that we hadn't left yet. Each one of us in that helicopter had a pair of night-vision goggles, enabling us to see more clearly in the darkness. On the "bird," as was our nickname for the Black Hawk, Grease checked his goggles to see if they worked. Apparently, the batteries were dead, meaning that he hadn't conducted a proper test prior to getting on the aircraft. While sitting there in the chopper, he told me to give him my batteries. I did, while thinking, *What a shit-bag platoon leader. Not only does he not have working bat- teries for his night-vision goggles, he's willing to leave me high and dry by taking mine.* Simon said I should not have given the lieutenant my batteries. Sure. As it turned out, we did a quick flyover of the designated areas, which appeared to be somewhat lit, not really needing any goggles.

In the meantime, while intermittently training to rescue Durant and doing flyovers, we stayed busy with weapons testing, guard duty routines, and armed-vehicle convoy escorts of United Nations supplies designated for certain areas of the city. We also rode around certain "safe" areas as a show of force. During one of our daytime drives around town, my squad leader, Clayton, absentmindedly dropped a grenade into the street. But the safety pin remained in it, thus avoiding an unwanted explosion. On another occasion, he borrowed gunner Mesh's 9-mm pistol to use as a sidearm, while manning one of the big guns atop the RSOV. Placed on the roof of the vehicle, it slid away without his knowing it. Mesh noticed the missing equipment and once again alerted Sergeant Matthew to it, as he had done with the firing pin back at Fort Bragg. In the short run, nothing came of it.

The usual route for armed escorts took us from our area alongside the airfield to the city "university," now serving as the UN's makeshift headquarters. It was all so sad, pondering over this area of the world and its failed attempt at what the Western world calls normalcy, things we take for granted. University life was nonexistent, Mogadishu's university being occupied and armed to the teeth by the United Nations; the commuter "airport" where we slept, a simple reminder of what could have been. Driving along the streets of Mogadishu, it was clear that the city's waste disposal units, if there ever were any, had long since ceased to function. The streets were paved with heaps of garbage. Women and children, in an effort to keep the sun's heat limited, wore sandless sandbags on their heads while rifling through the piles of trash, hoping to find anything of value. A few years later, in my community college days, a friend of mine at the time, Jason, summed up the ignorance and/or lack of interest that many Americans share about the outside world, "I don't need to go there [Somalia, or any other place for that matter], because I can see what it's like on TV." The horrendous smell and the day-to-day inescapable living conditions of the people are just some of the things that are filtered out of CNN's daily broadcasts.

Because of my "gung ho" patriotic attitude in high school, a friend of mine, Paul, was not surprised when I told him that I actually enjoyed being in Somalia. But it wasn't because of some noble cause that I was a part of, necessarily, or because I was hoping to experience combat while there, which I *did* have mixed emotions about. For financial reasons, I was glad to be departing for Somalia when we did. In early October, while I was already seriously short of cash, we left the States. The next payday wasn't until November. I had the bad habit (but fun as hell) of writing myself checks on the weekend before Monday's payday. For example, if it was a Friday and a few of us were heading out on the town, but payday was not until Monday, I would cash a check to myself that Friday afternoon, knowing (hoping) that the check would not reach my account until there was money in it (Monday). This plan usually worked. And sometimes my friends Tommy and Pete were broke as well, so I would cash a check big enough to cover all of us, and they would pay me back the following week. I had to pay a $20.00 service fee only a couple of times because of a bounced check. But luckily, I had a bank— Columbus Bank and Trust (CB&T)—that didn't notify your company commander if a check failed to clear. I know of soldiers who spent their Saturdays remedially writing checks for punishment/practice.

In Somalia, considered "hazardous" duty, we didn't have to worry about money. Our food was more than taken care of, as we enjoyed edible contributions from various UN members. Plus, crates of *Coca-Cola*—my favorite—were shipped to Somalia at tax-payer expense. On top of this, we were still being paid our regular salary, with an added couple hundred dollars for "hazardous duty pay." There were even rumors floating around that we might be staying for an additional five months. I started adding up the dollar signs in my head. A few Bravo Company soldiers, after spending two months there, came home and put generous down payments on vehicles of their choosing. We also had access to a TV with satellite dish, installed in Alpha Company's area upon arriving. After pulling an hour of joint guard duty one morning around three A.M., manning the 50-caliber machine gun on the rooftop, I watched part of a San Diego Chargers football game.

Besides the endless supplies of decent chow and cold soda, the expanding bank account and primetime television, Somalia, despite the garbage-laden streets, was a beautiful place in October. With its hot sun beating down next to the Indian Ocean, its climate and scenery were more preferable than the cold and rainy season of Scotland in the fall. As a weapons squad, we ran along parts of the secure beach area for exercise, getting partial (farmer) tans in the process. For security reasons, one of us ran carrying a rifle, while another carried a magazine cartridge full of ammo. I brought plenty of leisure reading with me (three novels) to Somalia, my favorites being Jon Land's *Blaine McCracken* series of fictional spy thrillers. I always got pissed off when being interrupted from reading to do some shit work detail, like reinforcing our indestructible concrete-living area with sand bags. We joked about "skinnies" (our nickname for Somalis) trying to breach our barbed-wire barrier. In the event that troops need to get across such an obstacle of flexible metal, and there is no time for a tactical and stealthy cutting of the wire, one soldier is supposed to quickly throw himself upon it, placing his weapon underneath him for some protection from being cut. Then the other troops have to run across his back, preferably stepping on a soft area as far away from the spinal cord as possible, so as not to get tangled up in the wire. Hence the expression: manual/human breach of the wire. Somebody, possibly Richard, simulated a "skinny" breach of the perimeter by laying a stick across the barbed wire—the stick being a "skinny." As we constructed First Sergeant Loony's brainchild—a reinforced sandbag outer barrier—some of us (lower-ranking personnel) not-so-subtly mocked it by warning against the possibility of an "8-hour 'skinny' artillery onslaught."

The evening before the Durant ultimatum expired, we rigged our vehicles for combat operations. I felt elated (whether real or imagined), knowing that this night could very well be my last one on Earth. Richard took notice of my "motivation" while he remained very cool in the meantime. We chatted a bit about what might lie ahead. He and fellow 3rd Squad member Jim had a "final" chat, just in case. Since the gunners from weapons squad were serving as one-man teams, we were responsible for carrying and maintaining our own ammunition. Simon, often setting the standard as usual, rigged his ammo box in the back of his vehicle in such a way as to prevent it from sliding around in the back. I considered this, but thought it would be a waste of time. What if we had to abandon the vehicles and take our equipment out? The next day, while waiting for a reply from the Aideed faction, we practiced our maneuvers one last time. With my ammo box sliding everywhere and tipping over on various turns of the vehicle, I hoped that I would have time to anchor the box to the vehicle before heading into the city. As soon as we returned to our quarters, it was announced, "They've agreed to release Durant."

Soon after hearing of Michael Durant's soon-to-be-release, within a day or two, we were told that our mission in Somalia was over. We would be heading back home after a couple of days. That is the point when First Sergeant Loony gave us a motivational speech (his only one) on the rooftop, telling us what an awesome company we were. Feeling like an integral part of the unit, once again, I turned to Sergeant Alexander and said, "I think I'm going to do it, Sergeant—get my tab and come back to battalion." Then we were "ordered" by Loony to relax during our last few days "in country," getting tans on the rooftop if we wished. I noticed that among some of the Bravo Company troops, the elation of having us (Alpha) around, since their battle, faded more and more with each passing day. As they enjoyed playing volleyball outside of their quarters (Loony prohibited us from partaking), their state of mind went from a joyous, "Boy, are we glad to see you guys" to a contempt-filled, "What do you know? You weren't here when the shit went down." And on our end, all that Sergeant Matthew could say was, "We would have done it better."

I was proud to be a part of what limited backup role we did play for Bravo. But unlike other soldiers from my company, I was not at all interested in hearing about their heroic antics. Initially, as I mentioned earlier, I was interested before the dust had settled, while thinking that we still might go "out there" as well. But I couldn't bring myself to crowd around the TV set among the others, with VCR attached, and watch actual footage of what had transpired only days ago. Part of me was a bit envious, because that could have been us, while at the same time, I took comfort in the fact that I didn't see any of my buddies perish. Richard remarked to me a year or two after the fact, "It would not have been worth it if you or Pete or Jim [or others] had died." But when is it *worth it* to die? As the late great Dr. Martin Luther King, Jr., said, "A life not willing to die for something is a life not worth living." I agree.

The night before heading back to the States, I sat on the rooftop of our compound just after dusk, watching one plane (filled with half of Alpha Company) take off down the runway. As I sat there observing, a soldier from another platoon sat not so far away, melodiously playing a harmonica. In the warm air of the Somali night, with comforting music in the background, I contemplated going home. "Tomorrow, that will be me on the plane, racing down the tarmac." I realized that I wasn't going to die here in Somalia. In fact, just the opposite had happened. I lived; happily looking forward to heading to America, I felt thankful. Like the helicopter ride over the jungles of Panama, it was an exhilaration I wished would last a little longer.

We arrived back in the States to extraordinary fanfare, a few of us questioning why all the fuss. Landing first in Fort Campbell, Kentucky, we were quickly paraded onto a field with a decent-size grandstand filled with welcoming onlookers. The whole thing seemed, and still seems, like an uneasy dream—partly due to the tremendous jetlag, no doubt. As if we were pawns appearing in an international chess championship, our moves were not our own to make, but we were heralded for the parts we were now playing. "Who are all these spectators in the bandstand?" I asked myself. Nobody in Alpha Company knew. "They couldn't be here for us," because we didn't know any of them. We were still a long way from Fort Benning. It must have been a big public relations ploy, officially welcoming the troops home for a job well done. To this, Sergeant Clayton remarked, "But we didn't do anything."

41-87

For Alpha Company's part in the Somali operation, we were each awarded the Armed Forces Expeditionary Medal (AFEM), entitling every participant to wear the *3/75 Ranger Battalion* scroll on the right sleeve of the uniform (a combat/hazardous duty signifier) for the rest of our time in the army, whether or not we stayed in battalion. I wore mine proudly from battalion to the DMZ in South Korea and onto the video rental shop during my final days of military service. Those troops from Bravo who were in "the shit" received the same, with Combat Infantry Badges (CIB's) to boot. A few of them were even awarded Purple Hearts and other distinguished medals—Bronze Stars for example—for combating Aideed's followers and other wannabees, or used-to-bees. One "B" Company medic, who was said to have been saved by his helmet, having been hit by bullets a couple of times, was still visibly shaken when he received his awards. "Never again," he stated.

Soon after being back at Fort Benning, I began counting the days until it would be possible to *41-87* (the number title of the document for requesting a change of duty station). My immediate post-Somali heightened sense of motivation for staying with the unit quickly rescinded. Since battalion was at least a two-year assignment, unless quitting early, I had two months to go before hitting my December two years of service anniversary. But I didn't have the gumption to tell anyone about my plans to leave, until I could "legally" do so, without officially being labeled as a quitter. For many, though, leaving battalion without a tab was the same thing as quitting. In the meantime, it was more of First Sergeant Loony's bullshit head games about the prospect of war and the need to remain vigilant—his justification for keeping us on an even tighter leash. At one point we were no longer allowed to stay overnight away from the barracks unless receiving approval beforehand. As Sergeant Alex commented, "So if you're dancing with some chick at the club, you have to be like, 'Sorry. We can't hook up, because I have to get back to the barracks.'" And up until then, having women in the barracks was never officially prohibited. It was a different sort of "don't ask, don't tell" policy. One time, I snuck up a friend of my roommate's girlfriend. Simon met her, saying to me, "Everyone does it." The only one to call me on the "policy" later, razzing me for having a female in my room, was of course, Phillip.

With Loony tightening the screws and Captain Silly letting him (who was really in charge?) it was clear that the barracks were *now* off limits to the fairer sex. On top of that, the legal drinking age of twenty-one was strictly enforced. In the past, underage drinking was also treated as a "hush hush" occurrence by our superiors. Most of us, if not all, had done it, often with our superiors present. My buddies from 3rd Squad later recorded me on video tape, ranting and raving about the unfairness of Loony's crackdown. Likening 3rd Ranger Battalion to "3rd of the Nazi Germany," I wore my beer-labeled T-shirt as a sign of support "for underage drinking," while downing a beer in protest. Sergeant Rural from another squad later saw my debut performance and wasn't too happy about it, calling me a shit bag on sight. Along with the new rules and regulations, there was plenty of cleaning to do around Alpha Company's AO. We had the prettiest rocks in all of battalion.

When December rolled around, with about a week or two to go before block leave, Sergeant Matthew wanted to send me back to Ranger school. This meant that I would not be going on leave with the rest of battalion. I mumbled to him and Squad Leader Clayton that I wanted to go home instead. After all, since I had missed the summer block leave because of pre-Ranger and Ranger school, it had been a year since I took leave and a year since I was home. I missed my mom. After bitching to others around me about higher-ups wanting to send me back to Ranger school, now of all times, Simon pulled me aside and scolded me, saying, "You're still a man. Act like it, whether you want to quit or not." The words still sting, particularly because they came from someone who is younger than me. But it must have been easier for him to say this since he already had his tab. This gave him leverage. Then Clayton gave me a bit of hell, rhetorically asking other privates if *they* wanted to go to Ranger school. Like matching parts stamped out at an auto assembly plant, the answers all came back, "Yes, Sergeant!" Then Clayton did something that was wholeheartedly human and totally unbecoming of him—possibly a reflection of his own short-time status in battalion. In a one-on-one chat, he spoke with me at a normal level, praising me for serving while expressing concern for my future well-being, "Look, you've given a lot to this unit, and if you don't want to go to Ranger school, that's your decision. But you'll regret it if you don't get your tab." And since that day, because he said that I would regret not getting a tab, I vowed to never do anything of the sort. In fact, because I don't believe in harboring regrets, I'm glad that I didn't get my tab. His "you'll be sorry" approach was another example of how higher-ups in the Service tend to make one feel, whether intentionally or not, that nothing exists outside of the "box." For many a lifer, life is the box or cubicle, depending on where you work.

Before heading out on block leave, I let it be known that I planned on leaving the unit. Sergeant Matthew told me to think about it over vacation. During our pre-leave photo-op, he asked me to pose with the platoon's guide-on (unit insignia flag) for the group shot, no doubt trying to stir the loyalty I possessed for the unit. It worked, but not to the point of wanting to stick around much longer. Lieutenant Grease tried questioning my manhood, asking in disgust, "You don't want to go to war anymore?" I told him that I would go right then and there if one were happening. But I knew damn well that that wasn't going to be the case anytime soon. He tried convincing me that it was just a matter of time. Besides, he wondered, "Do you really want to spend the rest of your days in the army as a clerk, sitting in an office somewhere?" *That sounds pretty good*, I thought, pondering over the amount of free time that would entail for extracurricular activities.

After block leave, I turned in my 41-87 to battalion HQ, requesting to head to the MP unit down the street where Tommy was working. The 41-87's, as with all types of bureaucratic paperwork, take time to process. Not only that, but a new place of duty had to be found for me. The MP unit wasn't taking any (more) former Rangers, so I was left open to worldwide assignment. Sergeant Matthew, though trying to give the impression of disappointment over my decision, was somewhat impressed with my rebound from the Ranger school debacle that nearly got me kicked out of battalion. "So you come back from Ranger school in disgrace, get back on good terms with the unit, and then put in your 41-87." It sounded as if I had planned it that way, which I hadn't. But I agreed with Matthew that that is exactly what happened. "Roger that, Sergeant." It was Phillip who accused me of jumping off a sinking ship, referring to the slide weapons squad had taken since he had left it.

While I waited for any duty station orders to come through, life carried on in battalion like "normal." I continued to cultivate my friendships with Richard, Pete, L-Man, and others, partying it up around the normal Columbus and Auburn hotspots. One night while Pete and I drove back to Fort Benning from some club downtown in his Nissan red pickup truck, Pete nudged me as I lay there passed out in the passenger seat. He said, "Hey, these girls next to us [in a car] want us to pull over." So we did. After chatting with them for a few minutes, we bought some beers and made our way to the trailer—no joke—of one of the ladies. Pete had his way with one gal and me with another.

In February 1994, during my final month in battalion, I turned twenty-one. The night before my actual birthday, I was out partying somewhere with Pete and another friend. Around 11:30 P.M. (a half an hour before my birthday), we ventured over to a club. The doorman looked at my *real* ID, asking, "Starting a little early, aren't you? Get in there." While shooting pool and getting more rambunctious with each consumed beer, a sergeant's girlfriend, with his initial approval, wanted to take me into the ladies' room because it was my birthday. I'm not sure exactly what she had in mind, but I said, "I'll go in there, Sergeant, if you want me to." Telling me at first to go for it, as I kept asking "Are you sure?" he finally let up with an uneasy, "No. Don't go in there." They eventually married, and when I left Fort Benning later in the year, for good, she had a little one on the way. This was the same woman who pulled a gun on him during their courting phase. For *Mardi Gras* celebrations in New Orleans, a bunch of us drove down there in Richard's newly purchased "boat," as we called it. Pete didn't come, saying that he was "all traveled out." We gave him shit for that expression, continuing to do so today.

Really though, he planned on hooking back up with the young trailer gal again and couldn't be bothered with heading to Louisiana.

There were a few of us in Alpha Company who had put in 41-87's around the same time. At one point, Captain Silly issued an order for all 41-87 pending personnel to be pulled out of their respective platoons and put in the "special ops" platoon, where they suffered humiliation for wanting to leave battalion. I'm still thankful to this day that Sergeant Matthew kept me in 2nd Platoon until my orders came through. Still short of qualified soldiers since the Juarez fiasco, he asked Captain Silly if 2nd Platoon's 41-87ers (meaning me) could stay with the unit, seeing as how it was shorthanded. While doing PT on the exercise field with weapons squad, as on any other normal day at the battalion compound, I witnessed the ops platoon being smoked beyond normalcy, as if the two years or more of service each one of these soldiers had given meant nothing. It was appalling to watch.

In late February, I performed my last airborne jump with battalion, it concurrently being my last jump in the army. I ended up with twenty-seven jumps, plus or minus one or two—the same number Jimi Hendrix had with the 101st Airborne Division. I became more of a fan after learning of this, never tiring of hearing his much-repeated songs blasted over the airwaves of any given classic rock station. My last jump was part of a one-night-only training exercise, where we jumped somewhere over Fort Benning, followed by a quick extraction upon hitting the ground. With my M-60 in hand, Sergeant Matthew barked at me when I asked him where I should set up. "Over there!" It didn't bother me. I knew I would be out of there soon. How right I was. As soon as we got back to the barracks, I was called down to the platoon HQ, where I was given my orders to report, in a few day's time, to the 2/11 Infantry Officers' Basic Course (IOBC) down the street, where I would work as an *ammunitions handler* for those cherry officers destined for careers, or attempted careers, in the infantry. My time in battalion, just a little over twenty-six months, was over. It's funny, now that I think about it, my obligation to Peace Corps takes me to just a little over twenty-six months of service—early June 2003 to late August 2005.

The Regular Army

In the spring of April 1994, about a month after being attached to IOBC, I received orders to report for South Korean duty in September. It was clear that Uncle Sam was getting every nickel out of me before my release from active duty, especially since I convinced myself the previous year during *Operation Team Spirit* that I never wanted to be stationed in Korea. While working at IOBC with many other ex-Rangers (quitters or expellees) and RIP dropouts and flunkouts, I came to see much of the "shit bag" regular army that I was warned about in battalion. Now I was part of *that* army. As ammunition handlers, our job was to supply the IOBC trainees the appropriate amounts and types of ammunition needed for their training missions. Though the job was often menial and monotonous, we did have ample free time for doing whatever. But we did have loopy sergeants in charge of us who made Ranger leaders look like distinguished laureates. Speaking of Ranger "leaders," I ran into Phillip on a couple of occasions outside of battalion.

As a sergeant living off the post of Fort Benning, Phillip was a neighbor of the marital L-man household (married personnel and non-commissioned officers—sergeants—qualified for *off-post housing*). On a visit to L-Man's place, I went to check out the pool of the apartment complex. Phillip was there hanging out with another sergeant, the one who nearly got shot by his fiancée yet married her anyway. Phillip was lounging in the sun, studying up for his next army promotional exam. Talking at me instead of with me, as he usually did, he said, "You'll have to do this too if you stay in [the army]." I was slightly intoxicated when I told him, "So I hear that you've been given a few army schools [to attend]." By this point, Phillip wasn't much liked by 2nd Platoon's other sergeants, except for Sergeant Matthew, who, mostly out of pity, became Phillip's newfound golfing buddy. And it was Matthew, being the platoon sergeant, who made the final determination about which soldier got to attend which school. With a grin on my face from ear to ear, I said to Phillip, "So how does Sergeant Matthew's dick taste?" He was speechless.

He didn't know what to do. What could he do? Not being in battalion I was no longer in punishing range of his reactionary whims. I relished the moment. Technically, he probably could have called my superiors at IOBC and say that I was being disrespectful toward a non-commissioned officer. But even he wasn't that much of a loudmouth. Leaving him stunned from my blatant disdain for him, I smiled and walked away. Score one very important one for me. About two years ago, during the initial U.S. campaign in Afghanistan, I heard from Richard that Phillip was down in Florida working in a Ranger school unit as a member of the training cadre. "Good riddance," I said. "He's out of harm's way and most importantly, everybody else's way." And supposedly, he and First Sergeant Loony (probably *Sergeant Major* Loony by now) are buddies working in the same unit.

Though I still hung out with my Ranger brothers whenever they had time (Pete 41-87ed to a next-door unit not long after I did), I developed friendships with some of the other IOBC lackeys. My roommate Dan was a RIP expellee who had been with IOBC for about two or three years. He also ended up going to Korea. He was a nice guy who smoked a lot of marijuana while in the service. Though I may or may not have used before coming in the army, there was no way in hell I would risk losing my army college fund just to get high. This happened to a roommate of mine in battalion. Beer and occasional harder liquor were fine with me. Dan and I often went to concerts around town, watching ex-popular acts who had been on the downward slide for awhile (*Bad Company, David Lee Roth, Loverboy,* some others). I even went with him to the annual "Atlanta pot festival," where he got high and drank some beers. I just drank some beers. We met a couple of ladies there, mutual friends, one who I really liked (more of an infatuation). I sort of felt that because I was no longer in battalion, perhaps I shouldn't be so carefree and diehard to stay single. I realized that my unbridled party days had died with my exit from battalion. I wanted more than polygamous one-night stands. Plus, I was scared to death every time I went in for an HIV test, which were mandatory in the service, especially before moving on to new duty stations. Though I believed in the idea of *safe sex*, I was far removed from actually practicing the concept. *Coitus interruptus* was my definition of being "safe."

Dan and I, along with Pete and another ex-Ranger, also went to the twenty-fifth anniversary Woodstock reunion up in Saugerties, New York. We rented a van and made the journey north, stopping along the way to and from the four-day event. This is something that would have been impossible to do if I were still in battalion—"boohoo," many would say to that. Another reason I left battalion when I did, what I told myself anyway, was because of my sister's upcoming wedding in September. It was to be a big, elaborate event with family and friends, and I was planning on being in the wedding party. But with orders to be in South Korea the same month as her wedding, it didn't look as if I would be able to make it. Sergeant Matthew had questioned my desire to go home for a sister's wedding. "What's the big deal?" he said, "I've missed a couple of sisters' weddings." "I only have one sister, Sergeant." Everything fell into place. I was home in San Diego at the end of August for three weeks of leave before heading over to the Korean peninsula. Four days after the wedding, I flew out of San Diego—Korea bound.

I arrived in Korea in late September 1994 with only thirteen months remaining on my four-year army contract, unless of course I decided to reenlist. The thought did cross my mind on a few occasions. But if I was going to *re-up*, I would be changing my *MOS* (Military Operation Specialty). There was no way in hell I would stay in the service as an infantryman. I had had enough of traipsing around God-forsaken patches of land in the dead of night, pretending to be in combat. I thought about becoming an MP, an air traffic controller, working in army intelligence, or working as an army photographer flying around in helicopters. In the end, I decided to get out completely (meaning not become a once-a-month reservist) and go to college. My attitude was: either I'm in as a full-time active-duty soldier or I'm a full-fledged civilian—none of this "weekend warrior" business. Though, because of an empty void I initially felt after army service, I did contemplate going into the reserves.

While in-processing on the Korean peninsula, I found myself in a room with about forty other soldiers, male and female, who were also there waiting for assignments. I had little to no idea where exactly I was being sent to in South Korea. Then my name was called, along with a couple of other male soldiers, where we were separated from the larger group and told to come into an adjacent room. That's when I learned I would be "heading North" to Camp Bonifas on the DMZ. Apparently, the DMZ recruiter for Camp Bonifas had the unwanted task of selecting newly arriving soldiers, based on our army records, and sending us North. He was not very liked, especially since he told DMZ-bound troops that it was a "volunteer" assignment, but when we arrived at the camp, the first sergeant told us that we were not considered volunteers, and that we had an obligation to remain there for the duration of our time in South Korea. It didn't really matter to me one way or the other. I knew that wherever I was stationed on the southern side of the peninsula, the work would be the same—so I thought.

Once up North, a few of us newbies were part of the "turtle" unit until being assigned to our respective platoons of the Camp Bonifas compound. We drank a lot during this weeklong turtle phase, so much so that subsequent groups of turtles were prohibited from drinking until being assigned to their permanent units. One guy in my turtle group, who sorely missed his wife back home (wives of lower-enlisted personnel were prohibited from accompanying their husbands to Korea), drank to a dangerous degree—to himself and others around him. In a drunken stupor, he became erratic and confrontational. In one instance, he took a swing at a corporal and was summarily sent "down South" to in-process with another unit. During my stint in South Korea, I developed a bit of a drinking problem, or worsened a pre-existing one, that followed me into civilian life. At one point, I even asked a sergeant who had been in Korea once before, if I would have a drinking problem once I was back in the States. "Yes," was his reply, while alluding to the fact that it would eventually come under control. That's only if I chose to make it so. On the DMZ, with little to no contact with civilians, meaning women, and faced with the reality of serving as "speed bumps" to slow an invasion by North Korea's KPA (Korean People's Army), many of us drank heavily when we weren't working. I was amazed by those very rare soldiers who didn't touch a drop, while at the same time being disgusted by our Korean allies who drank while on duty.

After my turtle duties, I was sent to the one American scout platoon on Camp Bonifas—at the time the only one of its kind on the DMZ. In conjunction with the other South Korean Scout platoons, it was responsible for monitoring a designated area of the border between North and South Korea. This involved conducting armed patrols along the DMZ, keeping a lookout from a guard tower, and monitoring the surveillance equipment that was supposed to report any enemy action along the MDL (Military Demarcation Line)—the border that actually separates the two Koreas. Each side had a slice of the DMZ up to the MDL, where certain weapons, including M-60 machine guns, were supposedly off limits. It wasn't long before I was performing border patrol duties on the DMZ with an M-60.

When I arrived at the scout platoon, as was the case with battalion, I wasn't exactly greeted with open arms. And as was the case with battalion, I didn't care to go out of my way to be liked. But this experience of being a newbie was much different; one, I wasn't a cherry private any longer and I had some experience under my belt; two, there wasn't a harsh indoctrination phase for welcoming new scout platoon members, especially for those who were not privates, as there had been in battalion. Nonetheless, I was met with a cold shoulder by a few scout members, including some privates, who thought they were more hardcore because they had more time in the scouts than I did. One guy of equal rank said to me smirking, "Oh, you're from California. The last guy from California didn't make it in the scouts." Confidently I said, "I'm sure I'll be all right," while thinking, *Are you a fucking idiot? Don't you see this combat scroll on my right shoulder?*

While in Korea, I never properly prepared myself psychologically for the prospect of dying, as I had in Somalia. While in the latter, I knew that I had at least a chance of surviving should I be involved in a firefight. In Korea, I knew that if the north decided to invade, we would win eventually, but long after the scouts had been obliterated. I did not want to die in Korea. Part of the reason we were there was a complete sham, many of us felt. We were there to pull security for the hordes of dignitaries and paying tourists who came to visit *Panmunjom*, where Northern and Southern representatives periodically meet to discuss the future of the Korean peninsula. One of the buildings on "Conference Row" is divided between the North and South, as well as the negotiating table inside.

As a scout platoon, we usually worked nine days in a row and then had three days off. The first three days involved manning the DMZ area north of Camp Bonifas, where each squad of the scout platoon had a designated responsibility—manning the tower and surveillance equipment along the DMZ, performing armed patrols along the DMZ, or manning the daytime quick reaction force (QRF) building in case of an alert. The next three days involved some sort of training operations on Camp Bonifas, while a South Korean scout platoon manned the DMZ area. And then for the last three days of our nine-day work cycle, we headed back up north. As a new scout platoon member, I was initially assigned to a SAW gun, which I wasn't too thrilled about. Up to this point, I had never used one on a regular basis. During our first trip north, I found myself manning a SAW gun in the back of one of our transport vehicles, a deuce-and-a-half truck (a two-and-a-half-ton army transport truck often referred to as "the Deuce"), with a private by the name of Christopher (Chris) manning the other side of the vehicle. As I noticed in battalion and was now experiencing for the first time, the SAW drum, which holds the ammunition for the weapon, kept falling off. Chris remarked later that I appeared to him at that time to be a shit bag of a specialist, since the SAW drum kept kicking my ass. I was soon saved from the physically lighter duties of being a SAW gunner when Sergeant Acorn asked me if I wanted to be an M-60 machine gunner. I jumped at the opportunity, since it was a weapons system that I came to know and like/love.

As a scout platoon M-60 machine-gunner, I like to think that I set the standard. Others, including my higher-ups and assistant gunners—Chris and then later David—remarked the same. I heard one sergeant comment to another, "That's the best gunner I've seen in a long time." Of course, I had been trained by the best. Everything I learned in battalion about the M-60 more than came in handy while serving in Korea—from how to clean it correctly to how to carry it on a road march. In battalion, letting someone else carry *your* gun was a major no-no. But in the regular army, it was common for someone to give the gunner a break and carry the gun for a while. During my first road march with the scouts, a mere eight-miler, my squad leader kept asking me if I wanted a break from carrying the gun. I kept saying, "I'm good, Sergeant. . . I'm good, Sergeant." Then finally, after he kept bugging me about it, I said, "Maybe at the halfway point you can carry it, Sergeant." "Halfway point?!" he retorted, "we only have a mile to go." I replied, "Well then I'm good, Sergeant." Afterwards, Chris, who has been serving as a full-time firefighter near Philadelphia for some time now and is a good friend of mine to this day, said that he was proud to be my assistant gunner.

With only a short amount of time as my AG, Chris soon went on to become our squad's deuce-and-a-half driver. After which, a newly arrived private by the name of David became my AG. I was at first pissed about this, because now I had to train someone else on the gun. David was also from California, but from further up north (around Fresno) way past San Diego. Chris and David, along with Corporal Toonman and Jeffrey (Jeff) from Kansas, became my better friends among the scouts. We drank a lot around bonfires outside of our barracks, talking about this gal or that one we knew back home. David was hardcore to the point where he didn't appear to be or try to play such a role. It goes back once again to the supported theory of that drill instructor in basic training: those who don't put on any airs will be the reliable ones in tough situations. With his laidback disposition and friendly mannerisms, he soaked up any bit of military knowledge that was explained to him. I taught him everything I knew about the M-60 and how to take pride in being a gunner. But the pride I felt in Korea was unprecedented and something I only periodically felt while serving in battalion.

While outranking many of my peers in the scout platoon, it was my responsibility to be the best gunner that I could be. But, as I often look back, my behavior as a leader left much to be desired. Drinking to excess in front of my "subordinates," becoming belligerent at times in the process, no doubt cast my willingness to be a proper leader in a less than ideal light. How does one make an ass of himself on Saturday and then command respect on Monday morning? Out in the field one very freezing evening during our three-day training cycle, David, my AG, gave me a pair of *his* gloves to help my hands from freezing up, and he did it with such calmness and cool-headed control over his own icy predicament. It was no surprise when I heard from him a few months back that he was a squad leader in a Special Forces outfit. I still feel proud to have served as his gunner way back when he was just a cherry private.

Jeff and I were basically in the same boat. We were both in our final year of service and ready to get the hell out. He had served in the 82nd Airborne Division for three years and was now ready to go to college. While in Korea, he bought an SAT college entrance exam booklet and was caught reading it by our lieutenant during an operation's order for that night's patrol of the DMZ. The LT was pissed and ordered the sergeant giving the op order to smoke Jeff. Jeff had planned on studying sports medicine in college, but switched majors when he found out how tough and boring it was. He eventually earned a degree in psychology and ironically went on to work for the U.S. Border Patrol, which has the semblance of army doctrines that he bitched about. Up until I came in the Peace Corps, we kept in touch periodically but haven't been in contact since, mainly because I forgot to put him on my e-mail list before I left the States for the Peace Corps. I hope to reestablish that contact.

As an M-60 gun team, David and I rarely went out on patrol. To the Bad Religion song that we often listened to, "No Control," we would sing "No *Patrol*!" And when my gun team was part of the patrol, I usually went out as a one-man team without him. One of my biggest highlights of serving in the scout platoon, if not the biggest, was the time when our squad, out on a daylight patrol of the DMZ, accidentally stumbled across the MDL and into North Korea. The sergeant in charge of this particular patrol, Team Leader Sturgeon, led the patrol while our actual squad leader supervised Sturgeon from the back of the staggered squad formation. It quickly became apparent to me and another member of the squad that we were in North Korea. I took the opportunity to relieve myself beside a tree, urinating on North Korean soil—score one for the good guys! The other soldier took a picture of the MDL marker from the Northern side. When it became apparent to our squad leader where we were, he rushed to where Sturgeon was and chewed his ass for what could have led to an international crisis. Once back at the barracks, Sturgeon lost his job with the scouts and was reassigned to a desk job on Camp Bonifas for the remainder of his time in Korea.

Another memorable moment for me occurred when the celebrity stars Don Johnson and Bruce Willis came to visit us near the DMZ. Though I am a fan as much as the next guy or gal, I did not froth at the mouth over the prospect of seeing these Hollywood greats. But what made their visit a special highlight was the performance of Bruce Willis's rock/jazz/R&B band, and the fact that I "sang" back-up to his back-up singers. As I stood there in the crowd of battle-dress-uniform-wearing soldiers, listening to the better-than-decent sounds of Mr. Willis's group, he invited a few of us up on stage. I, and about three or four other soldiers, jumped at the invitation. I soon found myself on stage next to Bruce Willis "singing" with his few back-up singers—some lovely ladies of African descent—and a couple of other soldiers, also of African descent, but not so lovely men. With all of us on stage, it was hard for me to get a note in edgewise. After a couple of songs or so, I exited the stage, unnoticed, and left a potential singing career withering in its cradle.

After six months with the scouts and being fed up with how things were being run, which was often my outlook no matter where I was, I volunteered to serve as the Camp Bonifas lifeguard at our dinky little summer pool. The original soldier who was assigned to do it became reluctant to do so, so I took his spot and he became the squad's new M-60 machine gunner. After he proved to be an uncaring gunner, my old squad leader remarked to me, "You know, Donayre, allowing him to be the gunner and letting you be the lifeguard was the biggest mistake I ever made." I was more than flattered. The same sergeant had asked me earlier on while I was still a scout, "Is your gun clean?" "Yes, Sergeant," I replied. "You know, Donayre," he said, "I can always count on you to properly clean your weapon." Barely inspecting the gun, he handed it back to me, knowing that it was clean. I would sometimes check my gun out of the arms room on my off time and clean it while drinking a few beers. I felt that we were sometimes not given enough time during the working day. Plus, I just didn't work that fast. I often needed the extra time.

Lifeguard duty during the summer was sham duty, but I was getting out of the service in a few months, so why would I care about what my peers thought? Some of them were envious, of course. Others razzed me because I was no longer a scout, but I continued to live in the scout barracks and party with them on their off days. Their off days corresponded with mine, unlike the other lifeguard/ex-scout, who had to work when they were free. Though I drank way too much, my bloated stomach being an indicator, I made some positive use of my excessive freetime as a lifeguard. I got back into good running shape by using a treadmill across the way from our barracks. On my last Army PT test, I maxed my two-mile run time, scoring 100 points. I utilized the small resource center on our compound, not only to play the video game *Pilot Wings* with Chris, but to introduce myself to the German language by using self-learning tapes. I was excited about my scholastic future and all of the possibilities that would go along with it. I also wrote a couple of opinion-editorial (op-ed) pieces to the U.S. Army-sponsored *Stars and Stripes* newspaper.

The first one I wrote was in regard to a recent news article about South Korean protesters wanting the U.S. Army out of South Korea, especially after U.S. Army servicemen were accused of raping a young Korean girl. I basically apologized to the South Korean people for any wrongdoings that such personnel may have committed, while saying that they "did not represent the best of the U.S. Military." And I concluded by stating that "if the U.S. Army pulled out of South Korea today, the next day, North Korea would roll through here like a 'Mac truck' while showing no mercy for their Korean 'brothers.'" Thus the U.S. Military, many South Koreans would agree, provided a very valuable service for the Republic of Korea.[xii] Word of this writing quickly spread around the camp. One sergeant came up to me, the one who had said that I was the best gunner he had seen in a while, and jokingly asked, "You're still here? I thought they would have sent you south by now." Then he told me that some of his Korean colleagues wanted to know who I was because of my published criticism of them. I had also stated in the piece that many of these Koreans serving in Camp Bonifas (KATUSA—Korean Augmented to the United States Army) appeared to be "spoiled rich kids who feel the same way those protesters do, unlike the real ROK [Republic of Korea] soldiers" who were seriously committed to confronting any northern threat in the future. The funny thing is: one of the harsher points I made was completely edited out of the final print. I mentioned hearsay "evidence" regarding our Korean "allies'" stronger inclination to turn left or right during battle and shoot an American soldier rather than turn their weapons on the advancing hordes from the north.

The other op-ed piece I wrote for *Stars and Stripes*, while not receiving as great of press coverage, focused on the fiftieth anniversary of the atomic bombings of Hiroshima and Nagasaki. The article I referred to in my writing, while mentioning the terrible results of the atomic blasts, dealt with atrocities committed by Japanese soldiers against their American captives. Basically, "should Japan apologize?" was the theme of the original article. In my centrist-right political leanings of the time, I argued that a "thank you" was more important than an apology. "Japan would not be where they are today [economically and socially prosperous, with a liberal constitution written by the U.S. occupation authorities] if it weren't for the United States of America."[xiii]

I think because of these early attempts at writing, some of my higher-ups treated me with a bit of respect. It was a great feeling, much appreciated at the age of twenty-two. A couple of officers—captains—chatted with me in a friendly manner as if we were old acquaintances, seemingly interested in what my post-army plans were. The first sergeant on Camp Bonifas, who coincidentally had the same name, and that is all, of Loony from battalion, once asked me what my plans were for the future. I told him, brown-nosing to a small degree while telling the truth, "Well, First Sergeant, I plan to go to college and then maybe come back in the service, perhaps in army intelligence." His reply, "Nah, you'll probably go on to do bigger and better things." Wow, such encouragement was heart-warming. Another boss of mine, a medical sergeant who was my superior while I served as a lifeguard, described me to someone as a "literary genius." Far from being a genius of any kind, I had a long way to go before writing some type of accepted literature, should I ever get there, or should I ever want to. First, I had to take Introduction to [Writing] Composition at my hometown's community college and make the uphill climb from there.

The Addiction of Knowledge

While ignorance might be bliss, as the old adage goes, there is one thing I have learned after seven years of formal university education and life experience between the services: *knowledge is addictive*–truly.

I was released from active duty in November 1995, but still had to "do" three years of service in the inactive ready reserve (IRR). On IRR, I never had to show up for any sort of training anywhere, but the army made half-hearted attempts to keep tabs on me. I was expected to fill out notices or changes of residency every so often, which I just ignored after awhile. Basically, being in the IRR meant you were one step below the reserves, who actually did some training. I knew that only if the world were ablaze would I be called back to service. On my flight home from Korea to the out-processing station in Washington State, I got blitzed over the joy of starting a new chapter in life. In fact, I was drinking so much–taking advantage of the complimentary alcoholic drinks available on international flights–I was cut off by the flight crew. Being somewhat belligerent, though non-threatening, I requested to speak with the captain, who backed up his crew. Then, trying to be comedic, I ordered a "screwdriver without vodka." Eventually, to what must have been the crew's and surrounding passengers' delight, I passed out until landing.

Through the state of Washington, where I officially terminated my employment with the federal government, I applied for Workers' Unemployment Insurance (Washington payments reportedly being among the highest in the nation), after which I received around $800 a month while living in San Diego, California, over the next six months–like clockwork. Of course, I always checked the "Yes" box identifying that I was indeed actively searching for employment.

I spent the next twenty-six months living at my parents' home in Imperial Beach and attending Southwestern Community College, attempting to set the standard among my peers, most of whom were younger than me, or at least make up for an abysmal high school academic record. Moving back home proved to be a greater challenge than I had anticipated. No longer was I a visitor on army leave, welcomed home as a temporary guest. Now I was an at-home son in his early twenties, who, if not studying hard was out with old high school buddies/acquaintances partying hard—too hard at times. On a few occasions, I drove my '93 Ford Mustang, purchased with funds saved from the army, while heavily intoxicated. I was involved in a minor fender-bender with a lady and her kids, though I played it off as if I were sober—the sign of an experienced drinker. As a result, we exchanged insurance information without police presence. The least of what could have transpired, my insurance went up. And my mother saw the damage to my car, as minor as it was, and rightfully chewed me out about "your drinking," as she called it. Though I did set the standard for academic performance in many of my classes, I didn't know how to handle school vacations and weekends free.

For the first time in over four years, I could do what I wanted and could go where I wanted without "Big Brother" looking over my shoulder. But now I was back in my parents' household. Though I could do what I wanted, I had to endure their nagging criticisms, with those from the rest of the family in San Diego, as long as I lived there. The hardest part: I knew that they meant well and wanted to see me succeed, no matter which path I followed. The more I've progressed in life since joining the army, the more encouraging and supportive they've been about my choices, while becoming less inclined to question where it is I'm heading. Regardless, I felt that in a few respects, returning home four years later was a bit of a step backward. I was happy to transfer to the University of California, Santa Barbara (four hours north of San Diego) after two years of community college, "branching out on my own (again)," as I explained it to my mother. And of course, she and the rest of the family were proud of this decision, assisting me with anything I might need or want.

As noted above, the first couple of post-army years was a period of major transitioning. The only thing certain to me was that I wanted to study history in college, having declared it as my major (and sticking with it) before the first day of college began. As far as future *service* of any kind, I greatly considered it, and even accepted it as the most likely career option. And being a veteran of the armed forces, I knew I could literally bank on my "preferential hiring" status with the federal government. But what could I do? Though the benefits were (and are) appealing, I wanted something more exciting than secure employment working as a clerk in some government building, looking forward to retirement down the road—twenty years later.

As a kid, I often thought of becoming a police officer and still considered some kind of law enforcement career while in community college. I briefly (very briefly) thought about working for the state of California as a highway patrolman—a CHP. The more college years I accumulated under my belt, realizing that I would earn a degree eventually, the more I felt I should obtain a job that required at least a bachelor's degree. Though I strongly believe in the notion of knowledge for knowledge's sake, I equally loathe the thought of doing something—five years of college— for nothing, meaning not utilizing the degree earned. But the latter could more easily be gotten over. (For example, I contemplated becoming a firefighter while in graduate school. To this, my mother said, "If you were going to do that, you should have done it right after the army." But the knowledge obtained, no matter where it takes me, is invaluable in and of itself—no regrets!) Federal law enforcement (DEA, FBI, CIA) had great appeal, though I can't say that I would have appealed to those organizations. The more months and years that pass by since army service, the more I appreciate not having to take orders from some jackass, as well as not having to run every morning, or any morning for that matter, if I choose not to. So the thought of chasing bad guys for the U.S.A. became less and less appealing for me personally, though I am in awe and appreciative of those who have made a career out of doing so.

While thinking about which career path to pursue and enjoying the process of learning in a formal community college setting, I was reminded of my veteran status, for good or bad, whether I wanted to be or not, almost daily. At times I felt isolated and alone because of dealings I had with friends and acquaintances who hadn't served, and who had no concept (in my eyes) of service, as well as a few unsavory encounters with other veterans. Part of these negative feelings I no doubt brought upon myself. Rarely did I boast about my army experiences in an arrogant manner. I tried consciously making an effort to be modest (even more so now) but yet remain proud at the same time. I usually became defensive (or offensive) if some idiot "friend" of mine made over-the-top criticisms about serving in the military, or took a shot at me personally. It sometimes came to a point where I preferred not answering questions about serving because of stupid questions thrown my way, "Did you carry a big gun?" for example. Most persons didn't understand or care to understand, so I rarely mentioned that I was in the service. (Here in Moldova, almost two months went by before the Peace Corps volunteers whom I trained with, having had daily communication with each other for ten weeks, knew that I was in the army. A simple question to me, "So what did you do after high school?" always does the trick.) But I was always more than willing to chat with someone who had a genuine interest in hearing what my experiences were like in the military. Once, I chatted with a roommate of mine at UC Santa Barbara about army life until four A.M., because the intelligible questions kept flowing.

As an army veteran receiving money for school from the government, every semester I had to take my official class schedule to the VA (Veterans' Affairs) office of the community college campus and show that I was indeed progressing toward a degree in my stated field of study—history. In order to receive full-time pay (a little over $800) a month, we were required to take a full-time study load of twelve units—four courses. Every time I walked into the VA office on campus, I had an uneasy interaction with the staff—composed of other veterans—whom I felt unwelcome around. Perhaps this uneasiness was due to my own insecurities about being a college student and the overwhelming desire I had to make the most of my army college fund and GI Bill.

On one of the routine trips to turn in my course schedule for the semester (near the end of my two years in attendance at Southwestern College) to the VA office, the young gal working behind the counter—a fellow veteran I assumed—noticed that I was taking fifteen units instead of twelve (one extra class). With a smug attitude she scoffed, "You know, you only get paid for twelve units." *What a shit bag*, I thought. It's persons with that kind of attitude who are lucky to make it out of community college in four or five years, or never. Her demeanor reminded me of a squad leader of mine in Korea, who had reenlisted in the army after being out for a while. He said that when he was initially discharged, he sat around a pool and drank beer until his $6,000 savings account dwindled down to zero. Then he re-upped, in the infantry of all sectors. I asked him, "Sergeant, didn't you have any aspirations to go to college when you first got out?" "No," he bluntly stated. Well, there you have it—another veteran (having previously been honorably discharged) counting down the days until retirement.

Two years of community college quickly rolled by, the last three semesters of which I worked as a copy consultant/nighttime shift supervisor at the world-renowned Kinko's Copies, once my Washington state unemployment insurance ran out. I was happy to quit that job, where the good workers there were underpaid and had to deal with both unruly customers and shitty co-workers. It seemed to me that those employees who knew they were going to be there only for a short while often pulled the weight of the Kinko's careerists. The worst time to work there, as can easily be guessed, was during the holiday season, when throngs of obnoxious and detestable shoppers, thinking that their Kinko's-produced family-portrait color calendars are more important than everybody else's, nearly beat down the door on Christmas Eve. It's a disgusting part of the American landscape, and yes, I am venting. I never got paid enough, nor would I ever, to take such shit from customers. And though I was always polite and courteous at work, as in life, I had no problem "raising my voice" at an ass of a customer now and again. The customer is not always right. But in a year and a half's time, I only had to get louder than normal on three occasions.

I began studies at the University of California, Santa Barbara (UCSB), in January 1998. At the orientation beforehand, we, meaning us transfer students, were warned about taking our studies too lightly. It was stated, "Transfer students often have the biggest problems, because they come in with this 'I've been in college already' attitude." There was more than a kernel of truth to this statement. I went from history courses where I had to read a book a month at the very most, to having to read twelve books on average during a ten-week quarter—if I wanted to excel anyway. In my first quarter at UCSB I received a measly 3.0 GPA—a "B+," "B," and "B-" for my three four-unit classes. This was appalling, seeing as how I left Southwestern Community College with around a 3.75 GPA. The one-week break between the winter and spring quarters allowed me to collect my thoughts and determine what I wanted to do in the future. I knew that if graduate school of any kind was to be in the cards, a 3.0 wouldn't cut it. From the next quarter on, I tried like hell to read every page of every book assigned for each class. This had generally worked as an undergrad but led me to nearly pass out on one or two occasions in master's history classes at the California State University, Sacramento (CSUS).

One of the first things I did at Santa Barbara, during the first week of my first quarter, was to call the university's student health center about assisting with some sort of volunteer program related to alcohol education. I knew that in order to keep myself from developing a serious drinking problem and wishing to avoid giving up alcohol all together (it's just plain fun and tasty to drink on occasions), I had to get involved somehow. Seeking help for one's self, if possible, and giving of one's self is the best way to avoid disaster. So I ended up, after sitting through a quarter of instruction about the effects of alcohol and drug usage, becoming a "peer educator" for a student organization known as STAR—Students Teaching Alcohol and other drug Responsibilities. The name is misleading. After the initial smirk received after stating the title of the organization, I had to overly clarify that "we are not an abstinence group." I have to say, the group probably did more for me than I did for it. As peer educators, we went around to different student organizations (freshman dormitories, fraternities, and sororities) and talked about "moderate and responsible usage for those who choose to use, while supporting those who choose not to use." I never really felt comfortable with this task of STAR. Personally, I was just glad to be part of an organization that discouraged drunken idiocy. Plus, we hung out every now and again, in meetings and in less than official settings. There were a couple of cute gals in the group, and seeing as how my nose was now usually in a book, "organized fun" was a much-needed break from time to time. But being a bit older (I turned twenty-five during my first quarter of study at UCSB) and a bit more serious than many of my peers, I often preferred talking to "Aunt" Judy, who was the staff director/overseer of STAR.

While contemplating graduate school as a first-quarter junior, I still pondered the thought of future federal service. If nothing else, focusing on diplomatic history and international relations intensified my desire to explore that which I had read so much about. At best, perhaps I would work in an international capacity—State Department foreign service officer (FSO) came to mind. (In fact, last April, 2004, I took and failed the foreign service written exam at the U.S. Embassy in Chisinau, opting not to take it again this year.) A year and a half of study in Germany, while technically still enrolled at UCSB (UC Education Abroad Program) fed my addiction for knowledge. The program consisted of one semester of enrollment at the University of Bayreuth in Bavaria (the home of Richard Wagner) and two semesters of enrollment at the University of Goettingen in the German State of *Nieder-Saxon* (Lower Saxony), where the future "Iron" Chancellor Otto von Bismarck was reportedly expelled because of his rambunctious behavior. "I'll show you!" he must have exclaimed, later ruling over the united German principalities in a few years' time.

While living in Bavaria on the Czech border, I ventured over to Prague no less than five times, where the beer and women were inexpensive. I was only adventurous to the point of staying "secluded" within the familiar surroundings of the Czech capital, knowing where my student loans would take me. One of my German roommates, Matthias, laughed at me because I kept going to Prague instead of trying somewhere new. I even took Maria—my German girlfriend at the time—there for her birthday once. I knew a man there, "Uncle" Anton, who always rented nice apartments to me and my friends/family for dirt cheap—five to ten dollars a person per night. In turn, I sent other vacationers from Germany his way for business. But I like to think that I did this more because he was genuinely a nice person I didn't mind providing free advertising for. While in Germany, it was my dream to do a grand tour of the capitals of Eastern Europe. I didn't do it then, but my position in Peace Corps has greatly helped out with this. I always tell persons, "If you want a great time for cheap in Europe, go east." But as is the case with Prague nowadays, since I was there in 2000 and even before, the tide of Westernism has engulfed the magnificent city. And it is continuing east. Next stop: Budapest.

After telling others that I studied history as a major, the standard reply was, "Oh, so you're going to be a teacher." "Perhaps," I usually said, really wanting to say, "No, I'm going to kill people for the United States government," just to see their reaction. I've long since come to terms with the reality that that is what history majors do; they teach. Certainly, there is nothing wrong with this. In fact, there is everything right about it. If in fact I do end up teaching as a career, and I just well might, I want all that an advanced degree entails. The "norm" was always less than desirable. It seems like nowadays, a bachelor's degree is a given. I wanted at least a master's degree for many reasons: greater knowledge for personal and professional sake, higher pay, a certain level of prestige, and increased opportunities. I never thought that the pursuit of a master of arts degree in history would ultimately lead me to the Peace Corps where I would subsequently write this book. That's one reason why it pangs me to hear things like, "Studying history is not practical. There's no money in it." This reminds me of a conversation I had yesterday with a Moldovan teaching colleague. She asked me what I planned to do when I returned to the United States. I said, "Perhaps I'll work in an *office* somewhere." (I used the general concept of *office* because Moldovans I often encounter tend to think in generalities when it comes to employment.) She said, "But you're a historian. What can you do in an office?" This goes to show: narrow-mindedness knows no boundaries.

Joining the Corps

As I mentioned much earlier, I often refer to the Peace Corps simply as "the Corps." I was told by another volunteer, something I had already assumed, that this special designation would not be looked upon so kindly by marines under arms, especially since a great number of them have recently seen action, or worse, in Iraq. Mainly because of my own military background and sense of humor to boot, the term is hilariously fitting. When I was getting ready to go into the Peace Corps, a fellow army veteran friend of mine—Christopher from Philadelphia—said that one day I'll be in a bar somewhere, talking with some old marine. And I'll be able to say, "Yeah, I was also in the Corps." If I had served in the marine corps instead of the army, I could have called this work, *What It Means to Serve: From Corps to Corps.* Oh well.

On the transatlantic flight out of New York for Peace Corps (PC) service in June 2003, I began writing what was a purely PC-based documented personal story; that is before the battery in my laptop was quickly drained of its power. One reason I chose to come to Eastern Europe was because of the extraordinary beauty I knew that the women here possess. Little did I know that the gal (Julia is her name) I was assigned to sit next to from New York to our stopover destination of Istanbul, Turkey, would become my loving girlfriend for the next two years, and then some. But of course, at the time I wanted an aisle seat, and she was happy to have the extra room from my vacant position, so I changed locations. After which, I began my PC story with a serious reflection as to why it is that persons join "the Corps." Earlier, I alluded to why it is that persons choose federal service in general—but why the Peace Corps in particular? I took a stab at the question, including some of my own personal reasons, while attempting to clarify how the Peace Corps functions.

Many people join the Peace Corps for a variety of reasons. "To save the world," a rather vague and superficial concept that usually resonates with a humor-filled

cynicism, is not a valid response. What's wrong with the world, ₍
saving it from? Some would argue that the world needs to be saved . ₍least
States of America, and since the "Corps" is a U. S. governmen
argument follows that Peace Corps volunteer action could never be
"saving the world." Then there is a practical reason of wanting to
percentage of humanity better its lot in life. That sounds reasonable. ₁
to note that the contributions made by volunteers in many developing regions of the
planet, whether in health and educational services, or in agricultural and environ-
mental assistance, were requested on behalf of local communities and sovereign
governments. And of course, volunteers are unofficial diplomats of the United
States, so positive volunteer action transcends into a favorable view of the
"American way of life." There is no better way of "saving the world" for yourself
and/or others than through diplomatic acts of kindness. A few dollars wouldn't hurt
either. Nobody goes into the Corps for purely idealistic reasons or for any one
self-serving reason. Just like nations and national movements throughout history,
individuals make choices with many motives in mind.

Speaking of history, my personal passion for history was a driving motive in my
decision to join the Peace Corps. In my M.A. studies at California State University,
Sacramento, I focused on twentieth-century European history, an infatuation I've
had since I was in the sixth grade. How could it have been any other way? Ronnie
was in the Oval Office and the Cold War kicked into overdrive. How was I aware
of this at age twelve? Thank God—no Cold War pun intended—that my parents
cared enough about being informed, letting the "CBS Evening News" with Dan
Rather broadcast nightly reports into our dining room. Why were there two
Germanys and why were the East Germans and the rest of Eastern Europe locked
behind the Berlin Wall and the "Iron Curtain"? These are questions I still
ponder, yet with a little more understanding and reassurance that I can give ade-
quate "answers."

Since writing this, I was disheartened to hear of Dan Rather's being forced into
retirement because of bogus reporting. Anyway, from day one of this Peace Corps
gig (the initial on-line application process), I had a specific job purpose in mind,
unlike many other volunteers who blindly sign up. I requested to teach English as
a foreign language (TEFL) at the university level in an Eastern European country.
"Ask and thou shall receive," though Moldova, which I hadn't heard of before,
wasn't exactly what I was thinking of when I said Eastern Europe.

When Peace Corps told me on the phone that they had a spot for me in
Moldova, I may have read the word Moldova at one time or another on some map
or heard about it in a news report about Europe. Upon hearing my choice [over
the phone], I immediately turned to my world map and thought, "Well, Moldova
is in Eastern Europe, next to Romania and close to Bulgaria"—two options I was
hoping to get. After [somewhat cowardly] leaving a message on my mother's
answering machine that I was going to serve in the Peace Corps in Moldova, she
called back and asked, "Where the f' is Moldova?" She is well-informed, keeps up
on many happenings around the world, like many of my friends and relatives who
also did not know where Moldova is. Why should they? Most Americans have at

ieard of the Soviet Union, and unless a person has committed to memory ie names of every former Soviet Republic, it is doubtful that he or she would know where or what Moldova is.

Regarding the "evil empire," my very first group e-mail home began with: "Greetings from the former Soviet Union"—*pretty cool,* I thought. After a short while of getting acquainted with my training village's "Internet Club" (composed of a dozen vintage computers where mostly young boys played graphically violent video games or watched vivid pornography), I received e-mails from family and friends referring to Moldavia (the Russian reference to Moldova—the former Moldavian Soviet Socialist Republic), Moldava, and Mongolia. My grandmother Lorraine was even worried for my safety when fighting broke out in the Liberian capital of Monrovia! When I went home last August 2004 for my grandmother's wake, I even heard my mom telling persons that I would soon be going back to Russia.

Another reason I came to Eastern Europe, a dream, some would say a twisted one, come true: I felt that I deserved a two-year, all expenses paid "vacation" after seven years of formal university studies. Plus, the experience of living within another culture and the opportunity of learning a foreign language can be career assets down the road. How can I effectively teach world/European history to American students if I don't have much-needed, first-hand experiences myself? Most importantly, working with motivated Moldovan students in and of itself has been the most rewarding part of this teaching venture, both personally and professionally. I can do without the unmotivated ones.

Core Training

With most new experiences in life, there exists a relatively short honeymoon period of heightened wonderment; a time when journal writing, if it happens at all, is at its peak. Moldova is no exception. When I was a student in Germany, I vigorously handwrote in my journal every day for the first week. Then it was two-three times a week for a period of one-two weeks, followed by once a week and on to once a month. Soon it was, "what journal?" I never understood how career diplomats and politicians could sit down at the end of a long day and seriously write in a diary about the day's events. In Moldova, my laptop has served as my "journal" and my word-processed letters home to friends and family have served as my "journal entries." Though I was often busiest during our initial ten-week summer pre-service training (PST) from early June to late August 2003, I wrote more consecutively about my observations and experiences than at any other time of my service. After training was complete and I became an official volunteer, I wrote periodically whenever something was fresh and exciting, which doesn't necessarily correspond to something good—usually the opposite makes for a more worthwhile e-mail home. The following letter is from that honeymoon period, when we trainees were all trying to adjust ourselves to Moldovan society, or at least certain aspects of it. We shared a commonality of being foreign/American, making many negative experiences, if there were any, seem rather tame:

Well first of all, the situation here in my Moldovan village of Costesti—pro - nounced CO-STESHED—is not as rural as I had imagined. The cold well water for my morning bath is right next to the house. I thought I would have to walk a mile or so to get it. And Yoga classes would have benefited my efforts to use an outside hole in a shed that makes for a toilet. The family I reside with is really nice and hospitable. The communication between us involves a skilled understanding of charades and the three phrases of Romanian that I know. My favorite: Cum se

*spune [in] romaneste? (How do you say that in Romanian?), as I point to some -
thing.*

Actually, now if I don't know something, which is still quite often after two
years, I ask: *Cum se spune in limba Romana?* meaning: How do you say (something) in the Romanian language? My comprehension of the Romanian language
has advanced slightly since training.

*Plus, I can say that I am a Peace Corps volunteer (Eu sunt voluntar in Corpul
Pacii). The [host] parents are in their early to late forties and there are two sons,
aged twelve and eight. The family is always smiling, laughing, and having fun. That
is a good thing. Well, if it is not at my expense anyway. The mother, Domnica
[Duna for short, pronounced Dune-ya], has an English-speaking nephew who
speaks English very well, so that helps out sometimes, even though I speak enough
English with the other volunteers. The house is a beautiful two-story home that has
a great view of the Moldovan landscape . . . I have my own room, on the aban -
doned second floor, with a table to work at. It's very posh. The family sleeps in
rooms on the first. All meals contain bread and some sort of cheese. There is often
a soup dish served (cabbage or chicken-type soup) with a piece of boiled meat in
the middle of the bowl. So far it has been chicken and pork ribs, I think. Domnica
makes a really great stuffed cabbage dish. I was never really fond of cabbage
before, but the excessive oil used gives it added flavor.*

And truthfully, I'm still not that fond of cabbage. Any novelty I may have had
for cabbage-laden dishes has long since worn off. Though I will choke them down
if served to me at a local inhabitant's house, I have discovered an array of tastier
soups served at the various dining establishments around the Moldovan capital of
Chisinau: cream of mushroom, cream of tomato, *solianka* (a better-tasting local
dish with a bit of spice and boneless meat).

Living alone in the capital, I tend to not eat as much of the traditional cuisine
as the majority of volunteers who live with host families in smaller towns and villages. Whenever I want a bit of nostalgia for Moldovan delicacies, I head to the
restaurant Sanatate (Health) with fellow city dwellers—other Chisinau-based volunteers—or with visiting relatives from the States. There are many different types of
edibles here that I find appealing, but there is one Moldovan entrée that we volunteers have agreed is overwhelmingly less-than-edible. That is *racituri*
(WRETCH-UH-TORE) or "gelatinous chicken" as we prefer to call it. It is basically composed of a cold chicken bone surrounded by a see-through *Jell-O*-look-
ing mold made from the fat of the chicken.

Though the focus of our first summer in the country was on technical (how to
teach) and language training, it was an important time for future volunteers to
adjust to living in villages and doing without the many comforting amenities known
back home. Most volunteers could count on moving to another village after the
completion of training. I knew that *university-level teaching* meant that I would be
living in a larger town/city for two years, which I was thrilled about. Though I did
not end up "roughing" it like many other volunteers who had a "real" Peace Corps
experience—something I never wanted—some villages were better off than others

in terms of access to basic resources for everyday living and for making the individual's job assignment less taxing.

Out of the forty-something volunteers in the entire group who met in Philadelphia, nine of us were placed in this village [of Costesti] for the ten-week training period. Supposedly it is one of the bigger and wealthier villages in the country. There is a disco (a.k.a. dance club) just down the dirt road from the house and an internet café around the corner. Granted, there are about six computers in the place and the connection "speed" fails to live up to its name. A couple of the volunteers have running hot water at their houses and one even has internet access at his.

What was most amazing, and amusing, was the fact that some village houses had internet access (and of course a computer to boot) but no running water. The complexities of indoor plumbing seem to far outweigh a seemingly simple electronic hook-up to the Internet.

Along with some maddening "sixteen hours a week of planned [Romanian language] instruction" and trainees adjusting to Moldovan rural life, it was a time for us to figure out if we really wanted to do this Peace Corps thing at all. If we planned on quitting, we were encouraged to do so within the ten-week training period, before settling into a "permanent" community and then deciding we didn't want to be here, which is our right to decide at any time as volunteers. Even now, as I near the end of my designated time of service, I could pick up the phone, call Peace Corps administration, and say that I don't want to be here anymore. Within a week, I would be home in San Diego. This amazes some Moldovans, most of whom must go through the laborious process of trying to obtain legal or illegal permission to work and/or study in the United States or other parts of the planet—a futile attempt for some. I only really contemplated quitting once, for all of ten seconds, when a minor blizzard set in during my first winter season here. I knew I could be home in warm and sunny San Diego by the end of the week. All I had to do was pick up the phone. It has been estimated that roughly twenty percent of every new group of trainings will not complete the two-year stated term of service. Our group, PC Moldova 11—the number eleven designating the eleventh straight year of Peace Corps presence in Moldova—is no exception.

We were not even out of the first week [of training] when we lost two trainees. They were a young couple who had been married for less than two weeks before coming to Moldova. During the training period, married couples are not allowed to live in the same village, but there are many occasions when they can visit each other. Plus, after the ten-week training period, they are placed together for the whole two years. She was in my village. So for whatever reason, they decided not to partake in the Peace Corps Moldova experience any longer. She came into the classroom after one break and said she was out of here. Two days later they were on a plane headed to the States. Coincidentally, they both have master degrees from my alma mater, California State University, Sacramento, and were slotted to teach at the university level here. All of us complain about some things here at one time or another, but HE was bitching about the program from day one. B-bye now!

As you can tell, I didn't care for this guy so much. Not only was he criticizing Peace Corps policies and procedures right out of the gate, including the type of survival language we were being taught—"*I am a volunteer in the Peace Corps*"—as if he knew better, he wasn't very friendly when dealing with other trainees. And supposedly, he and she didn't know that each spouse of a marital pair were to live in separate villages during the training phase. This probably put a strain on their ten-day old marriage.

During the progression of my Peace Corps service, I knew other volunteers, those whom I consider(ed) friends or friendly acquaintances, who *ET*-ed (early termination) or who were separated from PC for medical reasons. In fact, during my first semester of service I had three of what I call "ET dinners" with fellow volunteers at the same Lebanese-style restaurant—Class Restaurant—in the Moldovan capital. One of these dinners was with another young married couple—Brian and Nina—from the Berkeley area of California. I see with married couples that PC can either strengthen a marriage or strain it, the latter having happened with these two, who got married in order to be placed in the same PC location together—probably not the best reason to get hitched. They went home and called it quits after first quitting Peace Corps. Then there are my good friends—"Uncle" Patrick and "Aunt" Rosie—who have been married now for close to twenty years. Both in their early forties, they had talked about Peace Corps service a few years back and decided to finally make it a reality. Because of that decision, I've been fortunate enough to have had them as neighbors in Chisinau for a full two years.

Rosie was in my training village and Patrick was in my future girlfriend's—Julia's. As fellow "villagers," as it was with fellow soldiers in the same platoon, we bonded far more than any of us had planned or probably had wanted, personally speaking anyway.

The Americans here, all eight of us, often go to this bar across the street from our school after six hours of language classes on Tuesday and Wednesday. Moldovan beer from the tap costs about 30 CENTS (4 Lei) a pint [10-20 Lei in Chisinau—80 cents to a dollar sixty]. I exchanged a Ben Franklin the other day for 1400 Moldovan Lei, which should be enough spending cash for the next two months at least [two-three weeks in Chisinau, which is sad, seeing as how Moldovan university teachers get the equivalent of anywhere between sixty to eighty-five dollars per month as a salary]. We also got hooked up with Moldovan bank accounts. Though we will be volunteers, we will be receiving some sort of stipend to cover our expenses every month. I think it will be around a hundred dollars a month [more like a generous two to three hundred dollars per month].

Now that I am back in a European-esque country, of course I started hitting up the discos (a.k.a. dance clubs) again [what I did a lot of in Germany], where they close when you decide to leave. But since we have Saturday language classes (only for one more Saturday!) disco night is reserved for Saturday night. They have an "Americans get in free night," which, I think, is pretty much whenever we show up. [But then of course, we were expected to spend some green cash.] As I said before, the people in the village, for the most part, are really hospitable and inter -

ested in why we chose to come to Moldova, when many Moldovans [those who have the means] are deciding to leave the country in search of opportunities abroad.

Being American, in many countries, certainly does have its advantages. Despite the media's often negatively painted portrayal of the "ugly American," which itself has a kernel of truth to it, we are welcomed in more places than we are shunned. Many people here in Moldova are just curious to talk about life in the States and how it compares with theirs.

To retain an air of diplomacy when comparing Moldova and the United States, one must perform a balancing act. Americans in Moldova have obviously been to Moldova, but very few Moldovans have been to the United States. For the masses who have not studied or worked in the U.S., they "know" of America only from Hollywood blockbusters, the latest "gangster" rap songs/videos, or from filtered news services. As Galina—the Moldovan in charge of PC training of new volunteers—put it, "You are all kind of like celebrities." For many of us, this was fun and exciting in the beginning, until the constant unwanted stares (unless from beautiful women) and repetitive and single-minded questions about the costs of things in America became monotonous and stultifying. I didn't have as much of this living in the "big city" and having my own apartment, unlike my Peace Corps brethren living with host families in small towns or villages for a full two years. I could more easily blend in, which is what I wanted when going about town alone, especially when dressed in my business-casual work attire. More often than not, a local would come up to me and ask me a question in Russian—the unofficial first language of Moldova, "What time is it?" I always smile and say that I don't understand Russian (something I can now say in Russian). The person usually smiles back and then repeats the question in the "national" language—Romanian—if he or she knows it. But for a rare few volunteers, being "exposed" as an American/foreigner could/will lead to run-ins with unsavory locals who don't care about being good hosts for their American guests, who will always have life a little bit better; or at the very least, all of us volunteers are greeted with the same open-ended questions time and time again: How do you find Moldova? How much do teachers make in America? Do you like it here more than there?

Speaking of unsavory persons, hardly a week went by in training when we were not accosted by the town drunk(s) as we sat around outside on the patio bar, bonding over a beer or two ourselves, and venting and/or reminiscing about the previous days' activities. Usually he/they would talk incoherently and incessantly, while trying to make new best friends with us. The worst time was when one of them put his dirty mittens on a female volunteer, attempting to hug and kiss her, or trying to coax us into buying him/them more alcohol. Never before have I seen such a random display of sloppy drunkenness, often resulting in the crudest of behavior, as I've seen here during my two years of service. It's sad to say, but if there were an official national pastime in Moldova, drinking beyond excess would be it, myself and others having taken part on more than a few occasions. And this is even recognized by members of the Moldovan citizenry who would be viewed in the States as moderate and responsible drinkers, or from those who abstain altogether. From an early age, persons, especially boys, are shown that drinking is the obligation of men (I've known persons in the U.S. who believe this). Its part of the *barbat* (pronounced BAR-BOT) culture—*barbat* meaning *man*. Many of us volunteers continuously poke fun, or even go to dark humorous ends (myself included), at this aspect of Moldovan "culture." I know of one volunteer, living in Chisinau, who is working, or trying to work, with a Moldovan Alcoholics Anonymous group in the city. The problem is the lack of information or non-access to information that plagues Moldovan society, and not just regarding the consumption of alcohol, especially in the villages. That is one reason Peace Corps is here: to provide information.

There are times I see persons walking along the streets and I can't tell if they are seriously drunk or seriously handicapped, as they "walk" bumbling along, barely able to hold themselves upright. At my old residence in Chisinau, where I lived with a priest-headed host family—another story no less—for eight months, at any given morning during the week, men and women would be staggering about and/or rambling on incoherently, or they would be passed out in the bushes literally around the corner from my house. A few of us still refer to this old neighborhood of mine as *Zombie Land*. Because of this, and other reasons, I'm glad to be living in an eighth-story apartment in a relatively bustling, yet quiet enough, part of the city.

This drinking aspect of Moldovan society was clearly identified by Peace Corps administration during our training, especially during special "safety and security" sessions conducted by the PC medical office and the head security officer. We were warned about how volunteers who don't learn to say no run the risk of becoming problem drinkers themselves, and we were provided with past, yet anonymous, examples of volunteers who got into trouble, or worse, because alcohol consumption was involved in some form. If a volunteer has had any sort of *reported* negative run-in with a local, the PC administration's CIOA (cover its own asses) question is, "Was alcohol involved?" In training, if we didn't want to drink with a host family or other local, we were encouraged to say things such as, "I am a Baptist" or "I am on medication," whether these were true or not. Simply saying "no" was unacceptable for many a person, especially for Moldovan host families who pride themselves on their unrelenting hospitality. "If the volunteer says 'no,' just keep asking until he or she says 'yes,'" which generally works on some volunteers. I usually say yes the first time, unless I really have to get somewhere or have to do something that instance, but even then, "One drink never hurt"—famous last words. But before, during, and after training, Moldovan host families are briefed by PC administration about the do's and don'ts of interaction with American volunteers. Some take this seriously and respect the volunteer's wishes, and others, not so seriously.

During training, it seemed that whenever a volunteer initially had a gripe with a host family or member of it, the volunteer was reminded that the situation was probably just a matter of cross-cultural misunderstanding. But I've learned that there is a fine line between someone displaying a cultural difference and that person just being an asshole, which every society has more than one of. This is something Peace Corps didn't go out of its way to make a distinction between.

128

Being confronted by a "foreign" culture was an obvious reason why trainees tended to bond together; living under the yoke of the same ridiculous and seemingly Soviet-esque PC administrative policies, then and since, was a totally unexpected reason for commiserating. During training and beyond, we were constantly bombarded with the need to maintain cross-cultural sensitivity when dealing with the local culture. In fact, this was part of our official assessment. Failure to maintain cross-cultural sensitivity on paper would have resulted in our being sent home during training. In PC's defense of such information gathering on individual volunteers, if we didn't learn to at least tolerate the Moldovan culture and learn to accept, like, or possibly even love certain aspects of it, we wouldn't be able to effectively do the two-year jobs for which we signed up. But the techniques used were something none/most of us had ever dealt with.

There are only six weeks of training left before being sworn in [as official volunteers]. On Friday the fourth [of July], we had our first formal assessment, where we sat down with some of the Moldovan staff who work for the Peace Corps, to discuss our overall progress thus far. Just about everything has been documented on us from the beginning—Are we taking notes in class? Do we ask questions about Moldovan cultural practices? Basically, do we really care to be here and to do a good two-year teaching job and stay out of trouble?

Apparently, Peace Corps has had problems keeping teachers around for the full two-year stint. It seems that our every move is documented, from what color of pen we use in class to how many drinks we have at a village gathering. From what I have been told by one instructor, the teachers are not in favor of taking personal notes on Peace Corps trainees. It doesn't really sit well with students if they feel that their teachers are "spying" on them. Being in the former Soviet Union, I would make a joke about being written up by a teacher for displaying "bourgeois individualism" that threatens the "people's community." But the directive came from the American side, and as one Moldovan teacher stressed, "America is the land of freedom of speech"—something to that effect anyway.

In any case, my assessment went well and was relatively painless. My five-person panel wished that I continue to stay motivated while living and working in Moldova. I told them the Peace Corps said that I have to be motivated, so I have no other choice!

The panel laughed at this little quip I threw in. But if I and many of my fellow volunteers were "graded" today (fifty-four days before our departure from Moldova, according to Patrick and Rosie's wall calendar) on cross-cultural sensitivity, we would all fail.

When we weren't drinking at the local bar and/or fending off local drunkards, our summer training focused on preparing us for what we came here to do for two years—teach English as a foreign language.

Well, it's Wednesday, August twentieth, three o'clock in the afternoon, and tomorrow I will be sworn in as a Peace Corps volunteer. The last three and a half weeks have been pretty crazy, but they have also been the most productive ones out of this often ridiculous web of PC bureaucracy.

I completed a three-week "practice school" last Friday, where myself and four other trainees [including Julia—my girlfriend—and Patrick] left our villages every morning for fourteen days of practice teaching at a university here in Chisinau. The students were the best of the best—highly motivated and brilliant students who had the opportunity to take free English language courses on different subjects [definitely a caliber of student above and beyond the one we would generally deal with in our teaching assignments during the regular school year]. We were allowed to teach on any subject we wanted—something we knew or felt comfortable with. I taught an American Civilization course, focusing on history, politics, geography, economics, and current events. Since in college I chose to learn more about European civilization, I had a lot of preparation to do for my classes.

I had two periods in the morning. My first class averaged about twenty-five students and the second around fifteen. [During the year, on average, my courses ranged between four to twelve students.] My classes included issues dealing with the Constitution and the "right to bear arms," U.S. expansion in the 19th Century and today, American nationalism in comparison with other lands, issues leading to the Civil War, slavery, and Southern reconstruction. I would usually open the week with a history lecture-discussion on a topic, then we would often link it to the present—the gun-owning controversy or reparations for African Americans are two examples. It was important to have small group discussions and presentations, in order to get the students speaking English more effectively. Most of them spoke impeccable English and even those who had more trouble were easily understandable [I've had students during the year who could barely utter "my name is . . ."].

On the Thursday before the last day of classes, I had Moldovan students debating Southern reconstruction. It was beautiful. The scenario: It is April 1865 and the Confederate states have formally surrendered to the Union. My classroom was the meeting place for Northern Republican members of the House of Representatives. Half of the students were divided into the "radical" wing of the Republican party—those who wanted to treat the Southern rebels like conquered territory and administer the South accordingly until an appropriate time had passed when they could reenter the Union. Then there were the "moderates" who, despite the rebellion, saw the South as Union states that needed to be welcomed back as quickly as possible. Both sides had to deal with questions such as: What do we do about the freed slaves and how should the Southern states be governed until full-fledged readmission to the Union? One student really wanted to put the hammer to the South. I was convinced that she was a Yankee "radical" in 1865. It was awesome. Recently in Moldova, a decade ago, the Moldovan government had a "situation" with the separatist region of Transdniestria [in the eastern part of Moldova] that continues today. I wonder if that was being vented in my classroom.

I tried similar debates during my regular teaching responsibilities after arriving at my "permanent" university, with little to no success. There, only a handful of students are "practice school" material, but that's why I was there: to help lift the ones up who desired it.

Consequently, the day I wrote the above e-mail home was the same day Julia and I decided to give it a go. Though we were in the same overall training group, we lived in separate training villages. We became acquainted during this practice school phase of Peace Corps training. She initially called me on the phone to "discuss foreign language teaching ideas." Then, at the end of one of our shared rides home after a day of practice teaching, stopping in my village first, I asked her if she had "seen the fields behind the school"—not at all sly about my intentions. She said no, knowing full well what my intentions were, while being more than willing to walk beside me to see these one of a kind fields. Behind the school, with the garbage and glass-ridden "playground" of the school where my fellow trainees did their three weeks of practice teaching, she pinned me against the wall for a brief moment, her mouth finding mine. This August 2005 (marking the second year of our courtship), we will be moving to Boston together, where she will start a master of arts program in international education and I will be looking for work.

On August 21, 2003, after ten weeks of training in Moldova, I once again proudly took an oath to "uphold and defend the Constitution of the United States, against all enemies, foreign and domestic," as I had done when being sworn in as a soldier in the United States Army. But this time, I swore in as a volunteer of the United States Peace Corps. The Army and Peace Corps: opposite extremes?

Moldovan Society: Flexible or Organizationally-Challenged?

One thing that still amazes me about Moldova, among many things, is how a former communistic society, officially dedicated to the principles of organization and planning, can be anything but. Either Moldova as a whole has openly thrown off the shackles of the Communist monolith since declaring its independence from the defunct U.S.S.R. in 1991, consciously rejecting the stagnating planning schemes of the Soviet State at all levels of society, or the "benefits" of Communism, having *a plan* for example, were never realized, at least not in Moldova. Seeing as how the Communist Party, with hammer and sickle and all, governs Moldova at present, the former can be ruled out. The historian Eric Hobsbawm referred to the Soviet Union as having "pioneered the idea of economic planning"; [xiv] an idea no doubt accompanied by efforts at social planning. As such, when a national government prohibits activism from developing at the *local level* (Moldova) for over sixty years— not counting the Czar's heyday—while implementing plans from the *top* (Russia), it is little wonder why effective organizational planning, when it is happening at all, in matters of everyday life, is not the forte of the average Moldovan citizen.

Well, I was told to be flexible while residing and working in Moldova. Last Thursday, at our Peace Corps [swearing-in] ceremony, I met the vice-rector of my university: The State University of Tiraspol. After the ceremony, I was dropped off at my new host family's house in Chisinau. I was told that a car would pick me up on Tuesday at 9 A.M. The first thing I thought, "Awesome, four-day weekend!" After ten weeks of "basic training," it was a nice change. So on Tuesday at 8:50 A.M., while waiting around in professional ensemble and all, I got a call saying that I would not be picked up that morning, so we needed to reschedule [some volunteers didn't even get a call].

The next day, Wednesday, August 27, was impossible, because it is Moldovan Independence Day, which is a national holiday, certainly celebrated in the capital and most parts of Moldova. So we agreed that Thursday (today) at 9 A.M. would be good. This morning at 9:30, I realized that nobody was coming to pick me up. No problem. At a slow pace, the university is only a twenty-two-minute and fifty-one-second walk from my house. And I knew there was a faculty meeting at 10:00 A.M., so I headed over to meet my future colleagues, though I had already met two of them a month ago.

I arrived at my department's office at 9:55 for the ten o'clock meeting that began at 10:40. People kept straggling in at different times. The department I am attached to deals with foreign languages. I think it is the Philology Department or Foreign Languages Department [it turns out that I was attached to the Department of Foreign Languages for two years, but I periodically taught lessons for the depart - ments of philology, pedagogy, and mathematics]. So the "meeting" was basically a "who wants to teach what?" session, where the head of the department went down the list of possible courses being taught, and the teachers would say whether or not they wanted to teach a specific class. This took two hours. Earlier, while waiting for other teachers to show up, I spoke with one of the three male teachers in the whole department (three including myself [out of twelve colleagues] and no complaints here). So at our grab-bag scheduling session, he tried to volunteer me to teach English Literature. Shocking and all, but I know nothing about the subject and don't really care to start from scratch. At least our director asked me if I was qual - ified to teach it, and I quickly said no. She asked me what my expertise is, as if I have one. So of course, I said history. Well that falls under American Civilization, which I will be teaching alongside British Civilization and English Conversation of some kind. Basically, who will be teaching what over the course of an entire school year was decided on scraps of notebook paper in two hours—WOW! But I still have no idea what time my classes are and/or what days they are on. School starts Monday (September 1) or does it? I was told by the teacher who tried to hook me up with English Lit. that sometimes these things take a couple of weeks to iron out. Understanding my possible concerns, he said to just be patient—exactly what Peace Corps has been reiterating since day one!

Though I had declined this earlier offer to teach literature, I ended up teaching American Literature on three different occasions during my two years of service. It began with, "We need you to teach American Literature beginning *this* Wednesday," a message given to me by my English-speaking colleague and friend, Galina, who had translated the statement from the head of the Philology Department, who speaks no English and very little Romanian, mostly just Russian. My inflexible response, "Can I have a week to prepare [i.e., PLAN] something?" They said yes, so I did.

Because of my acceptance of this "call to arms," I was the big hero for a while, if I hadn't stopped being one after my initial arrival. But such challenges during my service were at first just that—challenges. What was once a "challenge" turned into an annoyance after time, eventually transmogrifying into a contempt-riddled atti-tude of the Moldovan university's, at least at the one I was at, total lack of planning and coordination among and within departments. At times, one department, right downstairs from another, would have me teaching a course at the same time as another course I was scheduled to teach for the other department, until I brought it to someone's attention. And the semesters didn't usually start when they were supposed to. Again—lack of planning. Courses that were canceled and/or changed didn't really bother me so much, as long as freed-up time allowed me to do other things, like work on this book. Though I became frustrated at times with how things were often run at my university, the two years (well the first year and a half anyway) spent there were truly phenomenal. And being intrigued by Moldovan history, even the name of the school made it an interesting place to work, long after the excitement of the work itself wore off.

The name of my university is Tiraspol State Univeristy [Universitatea de Stat din Tiraspol], and the capital of the separatist region in the East is Tiraspol. Often when I tell people where I will be teaching, they think I will be living in Transdniestria. The story I heard: During the civil war era (1992) between the Moldovan government and the Transdniestrian separatists, who sought, fought, and succeeded in maintaining an autonomous "nation" separate from the recently independent Moldovan state, there were those people in Transdniestria who did not want to be separated from Moldova. This included many professors and stu - dents at the university in Tiraspol. So these refugees left Transdniestria for Moldova and founded the Tiraspol State University in Chisinau. I will be the first PC volunteer to actually teach at this university. Including me, there will be four volunteers teaching at universities here in Chisinau. One volunteer has a year left to go in the Corps, one extended for a third year, and then Patrick and I were recent trainees.

Being a first-time volunteer at a site definitely has its advantages. I was not greet-ed by my colleagues and/or students with, "Well our last volunteer did it *this* way," meaning better, as Julia was initially confronted with by her students down in the southern part of Moldova—the State University of *Cahul*. But once she went above and beyond any and all standards the former volunteer may have set, they quickly forgot about the way the other volunteer did things. Some sites may even hold Peace Corps, and volunteers in particular, in low regard because of the trouble in keeping a volunteer around for the whole two years. This doesn't bode well for the site itself or for an incoming volunteer who is determined to see his or her service to the very end. Such volunteers are not expected to last beyond a year, often becoming treated as such by members of the community and/or workplace. Patrick's colleagues at the Institute of International Management (or as he calls it, the Institute of *Mismanagement*) were surprised when he returned after his first year of service, since the previous volunteer didn't. For some year-two returning volunteers, many are not treated with kindness or even with common courtesy until their intention of completing a second year has been made clear. And even then, maybe not.

In my case, being a first-time volunteer at Tiraspol State University, any teaching methods and teacher-student interactions I brought to the classroom were entirely new for my Moldovan students, except for the rare few who had a volunteer teacher in high school. But even then, the subjects we taught would have been much different. The English language taught at lower levels tends to focus more on grammar and on proper language construction; at the university-level, there is usually more of a focus on content knowledge and teaching communicative fluency. This is why I laugh when colleagues refer to me for grammar concerns they may have, as if I am indeed the expert on the English language. If something appears correct but doesn't seem "normal," meaning a standard part of American English, the volunteer trump card is, "That must be the British *variant*," the word *variant* being a favorite word used by English-speaking Moldovans.

Yet I find it comical that my university, where the professors and students are all technically adults, operates on a bell schedule, meaning that one of the key ladies at the front entrance of the university rings the bell (more like a buzzer), allowing everyone in attendance to know that it is time to either end class or begin class. But what is even more hilarious is how everyone depends on the power of a single *baba* (old woman) to kick-start the educational process. It doesn't matter that all of the classes, with the beginning and ending times clearly marked, are posted for all to see. "The bell hasn't rung." And the bell ringing at the beginning of an 11:00-12:20 class doesn't mean that class starts at eleven, it means that it is time for the students and the teachers to slowly drift over to the classroom.

During my tenure at Tiraspol University, I sometimes made my way over to the classroom a few minutes early in order to set up. Imagine that. One time I was met by a colleague with, "But you still have five minutes until the bell rings. Why hurry?" During my final semester, at a point when I was more blunt and less diplomatic than in the past, I arrived at a classroom where a colleague had just taught a course. He asked me if the bell had gone off. I said, "No, but I have a watch." So did he. Other colleagues would sometimes sit in the office long after the bell should have gone off, asking, "Has the bell gone off yet?" It was too much to ask students to be on time when all of their *other* teachers were never on time, even after I attempted to clarify my tardiness policy: "Try not to make tardiness a habit. It doesn't reflect well on your concern or respect for my class." Besides, they had all been conditioned to the bell system their whole lives. I refused to be a hard-ass about this and many other aspects of university-level teaching, except for testing, where I once ripped up a student's exam paper for cheating (or receiving "help" from another student, depending on whose lens you are looking through) after several warnings to her. So I adapted slightly, even on the testing front, where I would use the first few minutes of the class's "start time" to set up maps, dry erase boards, or any other materials I might have needed for the period.

It is one thing to be "organizationally challenged" in one's own life, as I find myself to be as of late, but it is another thing to have little respect for another person's time. Moldovans who follow through when saying they will be somewhere at a specific time tend to have experience working with Americans/Westerners—peoples generally known for punctuality and schedule-keeping. There are enough American and European supported/led organizations around the country (mainly in Chisinau) that expect their Moldovan workers to abide by the same time standards. Excessive tardiness is only a part of the general lack of urgency that engulfs

Moldovan society. Critics, some of whom are in my family, of Western/American values regarding time management, would probably argue that Americans could learn from the lackadaisical attitude that permeates life in Moldova, because we are in too much of a hurry and have lost sight of what is important. The argument could be made that such critics are often undependable people themselves who use such romantic sentiments to mask their own shortcomings.

And that's just it. When you are depending on someone to follow through on a plan that they don't care enough about to commit to in a timely and efficient manner, while at the same time expecting you to do the work they've asked for your help with, something is terribly wrong. The Peace Corps is supposed to be about helping persons help themselves, but more often than not, the Peace Corps is expected by local communities to get things done without the needed assistance of "muscle" from members of the citizenry. I believe that such attitudes are a holdover from the Soviet days—"back when things were better"—and the government took care of everything. Why think and act when the "vanguard of the proletariat" will do it for you? In matters of *realpolitik*, a Dutch graduate student by the name of Ruth explained so clearly, while doing research in Moldova on "conflict studies": "The Moldovans chose to be left to their own devices for the first time ever after declaring independence in 1991, subsequently becoming burdened with the hard realities that accompany nation-state status."

Part of the "hard realities that accompany nation-state status" is the need to develop, or redevelop (if things truly were "better" for Moldovans back when Big Brother was calling the shots), a decent public transportation system. I learned this reality soon after arriving in the big city of Chisinau once my Peace Corps training was complete.

Every now and again I have a "Moldovan" experience. For starters, let's take my traveling experience to the small town of Cahul a couple of weeks back. Cahul is the third or fourth largest "city" in Moldova and is about a three-hour rutiera (mini-bus) ride south of Chisinau. Round-trip it costs 60 Lei [about 4 dollars and 70 cents; the price went up to 70, then 80, now it's around 90 Lei round-trip, in two years time]. The departing point is in the "choice" location of a secluded and dead-end alley way behind a less than upscale hotel [after this trip, an easier hourly rutiera pick-up point was pointed out to me, which I gladly used for almost two years, until recently when the location and frequency of transport became an inconvenience once again]. People wait for the bus(es) to show up and literally rush the bus as it pulls to a stop. There is no ticket booth where people can obtain a stub that signifies they have a reserved seat on the next departure. Why pay someone to hand out tickets when the patrons can just as easily climb over each other and push the meek out of the way? There is hardly any, "Excuse me miss, you were waiting here first. Please, after you." As Patrick [often] says, "It's a clus - ter fuck!" a phrase I know all too well from my military days. During Peace Corps training in the summer, I received "top marks" on my evaluations for having given up my seat, on more than one occasion, to a woman. As I told my evaluators, it's not something that I do because I am in Moldova (the same thing goes for back in the States), and I certainly didn't know I was being evaluated on my use of public transportation. Granted, it's all good and well to give up your seat and stand when you are already on the vehicle, but now we're talking about just trying to score a ride. Plus, I figure that if I held back from trying to muscle in for a seat, it would not be a nice person getting my seat but some other jerk. Darwin's "survival of the fittest" is alive and well here. But that's not always the case.

The other day, on one of the rutieras around town, the driver helped an elder-ly woman onto his bus and a younger boy quickly gave up his seat for her. Then, though she tried to pay the standard fare of two Lei many times, the driver would not take her money. I thought, with a choked-up feeling of satisfaction, "There is hope." In fact, I have seen a lot of individual respect and admiration for older pen-sioners—those retired persons from the Soviet times who are now living on a fixed, and often appalling, amount of money per month—the equivalent of less than 100 dollars. I've also heard of ruthless babas (old women) throwing elbows and fists as they fight their way through crowds. So the one other time before this "cluster" when I went to Cahul, I walked right up and there were two empty mini-buses wait-ing for customers. No problem, I took a seat. I assumed it would be the same sit-uation during this second venture to Cahul. Never assume anything in a former Soviet Republic, I am trying to remember. But that is not to say that flexibility is a detestable characteristic in a people or peoples. It just takes some getting used to. God help anyone who ever tries to invade the United States, again. As Americans, the f'ing up of our schedules would be enough to cause their undoing. So I showed up this second time on Friday at about 2:40 P.M. There was one full rutiera getting ready to head out. Then another pulled up and it was rushed by a mob of people. "I see," I thought to myself, "I have to be aggressive." Well, this was close to three o'clock, and once again I falsely assumed that another rutiera would be here any second to pick up the remaining passengers. An hour went by and no rutiera, while more and more people start showing up for their southbound journeys. By four P.M., I am livid, cussing up a storm, upset that I am at the mercy of a mafia-con-trolled transportation system and having one of those thoughts, "Yeah, my coun-try is better than yours." One is never really certain when and if a mini-bus will show up. I know the wait was getting bad when locals were getting upset and ask-ing me if all of these people were heading to Cahul. I'm not even a citizen of this country and I felt like writing to members of the Moldovan Parliament, telling them how f'ed up their transportation system is. [Recently, from reports on the streets and from personal observations, the Moldovan president's son bought a few buses for southbound journeys, somewhat tightening the screws of domestic traveling, forcing the now considered "illegal" drivers to adapt somehow or find new jobs.] Obviously there is a DEMAND for travel to Cahul. Now let's get the SUPPLY side up and running. And throw those damn mobsters in prison for tak-ing advantage of the market. Being politically active in the affairs of the host coun-try violates Peace Corps policy. And I think it would be fun to have my students petition their government for a "redress of grievances."

Now, being an arrogant, optimistic, and determined citizen of the United States of America, I was getting on the next rutiera! The key is not to be aggres-sive, but to be MORE aggressive—do one better than the locals. Around 4:15 P.M., the next mini-bus bound for Cahul made its way toward the group of future patrons. The RUSH was on! As the rutiera began to slow down but continued in motion, I went straight to the passenger door and held on to the handle, escorting the vehicle until it came to a complete stop. I was the FIRST one on.

When I put it all in perspective, my frustrations with the Moldovan trans - portation system are pretty trivial. Families living in this region and elsewhere, have been torn apart by mass warfare and political turmoil throughout the past, espe - cially in the twentieth century. Moldova has been swapped numerous times between Romania and Russia/the Soviet Union, with disastrous results for many of the peoples involved. There I was, crying over the possibility that my three-day weekend with my girlfriend in Cahul might be shortened by an hour or two because of the transportation system.

For my efforts while working at Tiraspol State University, including my non-acknowledged dealings with "flexible" aspects of Moldovan society—traveling within the country for one—I am to be awarded an "honorary doctorate," but even that thus far has proved to be a bigger headache than it is worth. Don't get me wrong, I am thrilled beyond belief that the "university senate" would vote to confer upon me such a respectable and appreciated degree. It is a more than generous thank you for the work that I have done, or attempted to do, while serving here in Moldova. The head of the department—the Department of Foreign Languages—has been telling me about it for the past few months now. He even asked me when a good time for the ceremony would be. How about the end of May, I originally said, seeing how that is the end of the semester, minus the student exams that occur in June. He said *bine*, which means *fine* in Romanian. So the end of May approached and he said it would happen the following week, during the first part of June; then it was "set" to happen sometime before June 15. I, of course, had to be fitted for a cap and gown. This only took five trips to the local tailor shop. I didn't understand. It's a robe and a hat! Each trip I had to accompany the "special errand" person of the university. He wouldn't just let me meet him at the tailor shop, which would have been easier for me, seeing how it's on the way to and from my apartment. I had to meet him at the school each time, followed by a joint trol-ley bus ride to look at different types and colors of fabric, get measured and re-measured on a few occasions, be told that our order wasn't ready when it should have been (we could have called instead of showing up there), and do a final fit-ting. After the fifth and last trip to the tailor, so I believe, I told some volunteers of the Economic and Agricultural Assistance/Development Programs that I don't see how they collaborate, or be expected to collaborate, with locals for two years on different projects. I teach students and then go home. One of them asked, some-what joking, somewhat serious, "Collaborate?"

Collaboration between volunteers and Host Country Nationals (HCN's) is a core component of Peace Corps service in Moldova, and I assume, everywhere else in the world where the PC is located. But this is much more expected from other-than-English-teaching volunteers (health educators, economic and organiza-tional assistants, and agricultural developers) and less true for the English-teaching volunteers, who are expected to teach a minimum of "eighteen hours a week," which actually means nine eighty-minute classes at the university level (eighteen forty-five-minute classes at the secondary school level), equaling twelve hours a week of classroom instruction. A pair of university "hours" constitutes one eighty-minute class. That's "Moldovan math," as Patrick would declare. My teaching schedule never completely solidified, ranging anywhere from two hours a week (one class) to twenty-six hours a week (thirteen classes). For health volunteers, they were required to teach half of the hours that the English teachers did, but in Romanian and right alongside a Moldovan partner teacher—no thanks to both—while working at a clinic and/or doing other health-related activities. It's not that I would have minded working with a Moldovan side by side, as long as I had my pick of colleagues, something most health volunteers didn't have. I just prefer to work alone with students in general. I've heard horror stories of strange run-ins between *healthers* and their partner teachers, often with the volunteer becoming merely the token American within the community—something we all are to a certain degree.

For the other groups of economic and agricultural volunteers, often lumped together as if they are in the same do-nothing program, their schedules are even less set. Often times, they are supposed to find work in their communities once arriving at site, possibly working with a local NGO (non-governmental organization) or working in the mayor's office in some capacity or another. The worst case, or best case depending on how much free time one would like to have, is for a volunteer to be paired up with a Moldovan counterpart who has zero work for the volunteer to do. It seemed that a volunteer in one of these programs either had tons of work to do, making a difference in his or her community, or whatever work he or she was supposed to have was nonexistent, yet the volunteer's reading skills improved after leisurely reading dozens of books over the course of two years. Case in point: married friends of Julia and mine down in Cahul, Marc and Chrissy. EOD (economic and organizational development) volunteers, or as the joke goes, *out drinking* every other day (EOD). For a large portion of their service, Chrissy had regular work with two different organizations, while Marc stayed busy trying to continuously break his *Scrabble* record versus their laptop computer, impressively passing the 500-point line on many occasions. But in the end, to both be effective volunteers on a somewhat equal level, not that they were competing, they collaborated together with a host of outside interests on a thirty- to forty-something-thousand-dollar "Connect Cahul" project, designed to make the internet accessible in the mostly rural parts of the area's educational and social centers.

Another core component of the Corps' agenda, besides collaboration and cross-cultural integration, is *sustainability,* a buzzword always preached but seldom practiced. One goal of the Peace Corps, as I've stated earlier, is to help communities—local and national—help themselves. That's where sustainability comes in. What good is a Peace Corps-sponsored project if it is not sustainable? Put another way, will the project still be around, to be looked after and administered by Moldovans, long after the Peace Corps has left the country? Another joke passed around: the only thing that the Peace Corps has been involved with that is sustainable is the Peace Corps itself. If this is true, then the Peace Corps needs to stay in the country in order for any Peace Corps-sponsored/created programs to continuously work. I like to think that the English I've taught to Moldovan university students is somewhat sustainable, as I hope that many of them will go out into the world and use the language in one capacity or another, perhaps as English teachers, to affect positive change. But such hurdles of sustainability are hard to measure in the long run, nearly impossible in the short run. This is one reason why I think teachers are so underpaid compared to other professions, the whole world over. There is no immediate evidence that what they are doing will positively affect change, economically or otherwise. As a teacher, I was ecstatic to hear a student of mine tell me of the time she used a *Jeopardy*-style game activity, learned from being in my class, to teach her Moldovan pupils an English lesson. I personally would like to come back to Moldova, or go wherever my English-speaking students might be, in five years time and see if what I did for two years turned out to be sustainable.

A Tower of Babel

According to Moldovan folklore, God originally forgot to give the Moldovan people land to call its own (the Moldovans were late to the land-grant meeting of the Earth's peoples). Exercising divine benevolence, he decided to make up for this *faux pas* by setting aside a slice of Heaven—present-day Moldova—instead. What has not been written into the legend, as of yet, is the Moldovan Tower of Babel's subsequent, but timely, construction toward the Heavens. Demonstrating unquestionable omnipotence in the face of this sacrilegious abomination, the displeased Almighty unleashed his Holy wrath upon the Moldovan people, splitting one shared linguistic tongue into many; the end result being an array of used and abused languages spread out across the Moldovan landscape. Thus the Moldovan *peoples* were born.

The Moldovan "language issue," something that Peace Corps has told us to tiptoe around since day one, is a complicated tale of one national enterprise after another (ancient Romanian fiefdoms, Ottoman Turkey, Czarist Russia, Greater Romania, the Soviet Union, the Republic of Moldova) each trying to build its own "tower" of greatness, with the Moldovan land—formerly known as *Bessarabia*—as one building block in the fragile edifice that has made up Eastern Europe for hundreds of years. Stalin coined an expression about the necessity of imposing a country's own social system, including language, as far as its armies could reach. So went the development, or underdevelopment, of much of Soviet-dominated Eastern Europe after the Second World War, of which Moldova was, and still is, a part.

As Peace Corps trainees, the majority of us were required to study the official "state" language of Moldova—Romanian—while only a handful of other trainees, four out of forty (approximately 10%), were learners of Russian—the unofficial first language of Moldova—for obvious purposes of living and working in Russian communities within Moldova's borders. For an unabridged and historically well-written documentation of the complexities of Moldova's language situation, read Charles King's *The Moldovans: Romania, Russia, and the Politics of Culture*. The title says it all. For a somewhat biased and opinionated first-hand personal observation of dealings with a multiplicity of languages in Moldova during two years of living and working within the country, keep reading this book. I would personally read them both. In fact, I did.

While in training and throughout my service, I was part of the larger contingent of American Romanian speakers, though I never came close to mastering the language. But I did advance to a level that I never obtained while studying the only other foreign language that I had any previous familiarity with—German. At the end of our summer training program and before being sworn in as volunteers, we orally took officially recorded language proficiency exams in either the "state" language or the more frequently used "other" language—*limba Rusa*.

This past Monday, I took and passed my language proficiency exam, scoring "intermediate middle" for Romanian, but what is in a title, really? There were basi - cally four categories—novice, intermediate, advanced, and I think, superior. The average was "intermediate middle" but some people scored "intermediate low" or "intermediate high." A couple of people scored "advanced," I am sure. But it was nice learning a language in Moldova, in comparison with Germany. Among most of the Americans here, we started at the bottom together and because many Moldovans don't speak any English, there is forced adaptation. In Germany, I started out at the bottom [alone] and many more Germans speak English. A funny thing though, so I think, learning Romanian has forced me to recall much of my lost German. Often times, while being frustrated trying to find the correct word for something in Romanian, I would say it in German, since that is the only other for - eign language I have any connection with. I would sometimes accidentally slip German words into my conversation, especially when I was really tired. There are a couple of words or phrases that are applicable to both langauges, which are coin - cidentally my favorites to use. "Clar? Clar." (Is it clear? Clear.) I think it's spelled with a K in German though.

And now, when speaking German, which I've surprisingly found myself doing here in Moldova on more than one occasion, I often slip in Romanian words without thought. Though I officially did not advance above intermediate mid during my two years of service, I progressed far beyond anything I had achieved in German. And yet that did not make much difference when talking to members of the Moldovan citizenry who could barely utter, "Hello my name is . . ." in Romanian or in English. In fact, an outside "neutral" language was preferred if the setting called for it, meaning that there was no other way to communicate.

This morning a man from the Moldovan Electric Company came by [my host family's] to check the meters in the neighborhood for whatever reason. He is Moldovan [I assumed he was Moldovan, but he could have been a resident of Moldova] but doesn't speak Romanian or didn't wish to this morning. (Remember, Moldova became a part of the former Russian empire known as the Soviet Union after the Nazi and Soviet foreign ministers carved up parts of Eastern Europe at the behest of their leaders. Many people never learned Romanian—the national language today—or don't wish to use it.) Nor did this person speak English. No problem. We are both fluent in broken German—my second "con - versation" with a Moldovan in German. His part of our dialogue went from, "I have a friend in New York" to "How can you help me get out of Moldova?" in all of fifty-nine seconds. He explained to me that he had a wife and kid(s) and that he was willing to leave everything behind in order to get out of Moldova. I assumed this meant everything except the wife and kid(s). Though it is not uncommon for one half of a Moldovan marital unit to earn income abroad. [In fact, this is a com - mon theme. Estimates report that one out of every four Moldovan citizens lives abroad, often sending money home to help their families.] I also assumed that since he worked for the Moldovan Electric Company, his income was decent at worst and needs-meeting at best. He pointed to the latter, saying that all of his money went to the family. I attempted to make myself clear, again and again, that I did not work for the U.S. Embassy (Ich bin kein Diplomat) and that he would have to call the embassy himself to find out about getting a work or travel visa of some kind.

Still, he was resolved to e-mail and/or call me later to find out more informa - tion that I don't have and information that I am not going to obtain. The embassy is a twenty-minute walk from the house and is open for business, or at least they can answer questions about visas. It pangs me to know that here is a man willing to drop everything and head to a far-off land, wanting to make what he hopes will be a better life for himself; while in the United States, exchange programs at uni - versities are often threatened with closure, because students don't want to be sep - arated from their "friends" for a year.

Encountering Moldovans who do not speak the "national" language is a com- mon occurrence, especially in the capital and other larger towns, where Russian- speaking peoples seem to dominate the local political and social scenes. This is not a surprise, seeing as how the authority of the former Moldovan Soviet Socialist Republic (MSSR), King points out, was overwhelmingly dominated by non- Moldovan peoples (Russians and Ukrainians) for much of Moldova's pre-inde- pendence history, meaning before 1991.[xv] And at the very top:

> Until 1989, no first secretary of the Communist Party of Moldova ever came from Bessarabia [present-day Moldova], and indeed, immediately after the [Second World] war, a series of purges ensured that the under- ground communists from Romania would play no role in the new Moldovan republic.[xvi]

In 1989, after Gorbachev's *perestroika* and *glasnost* initiatives had already been spiraling on without end in sight for some time, the Supreme Soviet of the MSSR passed "Article 7," stipulating that "everyone in a position requiring com- munication with customers must speak" the state language as well as Russian.[xvii] Either this law was rescinded with the breakup of the Soviet Union in 1991 and the subsequent formation of a sovereign Moldovan Republic, or the law itself has been grossly ignored in recent years, seeing as how each one of us volunteers at one time or another has encountered employees in "customer service" sectors who speak less Romanian than I do—meaning none at all. An example of this is the Russian-speaking hair stylist I frequented every six weeks over the course of almost two years. But it was not a problem. After she cut my hair well the first time, all I had to tell her with every new visit was, "normal" (pronounced *normal*), meaning cut it like normal or like the last time. I wish all relationships could work out that easily.

At my official "Doctoral Honorarium" (*Doctor Honoris Causa*) gathering, which took place on June 23, 2005, an assistant of a Chisinau mayoral candidate, after being invited or after inviting himself, opened up the ceremony by campaigning on behalf of his boss, in *Russian*, for forty-five to fifty minutes to the assembled crowd of colleagues, administrators, and students from my university. It was a classic Moldovan scene; a testament to the historic domination of the Russian language, not to mention his hijacking of the proceedings. He began by speaking in shoddy Romanian, stating simply how he wanted to show the people in attendance that he does know the "state" language and had been studying it since 1999. According to Julia, who recently scored "superior" on her final language exam, he actually said *909* instead of *1999*. But the fact that he wanted to stress his knowledge of the state language, before rambling on in Russian, shows the political weight that Romanian speakers *now* have during Moldova's current attempts at democratic transformation. And besides, the Communists recently lost quite a few seats in this year's parliamentary elections, stripping them of majority rule and forcing a runoff presidential election. A rumor has it that the Communist authorities paid each of their opponents in Parliament a ridiculous amount of money to cast votes for the current president, President Voronin, who did successfully keep his office. A couple of months back, before the election, I read an online criticism through a Moldovan news source (*www.azi.md*) that most of Voronin's closest associates in the government don't speak the "state" language as a rule. And I've personally heard from a few Moldovan citizens how sad it is that some "Moldovans" have been here their whole lives and can't speak a lick of Romanian, yet we Americans are only here for two years and have learned to speak the state language, or in my case, have learned to at least communicate in Romanian.

But why do some Moldovans reference the official national/state language as *Romanian* while others call it *Moldovan?*—a controversy in Moldovan society at present that is not likely to go away any time soon. The latter term is used by a large percentage of persons who believe in the sordid Soviet-engineered idea that *Romanian* and *Moldovan* are two distinct languages, which would be like splintering the *American* language from its *English* roots and treating them as such. Part of the Soviet scheme of drawing *Bessarabia* (Moldova) further away from its western Romanian brethren across the Prut River was the artificial development of a distinct Moldovan culture and language. Thus the Romanian language of Moldova took on a Russian characteristic, being forced to trade in the Latin alphabet for the Cyrillic one. Yet during the Soviet Era, King points out:

The language that Moldovan intellectuals spoke in their homes, taught to their children and students, promoted through popular books and news articles, and hailed as the defining characteristic of the Moldovan nation was—to anyone outside the Soviet Union—known simply as "Romanian."[xviii]

Even today, many Romanian-speaking Moldovans, mostly elderly persons, know how to read and write in Romanian only via the Cyrillic alphabet. In Russian, my first name is spelled *Pobept*, pointed out to me by Julia after getting our travel visas for the Ukraine. Preferring to pronounce this spelling in English/American as is, Pobept—the *t* is sometimes silent—has become a nickname I have taken on during my remaining few months in Moldova.

Though the Peace Corps is officially a nonpolitical entity, the fact that ninety percent of incoming trainees are obliged to learn Romanian and not Russian has political overtones, if mostly subtle on the surface. First off, because the state language is of a Romanian character, learned by an overwhelming majority of volunteers, whether or not they would prefer to study Russian—viewed as more practical by many—the political support for the Moldovan authorities on behalf of the United States government is reinforced. But seeing as how the general nature of diplomatic relations among countries is cordial and full of compromise, there can be no other way around this language issue as far as the United States is concerned. The state language is Romanian; Moldova's independence was quickly recognized by the U.S., the second country to do so only after Romania. Though the Russian language tends to be used more frequently in various parts of the country, including the larger towns, there are many more persons in rural areas (where Peace Corps is most needed, though not necessarily wanted) whose first language is Romanian. On this last point, it's interesting to note that those who speak Romanian as a first language usually can and do speak Russian without problems. Not a surprise there, seeing as how Big Brother Russia was pulling the strings in this part of Europe and beyond for many years. But on the opposite side and for the same reason, if you were a descendent of Big Brother Russia, why learn that "peasant" language, as Romanian is referred to by some of the Russian-speaking Moldovans?

"The Transnistrian Conundrum," the title of one of King's chapters, sheds light on what happens when the language and cultural tensions afflicting Moldovan society are taken to an extreme level. A cause of, or excuse for, the *Transnistrian* attempt to maintain a sovereign independence, or idiotic stubbornness depending on who's talking, in the eastern part of the country, was because of the emerging Moldovan nationalist movement in the wake of the Soviet collapse, accompanied by the official sanctioning of Romanian as the state language over all of the territory that falls within Moldova's recognized borders, including *Transnistria*:

Every move in Chisinau that pulled the republic further away from Moscow was met by a countermove in Transnistria that drew the region itself further away from Chisinau. . .. For non-Moldovans, particularly many Transnistrians, the proposed language laws were clear evidence . . . of the shifting balance of power to the Moldovan majority and away from those groups that had traditionally exercised authority.[xix]

Transnistria had originally been a part of the Moldovan Autonomous Soviet Socialist Republic (MASSR), carved out of the Ukraine in the 1920s—its purpose to serve as a beachhead for annexing the rest of Romanian-controlled *Bessarabia* (present-day Moldova) to the Soviet Empire.

As Romanian-speaking volunteers, it is easy to see why many of us tend to identify more strongly with the Romanian culture of Moldova, while getting frustrated with persons who see themselves purely as Russian descendants. It has been more than annoying at times encountering Russian-only speakers, who often get huffy when they meet persons who don't speak their language. After a year and a half, I finally learned how to say, "I don't understand Russian" in Russian. But also, the few Russian-speaking volunteers who do exist, one whom I know of in particular, have acknowledged these people's "right" to speak Russian in the face of any criticism or disgruntled lamenting they may have been forced to endure. A couple of times toward the end of my service, I would become snippy when someone addressed me in Russian. "*In limba Romana, Va Rog!*" (In Romanian, Please!) Also, the volunteers have developed stereotypes, or learned preexisting ones, about both the Romanian and Russian speakers of Moldova.

Speakers of Romanian, especially women, tend to whine in a high-pitched tone when communicating with each other. The two sisters of the host family I lived with for eight months in Chisinau exchanged whines in this manner, driving me up the wall many times over. But this was not as bad as some of the Russian speakers, who seem as if they are yelling at each other, or at you, when speaking in their native tongue. This stereotypical aspect of Russian culture was even reinforced on *The Simpsons* a few years back, when Lisa gets lost and ends up in Springfield's Russian district. Two men are playing chess, and one starts yelling at the other, in Russian, as the yeller tips over the board. The translation below reads calmly and politely, something like, "Hey, that was a great game. Would you like to play again?"[xx] Igor, the same Russian-speaking volunteer and champion of *limba Rusa* whom I mentioned earlier, even lapses into a horribly heavy Russian-stereotyped accent, trying to score laughs from other volunteers, while remaining oblivious to any cultural sensitivities of nearby Moldovans. (He decided to go by the name of Igor instead of his real name—Stewart—while residing in Moldova, thinking it would be cool to do so. After which, some Moldovans in his own community have expressed confusion as to why he would think that Igor is a Russian-sounding name.) On my six-channel television set, what I call a Soviet-era monstrosity, five of the channels are in Russian and one is in Romanian, actually broadcast from Romania. But on the upside, or *Far Side*, where else in the world besides Moldova or Romania, can one watch an Italian or Spanish soap opera that has been dubbed in Spanish or Portuguese, and then subtitled in Romanian?

The study of these two Moldovan languages in such a way could be an interesting exercise in linguistics, as well as anthropological studies, but the results may be construed as culturally insensitive at the very least, subjectively racist at the very most. Romanian speakers themselves sometimes point out that their soft-spoken language is much more beautiful and poetic than Russian, referring to such poetry-writing Romanian (not Moldovan) heavyweights as Mihai Eminescu of the 19th Century. *Eu sunt de acord* (I am in agreement)—I do believe that it is a beautiful language. But Russian speakers will tell you that their language is much stronger and richer than Moldovan/Romanian. Well, it is acknowledged that Russian is much harder to learn than Romanian. I have befriended a couple of non-Romanian speaking Moldovans of Russian descent—really nice and hospitable persons I'm glad to call friends—who also speak English, and who have consequently spent a significant amount of time in places outside of Moldova, including western Europe and the United States. Coincidence?

In general, many Moldovans tend to talk at persons, especially persons younger than themselves, instead of with them. I find that it is often easy to hide the fact that I don't know Russian because Russian-speaking strangers whom I encounter often speak at me, pointing to something or another, while not looking for a reciprocal exchange of thoughts. I just shake my head and say "*Da.*" One time, when I was waiting for my kebab at one of the many new Turkish-run kebab stands around Chisinau, some lady, I think she was a bit mentally deranged, started barking at me in Russian. I calmly said that I didn't know Russian. Then she kept talking at me, saying something about me being Romanian or being a Romanian speaker. I finally said, "Romanian is the *national* language." This incensed her a bit, leading her to speak even louder, but she walked away soon after. I wanted to use this line of mine on others, especially creepy male Russian speakers (wannabe mafioso types) who think they are God's gift to—I'm not really sure—or who can spew out only a few profane words in English. It was probably better that I didn't do this.

During a "stereotypes" seminar run by my friends Patrick and Rosie at Moldova State University for Moldovan teachers of English, I participated in the discussion at hand. My assigned partner for the session, an English-speaking Moldovan teacher of Russian descent, and I worked together to list positive and negative aspects/stereotypes of Russian persons, while other pairs made lists about Americans and other groups. The positive side was very easy for her to work with, but when it came to the negative features, I stated, "Well, Russians are seen as very aggressive." Snapping back at me, she retorted, "No! They are not aggressive. They are very nice people." *Okay then*, I thought to myself, *my point exactly*. But later on, during the course of the activity, she acknowledged, "Well, maybe they can be aggressive at times." Perhaps this Peace Corps volunteer-led seminar worked. Hats off to Patrick and Rosie for getting the point across.

At some point in the middle of my service, I came up with a comical list for the volunteer community, entitled "You just might be a Peace Corps volunteer in Moldova if . . ." Pointing to God's displeasure at the sight of the Moldovan Tower of Babel, "You just might be a Peace Corps volunteer in Moldova if . . . when speaking the 'national' language [Romanian], you have been met with looks of confusion and/or contempt from members of the local citizenry." The situation here has reminded me a bit of a similar one in parts of the southwest United States, where the population of Spanish-speakers compared to the one that solely speaks English—English being the unofficial national language of the U.S.—is on the rise. Growing up in what appeared to be a Mexican-American-dominated community in San Diego (Imperial Beach), I was resentful of the primacy of the Spanish language among many of the local citizens, even though I had many friends of Mexican descent, including myself, and I was often accused of falling in love with every Mexican girl I laid eyes on. I don't know about every girl.

Along with Russian, Romanian/Moldovan, and even English and German, being parts of the lingua that make up Moldovan society, there are plenty of other languages that dot the country's landscape, including Ukrainian, Bulgarian, French, Arabic, signing for the hearing-impaired, and *Gagauzian*. This last one, being of Turkic origins, belongs to the semi-autonomous *Gagauz* region located in the southern part of Moldova. I know volunteers who have worked in this area and have dealt with students who don't know either Russian or Romanian. For these Moldovans/Gagauzians, their chances for mobility, should they seek to be mobile, within an already tiny country will remain minimal at best, unless they learn one of the two mainstream languages. Five of my best university students were from this region, having grown up using the Gagauz language at home while attending Russian-speaking primary and secondary schools. What amazed me about them was the fact that they were not the best speakers of English in my courses (in general, Russian-only speakers have a much harder time learning English than those who also know Romanian). English was not even their major, yet they came to class every week determined to improve their knowledge of English. Consequently, they earned the highest grades on my exams. I've had other students, nearly fluent in English, who were lazy and slacked off in preparation for the final exams. For these Gagauzian Moldovan minorities, university life was an adventurous trip to the big city—Chisinau—from their small towns and villages, having been few other places. I am proud to have been their teacher.

As noticeable English-speakers, though some of the volunteers try to blend in as much as possible (some better than others), many of us have encountered non-English-speaking knuckleheads at one time or another in one form or another, usually disgruntled young males who are upset by the global domination of the English language—a language they have never learned and probably never will. Such persons like to throw out such expressions as "fuck you," which usually comes out like "fac yu," because of their horrid pronunciation. My friend Rosie, of Patrick and Rosie, had young students at her school who would say to her, "Suck my fick." But such occurrences are more frequent in small towns and villages where the American volunteer is definitely one of a kind, unable to blend in if he or she tried. In the "cosmopolitan" town of Chisinau, where English-speaking diplomats and missionaries are in abundance, many more Moldovans speak, or have a basic understanding of, English. And more often than not, when my non-local status is exposed, locals are eager to chat and/or receive tutoring lessons, or they just stare blankly, wondering what planet I am from.

But even for those Moldovans considered to be advanced speakers of English, native speakers of English conversing in "tongues" (colloquial expressions and everyday slang) present a problem for even the most versed non-native speaker of English. This coded talk, used among volunteers when wanting to disguise conversations, especially when openly criticizing Moldovans or Moldovan society to a contempt-filled degree, often proved valuable when speaking English with one another. In a crowded *rutiera*, you can never know who is or who isn't familiar with English. It's best to speak fast and with as little proper English as possible. An example of an optimal time to speak in code: Trainee Kenneth lives with a Moldovan host family during the summer, and his host sister has a solid understanding of the English language, yet she is far from perfect. Ken had bought a beer and placed it in the fridge for later consumption. But while talking on the phone with a fellow American trainee from a different village, he notices that his host father has helped himself to the beer. Instead of saying, "My host father is drinking my beer," easily recognizable English by the Moldovan host sister, he explains, "My pops is sucking down my brewskie," thus securing the message in code.

Orthodox Duality

Moldovans like to celebrate. Who doesn't, really? But in Moldova, where restrictions on religious ceremonies have been lifted with the break up of *Uniunea Sovietica*, Eastern Orthodox Christianity has resurfaced, coated with all of the accompanying trappings, bringing with it a host of Saints' Days and Orthodox holidays, right alongside secular and Western celebratory traditions. For example, Christmas in the West as you know is celebrated on December 25, which is the date that some people in Moldova also choose to celebrate it. But Orthodox Christmas (*Craciun*), acknowledged by most Moldovans whom I've met, is celebrated on January 7, because the old Julian calendar (Orthodox), done away with by the Soviet authorities in 1918 in favor of the Gregorian calendar (the "Western" calendar used in most parts of the world today), actually puts Christmas on the 25th of December. It's a bit tricky, but remember, the Orthodox calendar is behind by thirteen days—an inferred commentary on Moldovan society?—so it makes perfect sense that January 7 is Orthodox Christmas and that Orthodox New Year's Day falls on January 14 (January 1 according to the Julian calendar system). Wow, I just figured this out while writing about it, and I've only been here for two years. Of course, I've asked myself before, why would Orthodox Christians choose to celebrate the birth of Jesus Christ on January 7, not realizing that on their traditional dateline, *it is* the 25th of December? That's one reason why in some history books, the 1917 October Revolution in Russia is explained as having happened in early November (on "our" calendar), which is late October in the world of Orthodoxy. It's one thing to hear information presented to you and another to retain and understand that information.

And of course, many of us volunteers have once again failed to live up to our cross-cultural "oath" by poking fun at the whole Orthodox duality that exists in Moldovan society. For example, after celebrating our regular birthdays, we jokingly celebrate our "Orthodox" ones. In May, the group of volunteers I arrived with

150

(Group 11) had our Close of Service (COS) dinner together with the Peace Corps staff, since we are leaving this summer (2005). But a week ago (July 3), Group 11 had what I call our Orthodox COS dinner at the Peace Corps director's home. On July 20, the day before many of us leave Moldova, we will have our second Orthodox dinner together at a local restaurant. I tried to explain to my students the "witty" concept of an Orthodox birthday, but most of them weren't having any of it. Well, one girl I remember did chuckle a bit. I have even had a few students who say that they do celebrate both the Western and Eastern holidays, expecting to receive presents on both Christmases. As well, the Peace Corps, and possibly even the U.S. Embassy, officially recognizes Orthodox duality by giving its staff days off for both American and Moldovan holidays. This has proved annoying at times for volunteers, who don't get sanctioned days off for such holidays as Memorial Day, when coming to the office for staff assistance and no one is there because of another holiday—Western or Eastern.

Here in Moldova, where every volunteer lives with a host family at some point while serving, Moldovan cross-cultural "sensitivity" often comes to the fore during the holiday season, for both Western and Eastern celebrations. Many volunteers, if choosing not to go on a winter wonderland vacation over Christmas (December 25)—back home or somewhere warm preferably—opt to stay put in Moldova or the surrounding area. If the volunteer does stay in the vicinity of his or her site, the volunteer may find him or herself celebrating with the host family, whether or not the volunteer has any desire to do so. During my first Christmas in the Peace Corps (2003), Julia and I decided to spend the holiday together in Moldova. Besides, we were planning on taking a week-long trip to Bulgaria at the beginning of January. (I never understood why other PC volunteers would come all the way to Eastern Europe and not take the opportunity to see parts of it, opting instead to go back to the States, or other places, as soon as they have vacation.) I believe it was Christmas Eve when the first heavy snowfall of the season hit. I was at Julia's site in Cahul, where she lived with one particularly unsavory host family at the time. We were supposed to travel from Cahul to her training village of *Mereseni*, where her host family from pre-service training (she was much closer in relation to all of her families than I was to one of mine) was going to celebrate our Christmas with us. Well, because of the snow, the flow in the transportation system slowed a bit, but we used the excuse of being "snowed in" to just lie low in Cahul for a few days, stuffing our faces with foodstuffs from back home. Julia, being the awesome cook that she is, decided to make us a fabulous Christmas dinner. And of course, her concerned host mother couldn't/wouldn't let us celebrate alone.

The day started off in typical host family fashion, for Julia's then host mom anyway, with pitchers of house wine flowing to an intoxicating degree. Both host parents liked me because I rarely said no to their offers of wine. But of course, I did not live there and saw them every other weekend at the most. Julia didn't drink much, and she had to see them all the time. They once told her that she must be boring for me, because she doesn't drink much. She drinks occasionally, but never to an idiotic degree. The host mom, with the host dad at work, decided to start early, tossing back a few glasses of wine around noon on what she had said was the anniversary of her mother's death. Twice that day she broke drinking glasses—once when she was having some wine and another time when she was having some orange juice. Her reasoning for this: her deceased mother also wanted some wine and then some juice. How about instead: I'm drunk and can't hold a glass correctly and/or the glasses are of poor quality? In the evening, while Julia was preparing a meal (I help cut stuff in general) and some cinnamon rolls for the next day, the mom invited herself to our dinner, deciding to contribute to our meal by preparing some type of chicken dish. In a Moldovan village (or small town in Cahul's case), making a chicken dish means going to the coop, getting a live chicken, killing it by chopping the head off, then gutting and cleaning it for kitchen preparation. While sweet-smelling dough was being kneaded on the table, the mom tossed a lifeless chicken head next to the soon-to-be cinnamon rolls. In the meantime, on the kitchen floor, where a bucket had just been filled with bloody poultry guts and entrails, the two somewhat domesticated cats were getting worked up into a feeding frenzy like sharks in blood-soaked waters. The younger cat was trying to pull the leftover chicken parts out of the bucket, looking like it was stuck chewing on a piece of beef jerky. Needless to say, the chicken, once prepared, was delectable. So too were the homemade cinnamon rolls.

After having dinner, the mom, with a drunken glazed haze over her eyes, wanted us to get into the spirit of Christmas by singing some Christmas carols. In her nonexistent English, she decided to kick-start the caroling festivities. Feeling her well-endowed breast area up, while moving both hands in a circular fashion, she began singing, "Ringle rells, Ringle rells." Afterwards, she knocked on the kitchen/bathroom door a few times, asking for "Santee Claus? Santee Claus?" Then in Romanian, "Please make sure that Julia and Robert stay together." It was a Christmas like no other. On Orthodox Christmas (January 7), we arrived back in Chisinau from our Bulgarian excursion, where we spent the day without host families. Mine was off celebrating with other relatives in a nearby village. I was glad. I lived with my host family for eight months (September 2003-April 2004), two months longer than the six-month Peace Corps-stipulated requirement. There was little celebrating to be done with them while I resided there, and none since.

My host family is nice and all, but we don't get along very well. I've felt like I've been walking on egg shells since I've been here, as if I'm constantly in the way, though I shell out 1400 Lei (a little more than $100) every month, when the average national salary is much less than that. There are anywhere from three to eight people in the house at any given time. The dad, whom I've mentioned before in the past, is a priest in the Orthodox Christian Church. And as my tutor of Romanian told me, just like many religious "rackets" in most countries, the priesthood is paying pretty well these days. Though Moldova is a poor country in many respects, I knew my family wasn't hurting for cash when, on the day after I paid them rent, they went out and bought a brand-new Panasonic cordless phone with answering machine. [If they were really hurting, they would have bought something else, like food.]

The only food I eat is food that I make, but usually there are a few people running in and out of the kitchen, so I often go to one of the many pizzerias in the

Chisinau area. Peace Corps states that we are to pay our families an average of 25 Lei ($1.95) per meal, but when my family makes a big vat of potatoes, rice, or soup FARA CARNE (without meat) for the entire family, and I am still expected to pay 25 Lei, I can get a large and tasty pizza with meat, bread, vegetables, and cheese down the street for 22 Lei—less expensive and more hunger-satisfying. There is one teenage girl (the younger sister I never wanted) who is constantly hovering around the phone, keeping it in her room instead of putting it on the charger where anyone can get at it. In the mom's defense, she is always nice and cordial with me, but usually stays in Transnistria in the East four days out of the week, conducting church duties with her husband. She is the only one in the family who drinks coffee. Perhaps that's why we get along the best, though I don't talk with her that much. Oh yeah, the oldest brother, out of five children, recently got married, and he and his wife often stay at the house. She's not one to crack a smile. Now that he has a wife, he will try to get a gig with the church (marriage is a requirement to be a church priest here).

I was actually invited to the wedding reception (*nunta* in Romanian) of the oldest brother, having been told the day beforehand by the youngest host sister, Maria, "There will be a lot of people here tomorrow for a big party. You are welcome to come if you like." To this I asked somewhat rhetorically, having overheard, and impressively understood, the plans being fomented by the family over the previous few weeks, "Is somebody getting married?" She replied, "Yeah, my brother." Julia and I attended a part of the wedding reception at the house. We really had no other choice. Our seeing-each-other rotation landed us staying at my house that night. So we made an appearance, somewhat star-striking some of the other guests with our American-ness. We were approached for pictures and casual conversation, not a seldom experience at Moldovan celebrations. The unsmiling bride eventually brought us cake, thus practicing her recently accepted eternal duties as the wife of a Moldovan priest. (My students, during a lesson on "American wedding traditions/practices," had trouble answering the question: Why is the [American] wedding day often called "her day" or "the bride's day"?) It is hard for me to believe that this woman had her entire future planned out at the age of nineteen.

At one point during this host brother's *nunta*, when the basket of money was passed around, and friends and family members are expected to make a cash contribution to the basket while vocally stating the dollar/euro/lei amount given, I contributed "*cincisprezece* [fifteen] *dolari Americani*" (about 180 Lei) on behalf of myself and Julia. It may sound cheap to a Westerner, but to a Moldovan, it's a good chunk of change, which I felt to be true by the round of applause we received. But the ten-dollar and five-dollar bills I put in were ratty by Moldovan standards, not to be accepted by most Moldovan banks, yet good enough to be used at any podunk *7-11* back home. Oh well, those in attendance didn't know, and I was the big hero for the moment. The two hours of attendance at the twelve-hour wedding reception was the most time I spent with the family at one stretch. I moved into my own apartment six months after this celebration (May 2004) and never looked back. As far as host families go, I adopted Julia's second (after the drunken "ringle rells" singing family), and permanent host family as my own. Julia and I celebrated a few joyous and memorable holidays, Orthodox and otherwise, with Alexandra, Nicolai, and their nine-year-old son, Sandu.

Easter is even more difficult to understand. This year, it was celebrated in early May, more than two weeks after Western Easter, but last year, it was celebrated on the same day, yet it also comes in pairs. There is Easter, then there is what we volunteers refer to as the "Day of the Dead," when Moldovan families visit the gravesites of their relatives on the Sunday after Orthodox Easter, often bringing enough food and spirits for a full-fledged *masa* (celebration). And it's sort of like a Moldovan "Halloween" for the kids, who run around to different graves with their bags, asking for different types of treats—candies, cookies, *bani* (money). The one time I went to such a gathering, there was no crying to be had, but plenty of laughter heard while drinking *vin de casa* (literally meaning *wine of the house* or simply *house wine*). It is not an understatement to say that every village home produces vin de casa, or vodka de casa, in some form or another. Of course, some families make it better than others, but all will tell you that theirs is the best. I like the sweet-tasting house wine for the most part, as long as it is not too sweet, and I have been hammered on it more than a few times (house wine is not sipped as one usually would with a bottle of *pinot franc* or *cabernet*. It is shot back in gulps like the moonshine that it is). Now house vodka is a whole other story. I don't usually prefer vodka in general, but I have drunk some of the factory-brand stuff—*Perfect* for example—in Moldova on a couple of occasions. The first time I took a shot of homemade vodka (one out of the three times in my life), it took thirty seconds to work its way down, burning the whole time, and then I spent the next ten minutes burping it up, a fiery pain with every belch.

Along with the major holidays, there are plenty of other religious (Saints' Days) and secular holidays (International Women's Day, Students' Day, Teachers' Day, Valentine's Day, and so forth) that are acknowledged and/or celebrated throughout the year. Not all of them are days off from school or work, though celebrating persons may take a day or two off, and therefore, they are not official excuses to have a party. Women's Day (March 8) is a major holiday in Moldova, where students at all levels have the day off. The men of the households are supposed to cater to their wives' and/or daughters' whims. It would be a good holiday to celebrate in the United States, but as I told my students, "Every day in America is women's day." I think that for political reasons—March 8 being late February on the old calendar system (Orthodox), when women in Russia protested food shortages and their men were at the Great War's front, sparking what would later become the November (October) Revolution of 1917—it was not acknowledged in the U.S., especially during the Cold War. Why would you celebrate a day held in high regard by the Communist world? The same goes for May 9, which is celebrated here as Victory Day, commemorating the defeat of Nazi Germany by the Soviet Union, of which Moldova was officially a part. But also, the Germans had already surrendered to the Western Allies, General Eisenhower in particular, on the previous day of May 8. Stalin wasn't having any of it, demanding that an official surrender ceremony take place the next day (May 9) in front of all of the major Allied powers—a seemingly reasonable request.

Not only are national holidays in abundance, but local ones are as well. Throughout the year, every little town and village, on up to the "big" cities of Chisinau and Balti, celebrate a day that is called *Hram*, simply meaning *festival* according to my Peace Corps-issued English-Romanian dictionary. The dates for each *Hram* vary, and the determination of the date of a site's annual Hram ranges from the signifying date of when the town/village/city was established to the day when the location's first Orthodox church was declared complete. At least, these are the reasons I've heard. *Hramul de Chisinau* or *Ziua de Chisinau* (the day of Chisinau)—October 14—is a huge day, celebrated by persons all around the capital and visitors from other areas of Moldova. Being a not-so-politically charged holiday, unlike Moldovan Independence Day (August 27) and National Language Day, meaning pro-Romanian language day (August 31), everybody can celebrate Chisinau's day. Of course brew flows at various beer tents around the city, at a fraction of the cost back home, plus the beers are twice as large, are much more potent, and drinking one does not prohibit you from legally moving freely about town with beer in hand. I took advantage of all of these beer qualities that Europe has to offer during my first Chisinau Hram, ending my night at one of the few dining establishments around town, and in the world, that epitomizes "tasty efficiency."

Well, I broke down yesterday and had my first Big Mac in Moldova. After a few beers, the question, "Where can I get some decent and FAST food at this hour?" is easily answered by the Golden Arches, though McDonald's is actually an expensive restaurant for many locals. The 14th of October is the "Day of Chisinau," celebrating the anniversary of the capital. It is one of the many holidays celebrated. I believe that every town and village has an annual HRAM, meaning anniversary festival. Many exciting encounters happen at Mickey Dee's, usually involving one or more volunteers. A couple of weeks ago, a less than appealing young Moldovan gal asked my married friend Pat and me, in English, if we would like to get together and "do some crazy things." At first she asked me, as Pat was getting ready to leave. I started to laugh and told her to go tell my friend that, just so I could see his reaction. Needless to say he smirked, as if to express, "Yep, I'm in Moldova." [After he told her he was waiting for his wife, she went and chatted with another McDonald's patron.] He is referred to as "Mr. Cultural Sensitivity," mostly by me, because he is often NOT that, but hilarious nonetheless! He is also "Mr. Wall Street," because he used to work in the market in one capacity or another. ["Mr. Wall Street" was actually never used beyond this letter. I figured I would use it in conjunction with "Mr. Cultural Sensitivity," which was an expression sometimes used.] There are many volunteers here with a variety of dynamic backgrounds. And of course, there are a few "kids" right out of college.

Any American who says that he or she will never eat at a McDonald's in Europe is probably an American who has never spent a significant amount of time in Europe. It's not that, for me anyway, I crave a tangy and saucy meatless Big Mac, or the one-of-a-kind salt-laden French fries served crisp. Though these are sometimes compelling reasons for running to the Golden Arches for a taste of

Americana, there are hardly any places around town that can serve burgers of any kind. The draw of McDonald's often has more to do with the symbol of things like customer service, perhaps in the form of a smile from the cashier when you place your order, something seriously lacking around the country. Plus the choice real estate location of Ronald's houses (he has three of them in Chisinau and nowhere else in the country), make people-watching (scantily clad women in see-through clothes) under his outdoor umbrellas a favorite pastime among Peace Corps volunteers. And if burgers and/or fries are not your forte, McDonald's has some of the best, and cheapest, ice cream in the country. It's funny though how McDonald's in Chisinau has adopted what might be considered Moldovan practices. There is an attitude among many Moldovans, a sort of "this is how we do it in Moldova" and therefore everybody should do the same. At McDonald's, everyone gets a tray, whether you ordered three combo meals or a cup of coffee. There seems to be no room for employee-flexible considerations. Does the customer really need a tray? He only ordered a 2 Lei [about 18 cents] ice cream cone? Of course he does. Everybody gets a tray in Moldova.

Thanksgivings were perhaps the biggest celebrations involving all of the Peace Corps volunteers and staff, as well as other invited dignitaries from around Moldova. For me personally, it wasn't a big deal to be away from the States at this time of the season, seeing as how one of my Thanksgivings in the past, I spent part of the day in a guard tower facing North Korea. Still, it was nice to be with fellow Americans, many of whom I call friends, during this joyous occasion. And being in Moldova, as one can imagine, our Thanksgiving celebrations were like no other.

There was a massive snowfall on Thanksgiving here, which finally melted away today (Saturday). Last year it did not snow until Christmas Eve! We had quite the celebration here with over a hundred volunteers, a few PC administrators, and many other guests (dignitaries) from around Moldova. Julia and one other volun - teer [Jennifer] led the cooking extravaganza for over 200 persons in attendance! And it was awesome, of course. I made two cheesecakes that lasted less than five minutes once being put out—a peanut butter and chocolate one and a chocolate-caramel toffee hazelnut one. The next day, another volunteer told me that the peanut butter one was the best dessert of the evening. You [Mom] would have been proud.

After the dinner, we had a turkey show, where volunteers and/or administra - tors could perform an act on stage (sing a song, perform a dance, act out a skit, etc.). I was part of the three-man MC committee. We introduced the acts and kept (most of the time) the audience entertained, with outside help, while the acts were prepping themselves to perform. Our acts were "fillers." It was a fun time. One of the acts that I wrote was Sater Camp (from the Romanian word "Sat," meaning village), where a volunteer who lives in a village is retraining us big city/town folks (those with an indoor toilet) how to re-use an outhouse. We were awarded "the best use of asses" in a skit. In another filler, myself and the head MC, Ken, came out on stage in speedos (common attire for men here in the summer, I call them manties instead of panties). When asked what we were

156

doing, I hunched my shoulders, looked at Ken, and he said, "We're just going to the beach." Then we walked off the stage.

One of the "acts" was a slide show put together by a recently arrived group of volunteers. They (about five) were serving in the Peace Corps in Nepal, when a Civil War supposedly re-erupted there. So of course, they were pulled out of Nepal and had the choice of serving somewhere else. Their slide show was about their time spent in Nepal. I didn't see it since I was backstage preparing, but heard that it was a real tearjerker.

An Upstart among Nations

On December 30, 2003, I left Moldova for the first time since arriving in June. And let me tell you—WOW! Though it was a nine-day vacation of frolicking, eating, traveling, having a drink every now and again, taking in the sights and carousing around parts of Romania and Bulgaria to the west and southwest of Moldova, it was an eye-opening culture shock. My fellow Peace Corps volunteer and "traveling partner," Julia, and I felt bad for volunteers who went home to the States for the holidays and then had to come back to Moldova. Now that I think about it, I shouldn't have felt bad at all. Some volunteer(s) often opt not to come back from vacation in the U.S. A couple of recent English-teaching volunteers decided not to complete their final semester of service and stayed home. I was in the Romanian capital of Bucharest for no more than six hours when I caught myself dreading the prospect of going back to Moldova. Granted, part of this "dread" was the natural impulse of many vacationers not wanting to go back to work—a universal feeling if you will. But I began to empathize with those people of the Moldovan citizenry who feel confined to their lot in life, especially when many of us have been taught that the "American Dream," however one defines it, at the very least fosters a real sense of social mobility.

The first thing I noticed in Romania was that people seemed to be more cheery than their neighbors to the East. Even the Romanian border guard on the train flashed a smile as if to say, "Welcome to my country and enjoy your stay." In Moldova, I have been "greeted" with "Why are you in my country?" and "Why did you leave America to come here?" Being used to superficial niceties, I much prefer a smile. Walking along the streets of Chisinau, I have rarely encountered a passerby willing to offer up a courteous smile. So this makes me not want to smile either, which I rarely do now when walking down the streets unaccompanied. As a foreigner, I often stand out as it is. For safety reasons, I try to blend in as much as possible. In the summer, during training, one of our Moldovan directors who works for Peace Corps told us that we should smile at people in our villages and greet them with a buna ziua (good afternoon), which I often did. Later on, I asked my Moldovan host cousin if this was acceptable to do. He said that if I greet strangers passing by in this way, they will think that I am crazy! I may have looked like a foreigner in Romania, but people didn't seem to care. Foreigners come and foreigners go, leaving money and smiles in their wake.

In a research interview—"The Moldavian Immigration to Milan" in *The Romanian Journal of Society and Politics*—conducted by Adela Popa of the Polytechnic University of Bucharest, a Moldovan woman living in Italy explained: "There is a psychological gap between people in Moldova and the people living in Italy." The woman went on to clarify:

> After one and a half years [of living in Italy] I went to Moldova, and when I saw that there were so many persons that were not open, that would not answer my smile, I said to myself that I had made more friends here, in Italy . . . I would like to go and live on the land where I was born, but I realize that I could not live with the people who have never been abroad . . . I was born to belong to more than just a small corner of this earth.[xxi]

This is a sad commentary on the economic, political, and social situation of the Moldovan nation, seeing how a reported one out of four Moldovans lives in another country, whether legally or illegally. After having taught a group of students the historical expression, "The sun never sets on the British Empire," a student poignantly remarked, "The sun never sets on the heads of Moldovans," because they are all over the world, trying to escape a dismal situation in their own country. By far, the biggest advertising campaign in Moldova must be that of Western Union, with billboards in every large town and Chisinau, letting Moldovans know that the quickest way to receive money from a loved one abroad is through its services. Usually, on the one side of the advertisement is a man working hard, possibly in a construction job and certainly not in Moldova, while the other half of the ad shows the wife and kid relishing in all of the material comforts that daddy's work has paid for. And of course, everyone is smiling. The ads appear to be a bit misleading; one, most of the Moldovans abroad, who I know about, are women with less than ideal jobs; second, it's not all smiles when one half of a marital unit lives in another country, especially for the parent who has to look after a child on his or her own. And it's not just persons needing to support a family who are making the journey abroad, or attempting to do so.

I asked a student what she wanted to do after graduating from the university. There was no, "Perhaps graduate school or law school" or "I've always wanted to backpack through Europe," nor an alternate universe response of, "I will work for the Moldovan Peace Corps, teaching Romanian in America." She stated succinctly, "I want to get as far away from Moldova as possible." After hearing such grim responses, I was left a bit confused and unsure of what to say in return. What can you say? I often thought that instead of jumping off this sinking ship, locals here should contribute to the betterment of their country—easier said than done. What *would I or anyone else do in this situation? There are many expatriates from the United States who live in other countries for various reasons, but I'm certain that most of them have little intention of renouncing their U.S. citizenship. One of my Moldovan language instructors from last summer had, at one time, studied in Romania for a short while. She often spoke bitterly about Moldovan society and said she would gladly become a Romanian citizen in order to pursue doctoral studies in Romania—for that and other reasons.*

On the other hand, though, there are students of mine who've said that they do not want to leave Moldova, and are determined to make of themselves whatever is possible in their own country. For these Moldovans, staying close to family and friends is more important than exerting energy trying to leave it all behind, even if only for a short duration. I should know. I provided this particular group of students with U.S. Embassy-written information about studying in the United States. None of them applied, a few of them making excuses as to why they didn't bother. But for countless other Moldovans, including many of my students, how did Moldova become such an abysmal state of hopelessness?

It is in the outlook of Romanians and the historical development of Romania that one can begin to understand the confinement of the Moldovan "nation." Up until ten months ago, when the Peace Corps told me on the phone that they had a spot for me in Moldova, I may have read the word Moldova at one time or another on some map or heard about it in a news report about Europe. Upon hearing my assignment, I immediately turned to my world map and thought, "Well, Moldova is in Eastern Europe, next to Romania and close to Bulgaria—two options I was hoping to get." After I left a message on my mother's answering machine that I was going to serve in Moldova, she called back and asked, "Where the f' is Moldova?" She is well-informed, keeps up on many happenings around the world, like many of my friends and relatives who also did not know where Moldova was. Why should they? Most Americans have at least heard of the Soviet Union, and unless a person has committed to memory the names of every former Soviet Republic, it is doubtful that he or she would know where or what Moldova is. But Romania and Bulgaria on the other hand, even though they were part of the Soviet sphere during the Cold War years (Bulgaria much more so), were nations with national histories.

In the little Bulgarian border town of Ruse, on the Danube River that splits Romania and Bulgaria, there exists a "pantheon of the national revival," com - memorating Bulgaria's past fight for independence from Ottoman/Turkish rule, which I believe was achieved in 1908. Within its walls are located marked gravesites of Bulgaria's most recent "national heroes." Moldova's national hero, Stefan cel Mare (Steven the Great) existed some 400 or 500-plus years ago. He was some kind of important ruler who lived in this region of the world at one time or another. There is a statue of him in Chisinau and many towns' "main avenues" are named after him. [Also, 2004 was declared by some organization, the UN perhaps, as the year of Stefan Cel Mare. Incidentally, the Romanian president at the time criticized Moldova for adopting Stefan as their own, seeing how he is a historical figure of the Romanian peoples and is not solely Moldovan.] But within the

Moldovan nation, there are semiautonomous regions, such as in Gagauzia and Transdniestria, where statues of Vladimir Lenin stand in all their splendor. Though Bulgaria and Romania are relatively young nations in the truest sense of the meaning, and were carved from empires not too long ago, Moldova as a sov - ereign nation has existed for little more than a decade. With Romania poised to enter the European Union before this decade is over, and Bulgaria perhaps some time after that, it would be reasonable to assume that many of the people of these Balkan countries have a sense of purpose, or at least an understanding of where their country is heading, for good or bad. In Moldova, where the separatist Transdniestrian region in the East is propped up by Russian military forces, it is an uncertain future. There are many who wish for a reunification with Romania, some who wish for stronger ties with Russia, and possibly the majority who are indifferent.

My tutor of Romanian said that one problem in Moldovan politics and society is that there is not one political party that appeals, or attempts to appeal, to view - points of the middle. The choice is either one extreme or the other. There have been many recent talks about a federal state for Moldova, incorporating Moldova and Transdniestria under one federal constitution, but from what I have read, the two sides can't even agree on what to call the future nation. The former wants "the Republic of Moldova" and the latter wants "the Federal Republic of Moldova." At this point, even if Moldovan unification with Romania were a viable option, Romania's hopes for future member status of the EU would be diminished over the Transdniestrian quagmire. According to a recent news report, Romania's "brethren" in Moldova may soon be required to obtain a visa in order to cross over into Romania. And so the clock ticks on.

On the day we left Chisinau for our winter wonderland adventure, we were amazed at how beautiful and decadent-looking the Chisinau train station appeared. There was marble tiling and magnificent light fixtures everywhere, and it was warm inside! It is definitely one of the more beautiful man-made structures in all of Moldova. Yet as is often characteristic of Moldovan society, the frumos (beauty) factor [coined by Julia] of the train station far outweighed the efficient and practi - cal aspects of the Moldovan capital's main transportation hub. There were a cou - ple of track lines for the entire station, customer service was nonexistent, and there were more "transportation police" than there were patrons. We were stopped by a police officer upon entering the station. After pondering over our passports, he made sure we knew what time the train for Romania left. There was no sign direct - ing people to step onto their destination's platform; there was only another officer asking to see passengers' tickets.

This contrasted with both the main hub in Bucharest, Romania, and with the one in Sofia, Bulgaria, where the bustling stations were unattractive and cold, yet were for the most part, except the Cyrillic alphabet used in the Bulgarian language, easy to navigate and thrived with necessity-providing infrastructure, such as a hot coffee while you wait. Okay, coffee is not a necessity, many of you would argue otherwise, but you get the picture. And, no matter how much of a "little hole in the wall" a place appeared to be in Bulgaria, it was brewing up real cappuccinos anywhere from 75 U.S. cents to $1.50. The higher-end establishments in Chisinau have the real deal, but most places tear open the instant packs. [Since I first wrote this letter, a year and a half ago, the train station in Chisinau has been upgraded from a serious lack of efficiency to aspects of efficiency. Still no real cappuccinos though.]

I honestly feel that after having been to Romania and Bulgaria, if Peace Corps is needed or wanted anywhere in Eastern Europe, Moldova is the place. There are volunteers working in all three countries, ranging from teachers of English and health educators to economic and agricultural developers. We met one volunteer in Bucharest who lives and works in a Black Sea coastal town in Romania, kind of where I had hoped to be. Nevertheless, I am fortunate to be in Chisinau. Most of my students are highly motivated, intelligent, and nice people, as well as the major-ity of my teaching colleagues. The same goes for a few casual acquaintances I have met. Moldova is known to be one of the poorer states in Europe, so leisure travel to surrounding countries is not a possibility for many Moldovans. Yet some of those who could travel would rather spend their money on an exotic new rug for their wall or on a new set of pots and pans from Romania—once again champi-oning the frumos factor above all else. But then again, many Americans and peo-ple in general, who can afford to choose, favor the frumos factor above all else.

As our train chugged on from Bucharest to Sofia, the snow began slowly melt-ing away with temperatures reaching the mid-thirties—a short-lived thaw in the weather. I looked out of our compartment window, imagining what it must have been like traveling this route during Soviet times, especially during Stalin's reign. Was there much leisure traveling done? I could only imagine "special permission" trips for Communist party functionaries or for workers needed to fill manpower shortages in parts of the Eastern Bloc. At various stopping points, guards with rifles slung over their shoulders searched each wagon with K-9s, only too happy to come across a passenger without proper papers. How about during the war years? German soldiers from the Eastern Front at the zenith of Hitler's empire, heading home on a furlough from combat, wondering why they should not ask too many questions about the boarded-up train wagons, filled with "prisoners," on the oppo-site track line. There we were, having a picnic and enjoying the warmth of the com-partment and the picturesque scene outside. On the overnight train from Chisinau to Bucharest, we played Scrabble part of the way.

It is more than apparent that Moldova does have its hardships, and locals are always prepared to tell you how poor their country is, but they are just as quick to point out how wonderful things are in Moldova. "The wine is better. . . things are more natural here . . . you should get married in Moldova, because you'll make a lot of money at the *nunta*." While eating watermelon at a local's house, I was asked if California has watermelons. I said that it does, wanting to say that we have everything Moldova does multiplied by 100, in terms of quantity and quality. I have been in numerous conversations with locals wanting to compare the eco-nomic situation of Moldova with that of the United States. I'm still not sure which floors them more: hearing that starting teacher salaries are at a whopping $35,000 a year, or hearing that a loaf of good mass-produced bread—*Oroweat* multi-grain comes to mind—costs over $4.00. A loaf of the three-day-old 99-cent stuff costs a third more than that of a fresh-baked out-of-the-oven loaf in Moldova (4 Lei, about 66 cents).

The volunteers have agreed that Moldovans are generally not poor in basic life necessities, such as food. Most *masa* gatherings include enough food to feed the guests for at least two days, long after staleness and spoiling sets in. But this also has to do with the unmatched Moldovan hospitable spirit. It is better to go broke than to be a "bad" *gospodina* (housekeeper, but meant as *host*), especially in a small village or town, where your business is the neighbor's business. On one occasion, when confronted by a colleague about Moldova's economic plight, I asked him, "So how does Moldova compare to some places in Africa, where people are starving to death or don't have enough shelter?" Becoming a bit defensive, he said, "Oh, well here there is a kind of civilization," meaning that parts of Africa were without the enlightened civilization that has embraced Moldova. And when I asked him about all of the Moldovans in the capital, *gumba* types, driving Beamers and Benzes, he said that some people probably buy them used from other parts of Europe. So when Moldovans say they are poor, they mean in comparison to the United States and Western Europe, and possibly parts of Asia—Japan. And as the BBC online "country profiles" section will agree, "Moldova is one of the . . . poorest country in Europe."[xxii]

Though Moldovans do not generally die of starvation, there are many other factors that contribute to an appallingly low, in Western terms, average life expectancy, which hovers around the age of sixty. (I think that nowadays, in the West, dying before the age of eighty is a short life.) Part of this I would say has to do with the excessive consumption of alcohol over a period of time, combined with the total lack of healthy water intake, especially in poorer rural areas, where the only source of water comes from filthy, contaminated wells. Either no water is being drunk or the non-potable kind is. Some of the health, economic and organizational development (EOD), and agricultural volunteers have been involved with projects designed to better the drinking-water quality of certain areas, or at the very least, they have provided information about proper water consumption and reasons for hydrating oneself. And that's just it. A major problem here, that I've seen and many of my fellow volunteers would agree, is the lack of information about the basics of life—something we in the U.S. often take for granted. Though the internet has spread and will continue to spread throughout the country, people aren't yet running to internet cafes/clubs to find information about proper hydration techniques. Kids are usually looking at pornography or playing the latest blood-spattering "Grand Theft Auto" game. Julia's old host family—the "Ringle Rells" mom—once told her that you can just as easily hydrate yourself by eating watermelon, but never eat watermelon and drink water at the same time! For whatever reason, that potent concoction will be the end of you—something about *too much* water intake.

Another irony about being in the self-proclaimed "poorest" country, people here know what is best for you. Based on what sources they are accessing their information from, I'm not sure. One would think that because of the poverty here, the locals would be more open to accepting differing opinions and ideas about life. There are a few superstitions here that defy scientific logic, creating health problems of their own—both physically and psychologically. One is the *curent*, what we would call a *draft* or a *breeze*, which occurs when one or more windows and/or doors on opposite sides of a room from each other are left open. Thus the *curent* is generated. If a person gets stuck in the *curent*, there is a better-than-average chance that he or she will become sick, possibly bed ridden or worse. And the catcher: the *curent* is more dangerous in the summer months, when the heat inside of an old Soviet concrete-bloc apartment is magnified ten times that of the actual temperature outside. When it's ninety degrees outside, I can't wait to get the *curent* generated in my apartment. After gesturing that my back hurt in the presence of my Moldovan landlord, she said that my back hurt because I had the *curent* going. I tried to tell her that I carried a lot of weight in the Army.

In a class I did on superstitions with a group of Romanian-speaking students, I asked: "Why don't Americans believe in the *curent*?" One gal pinned it: "Because Americans have access to scientific information which says it doesn't exist." Bingo! With my Russian-speaking students, many of them said that it was indeed absurd to believe in this "*curent*." I thought the belief was a universal Moldovan thing, one held by Romanian and Russian speakers alike. In sweltering *rutieras* (mini-buses), drivers sometimes will only have one window rolled down, his, while all of us sit in the moving sauna, waiting impatiently to get somewhere. And moms have their babies fully wrapped as if they're getting ready to go on a snowy hike in the Himalayas. As Patrick had once said at the beginning of our service, "In Moldova, just take what's logical and do the *opposite*." "In other words," I coined, "It's *Opposite Land*."

I had not planned on going back to the States during my two years of service. But I also did not plan on my grandmother Lorraine, my mom's mom, dying while I was in Moldova. It was not a total surprise. She had had health problems for a few years, and her life companion, my grandfather Shakes, had died just over a year before her time came. But it was still an emotional shock nonetheless. So I went home in August of 2004, shortly after Julia and I got back from an awesome three-week vacation through parts of Eastern Europe and beyond. We saw parts of Hungary, including a five-night stay in Budapest; stayed in Bratislava, Slovakia a couple of days; strolled through the streets of Vienna, Austria, with Starbucks coffee in hand; met up with Julia's mom in a Bavarian resort town where we stayed for almost a week; ventured to Krakow, Poland, for a couple of days, taking part in various aspects of the Annual Jewish Cultural Festival and visiting the terrifying historical site of nearby Auschwitz. Many Americans, understandably, opt to go to western Europe if they come to Europe at all. But I often tell people, for a fraction of the cost to see as many, if not more, wondrous tourist and historical sites, go *East*.

I was told by my mother soon after getting back to Moldova from the primarily Eastern European excursion that Grandma had died while I was on vacation. Of course, my mom didn't want to just shoot me an e-mail alerting me to the fact. So she called me at my apartment in Chisinau, once I had returned. I still hadn't planned on going home, but my mother eventually asked if I wanted to come home for the party-like wake to be held in August (2004). *What the hell*, I thought. *It will be great to see the family. I have plenty of vacation days left [volunteers get twenty-four days a year of vacation time.] School doesn't start until September. And my parents want to pay for my ticket.* So I went home to the States for a week after spending a little more than a year in Moldova, experiencing in the process what many would describe as *returning* or *reentry* culture shock. From the United States, I explained this to a few of my fellow volunteers in Moldova.

Well, before I was home, I was "home." I was sitting on the plane from Bucharest to Paris, waiting for the plane to take off, when I overheard a stew-ardess/flight attendant having a little "chat" with an older American lady (fifty-something) and her daughter. Somehow this lady was able to sneak on her dog, or her "baby" as she identified it, in her carry-on luggage. [I don't know how the hell this was the case, thinking that maybe I was hallucinating.] She was going on about how she and her daughter had been falsely lured there (Romania?) with a promise of a teaching job, but instead, their money was stolen by THEM. *So now they were heading back to the States with their baby/doggie whom the person at check-in, said the woman, allowed them to carry on the plane. The attendant kept telling them that the dog would have to go under the plane with the baggage, and the flight crew even radioed in for a person to come aboard with a carrying cage for the canine. Finally, and reluctantly, with tears in her eyes, the older American agreed to part with her "baby" for the duration of the flight and allowed it to be stored with the luggage. It was either that or get off the plane. This scenario delayed our take-off by a good thirty minutes. [Even after two years in Moldova, it is hard to relinquish my "American" need for immediacy.] What made the situation all the more comical was that the fifty-something-year-old had a thick southern drawl. "Are you freakin' kidding me?" I thought to myself. "If you (FILL IN HERE), you just might be a red-neck."*

At the Customs point in Los Angeles, what appeared to be an American man, his French wife, and their two children were the next ones in line to clear Customs. One of their kids was a little boy (about four years old). He decided that he didn't need to clear Customs and walked past a Customs official with his toy suitcase, scampering through a different line than the one with his parents. The dad told him to come back, and the kid said "no" and started running faster. So the dad was given permission to track down his son, finally bringing him back to join the rest of the family. But he didn't care for this and started screaming—LOUD!

My father met me at the airport in L.A., where he lives and works Monday to Friday. He most often stays at my sister's in San Diego on the weekends, where he lives the good life playing golf. Once I cleared Customs, I had exactly two hours before my connecting flight left for San Diego. In an e-mail a few weeks back, I wrote to him that I would have a layover in L.A., and perhaps we could meet for lunch in the airport. He replied, "No problem. Burgers or Mexican?" Well, you [volunteers] all know, thanks to all of you, that we get pretty damn good Mexican food in Moldova [usually prepared with spice packets from the States], so I chose burgers. My dad is an airline mechanic in L.A., so he knows the airport. He

165

thought it would be great to leave the airport, have lunch nearby, and head back. "Cool," I thought, but was sort of concerned about time, especially since I had to check a bag to San Diego.

Needless to say, we had incredible blue cheese bacon burgers!—ghhaaaaahh (frothing at the mouth). Plus I had a 32-ounce Firestone brand microbrewed beer from Santa Barbara, California. Take that Vitanta . . . Premium! [Vitanta is the "classic" of the Moldovan beers]. During lunch, I inquired whether or not we were good on time. Sure we were. So I got back to the airport with about forty-five min-utes to spare and faced a rather lengthy line at check-in. That took a good twenty minutes, followed by another ten to get through security. Then I walked, fast, to what I thought was my gate. But it was just an exit to the six-minute shuttle ride that took me to my actual departure gate. So I arrived at the gate's counter with seven minutes to spare before the 3:45 P.M. departure time, so I thought. From the air-line employee, I received a cold and indifferent, "Yeah, the flight left." "But it's not 3:45 yet!" I exclaimed. He said, "You have to be here ten minutes before the actual departure time," explaining that the wheels go up at 3:45 on the dot. "Where were you?" he asked. "I was checking in," of course. Then I started to give him my sob story about how I had flown from Bucharest, Romania, to Paris, then on to L.A., as if he had ANY power to call the plane back to pick me up. So he reissued me a ticket and said, "You're on the 6:00 P.M. flight." As my father told me later, they should have waited, since it was in the computer system that I checked in and was on my way to the plane. The funny thing: persons on the Bucharest-Paris flight were scrambling to get off the plane in Paris and connect with their flights to Cincinnati, of all places. They had about an hour to get to the plane, and I told one American lady, "Ah, don't worry. They know you're coming and won't leave without you." But then again, there probably wasn't another Paris-Cincinnati flight heading out two hours later.

Waiting at the L.A. airport for my 6:00 P.M. flight to San Diego, I called my father to tell him what had happened. But, assessing my priorities and putting them in their proper order, I first bought a venti mocha from Starbucks, using a portion of the money Ken and Danielle gave me to mail their computer [from inside the States, after having lugged it from Chisinau, Moldova], since I didn't feel like paying $2.50-$5.00 for an ATM withdrawal service charge. [That's about the price of the coffee.] As I was trying to remember my father's correct cell-phone number, a man from India (I think) said that he was not from the States and need-ed help using the pay phone to call a long-distance number within California. He wasn't too sure where the quarters went in the phone or how much the phone call would be. I looked at the area code of the number to be called—916—and imme-diately knew it as my old stomping ground up in Sacramento, where I did an M.A. program. So once I got him squared away, I finally got hold of my father. I would have called my mother at home, but she was already at the airport in San Diego, seeing as how she thought I was on the 3:45 flight and the flight is all of thirty-nine minutes. So after I told my dad what happened, he said, "Your mom is going to be pissed." This was an understatement, I found out later. So my father decided to take the night off (he works the graveyard shift at the airport) and drove me down to San Diego. I, myself, in a loopy jetlag-filled haze, was a bit ticked off that I saw my mom and other family members three hours later than I would have if I had made that flight. I'm only here for a week!

The week came and went. The party celebrating Grandma Lorraine's life was great, except that the jetlag seriously hampered my ability to hang with the party during late night hours.

Before I knew it, I was back in Moldova, ready to start my second year of teaching and deal with any other mad-capped hi-jinks that were waiting for me, including visiting members of my American family, in this ex-Soviet Republic. Within a day or two after returning from the States, Sandy, my only sibling, and our cousin Mary came to see what my life, and life in general, was like in Moldova. Of course they only had a week to do it, as my sister explained in an e-mail from Moldova.

Today is my last day and we are off to the village to meet Robert's host family. I am so happy that I came here. It has really meant the world to me to see what my brother's life is all about. Mary and I have had a wonderful time traveling abroad together. We have eaten well, rested well, and have drunk very little (maybe two to three beers in the evening with dinner). We have done and seen more in the last six days than I do not know what. Robert is a great host with great friends, too. We, too, have made lots of new friends. During the first day back to school (work), Robert had both Mary and I speak in front of his classes about being women from America in their forties—single, with careers and no children. [This was great, because about 95 percent of my students are female. For 99 percent of them, it is inconceivable that a woman would choose to do anything that didn't involve child-rearing.] It has been an awesome trip.

We went to the town of Soroca for my birthday [September 3]. It is about two hours away by rutiera. It is more quaint than the Chisinau. [Students here tend to make the mistake of saying the Chisinau or the New York when referring to cities.] Anyway, Robert has some friends, Ken and Danielle, who are a married couple in the Corps also. Soroca is also known for the gypsies. However, they are not your typical [wandering] gypsies. They made Soroca their home and are quite well off. As we were walking through the town past the Gypsy King's home (King Arthur) he was also walking and stopped all of us, inviting us in to his home for a beverage (fruit juice). We met his family: wife, and daughter Angela. The King then played the accordion while his little girl danced for us. Then he played the piano and sang a song to me. As we were leaving, his wife wanted to read my palm and of course I let her. It was quite exciting. She said to me that I have no enemies and I have lots of love from God. I have had good luck throughout my life.

"The Police Republic"

The other day, I was followed by the police into my apartment building and I ditched them. It was a beautiful move. I don't think I've really commented on the police here. Those who walk the "beat" usually do so in threes, and these keystone coppers, I call them, look all of sixteen years old. [There is a joke here among Moldovans about this "tripod": one of them can read and write, while the other two pull security for the "educated" one.] They walk around the streets with billy clubs at their sides, stopping for anything or anyone that appears to be "abnormal." As Peace Corps volunteers, we're required to carry our "Green Card" with us at all times, in case we get stopped. The only times I've been stopped were when I was with other loud Americans. I never had a problem. Usually you just show them your permit and you're on your way. But for some volunteers, usually if they're approached alone, the police have given them a hard time, expecting some sort of payment. This happened to Patrick one time, when he was walking through the park and some cop tried to say that he needed to have additional documenta-tion. So then he used his cell phone to call Alex—the Safety and Security Officer for the Peace Corps—who was also once a Moldovan cop himself. Patrick told the policeman, "Here, it's for you," and the cop said abruptly, "Have a nice day," and then took off in the other direction, without first talking to Alex.

Last Friday, I was wrapping up my morning run when I saw three keystone coppers walking in my direction. I didn't have my Green Card on me, technically making me "illegal"; only my Peace Corps ID card in case of an emergency. The moment I finished running, I said, "Oh shit" or "Oh f***," as I noticed we were approaching each other from opposite directions alongside my building. As I said before, they tend to stop people who are not part of the "norm." When I'm dressed to teach—business casual—I can more easily blend in with other members of the local citizenry in Chisinau. But here I was, dressed in blue workout clothes and drenched in sweat—definitely abnormal because most people in Moldova *don't go running around the streets for exercise. As I found myself walking in their direction, knowing that they had spotted me, I knew that an abrupt about-face was out of the question, because then I would have looked really suspicious. I've run by a few of these coppers in the past, and it's never been a problem while running, because they never seem to be interested enough to catch up to me and ask me for my documents. And the thing with me is, even though it probably wouldn't be a big deal to be stopped, I would just rather not give them the pleasure of try-ing to intimidate an American/foreigner. Therefore, it is a big deal.*

As we approached the area where the opening to my building is situated, I sped up my pace a bit, since it was obvious to me that I would be nearest to the entrance first. Usually after running, I hang outside for a couple of minutes, catching my breath and petting the communal cats, before walking up the eight flights of stairs to my apartment (there is an elevator, but after runs, I walk up the stairs for added exercise). On this occasion, I immediately took a sharp right into my building and began to ascend the eight flights of stairs, acting as if I didn't see the police. While stepping out double-time—two steps at a time—my leg muscles screamed in pain. Approaching the second floor, I heard the three coppers come into the entrance-way, one mumbling something in caveman fashion, "Ey." So I kept going up the steps, not looking back, determined to continuously lengthen the distance between me and them. When I got to the fourth floor, I was exhausted and had to take a quick break. As I bent over, trying to catch my breath, I heard the loudness of the elevator resonating, as usual, throughout the whole building. Then I thought, "Okay, maybe I'm just being paranoid. Maybe they're not following me." So I looked down over the stairwell and noticed that one copper was indeed a couple of flights below, gradually progressing up the steps in pursuit of me. "Why only one?" I thought. Well if they had any brains, one or two of the others would take the elevator to the ninth floor and walk down from there, trying to trap me. There must have been at least one of them in the elevator that I just heard. So I walked up to the fifth floor, called the elevator with a push of the button and rode it to the eighth floor. Then I ducked into my two-door secure apartment, thus avoiding any unwanted dealings with the police. After cleaning up and relaxing for over an hour, I left my building and they were nowhere in sight. Score one for the good guys!

Though my "run-in" with the Moldovan police was a bit comical, and I was at the most highly annoyed, other volunteers have had serious dealings with the police, bordering on harassment or even oppression in some cases. I believe Alex, the Peace Corps Safety and Security Officer, when he says that he meets with Moldovan police representatives on a regular basis, informing them of Peace Corps presence in Moldova, including the diverse make-up of volunteers. But I would also bet that for many officers, things said in one ear often go out the other. There is an African American female volunteer in my group who has been stopped by the police a ridiculous thirty-something-plus times during her first year of service! On an occasion or two, she was even pulled off the transportation she was riding so the police could examine her documents, while her accompanying volunteers were not obliged to do the same. I see two ironies here. As a black American female, she surprisingly said that she was never racially self-aware until coming to Moldova. Granted, she is the daughter of a diplomat, having lived in different places around the world, and spent a portion of her life living in the multiethnic Miami, Florida, area. I think that a large percentage of African Americans are aware of their racial identity, hopefully not because of present day harassment that they deal with, but because of the history of race relations in the United States. But I also tend to believe that it is a good thing if a black American sees him or herself as a citizen of the United States of America, and not as a minority pushed to the outer fringes of American society.

The other irony I see is on the Moldovan side, where this ex-"socialist" Republic of the Soviet Union, indoctrinated with the communal acceptance of all peoples, is anything but accepting of noticeable differences. Again, perhaps with the dismantling of the Soviet system, the people here made a conscious effort to throw off the shackles of Communist ideology. But since that would involve making some kind of well-informed decision, that's probably not the case. Then one must conclude that the communal front of the Soviet era was just that—a front. How many neighbors spied on each other for the "good" of the community as a whole, making reports to the KGB because someone next door was being different or exercising a "bourgeois individualism?" It's well documented that in the former Soviet-backed East Germany, some spouses reported to the state security police (*Staatsicherheitsdienst* or *Stasi*) on the activities of their partners. I assume that the same happened in the Soviet Union, back "when things were better."

In Moldova today, black people are often first seen as illegal refugees trying to hide out among the mostly white Moldovan citizenry. This is where the police come in to check for proper identification. Gypsy (or *Roma*) peoples are generally viewed as thieves and untrustworthy people. Yet in the northern town of Soroca, next to the *Nistru* river that divides Moldova from the Ukraine, where my good married friends and fellow volunteers Ken and Danielle live, many gypsies earn more money in a year, doing whatever kind of work, than some Moldovans would in a lifetime. The Roma there are not the wandering hordes of thieving bandits that many Moldovans have come to associate with gypsy culture. The black volunteer— Ahmindi— was kind enough to talk to my university students, who had previously learned a bit from me about diversity in the United States, about being a black American female in general, and being one in Moldova, in particular. This was great information for the students to have. Again, going back to the lack of information in Moldovan society, or misinformation in some cases, many people here only associate black Americans with rap music or with Hollywood films, which are more often than not, at least the ones Moldovans have seen, negative portrayals of black Americans.

A local neighbor came over to my Chisinau host family's house for dinner one night. He asked me what I though of blacks in America, because in films he has seen that they are "bad" people. I said that many black Americans don't like films about black Americans, because they are often negative films about blacks. Then he asked me what Americans thought about Judaism. I said that there are tons of religions in America, including Judaism, so most Americans don't really think twice about this religion or that one. A student of mine kept bugging me about music in America, with continuous questions about which rap artists and songs I liked most. "How about *50 Cent*? Do you like *this* song from *Tupac*?" One time, he said he encountered a black American in Chisinau, and he asked the man an idiotic, "Are you a gangsta?" Then the student told me that it's normal to ask such a question. "No, it's not normal," I said back, obviously annoyed. Then I tried to explain that most black Americans are not rap stars. They are police officers, judges, teachers, etc.

One of the worst examples of police harassment I've seen in Moldova involved five police officers and one *baba* (old woman). I came home one day, possibly from work, jumped off of my bus and saw five police officers in an arch-shaped formation, surrounding an old woman who had a stack of eggs almost as tall as she was. As one cop addressed her, she was yelling at another. One of the officers, the only noticeable female, was on her radio, probably calling for more back-up. I first thought to myself, *Perhaps she's illegally selling eggs or they are bad/poisonous eggs.* But then a more intense thought popped into my skull, as I began to feel sickened by the scene I was witnessing, *I don't care what the hell this old woman is doing. It doesn't call for five uniformed and armed police officers to surround her in an intimidating fashion. I know that Moldovan babas are tough, but this is ridiculous!*

Yet there have been more serious incidents of police brutality, that of a politically violent nature, reported by prominent Moldovans themselves. The Moldovan news source INFOTAG quoted Moldova's former prime minister and ex-Independent candidate for the Chisinau mayoral election, Dumitru Braghis, "Moldova is degrading into a police state." In competition with the dominant Communist Party and other less popular parties before his withdrawal from the race, Braghis claimed that police working on behalf of the entrenched Communist authorities dragged one of his own party representatives out of a car and "beat him black and white" [blue?]. While such actions, including the detaining of other Braghis affiliates, were being perpetrated by members of the Moldovan police force, the same police "were tenderly protecting [the] Communist Party's campaign agents." Braghis concluded, "If things continue in that way, I guess our country will have to change its official name into something like 'The Police Republic of Moldova.'"[xxiii]

It is common knowledge that corruption in the form of monetary payments is the norm in many sectors of Moldovan society. The police force is no exception. This is most noticeable among the "transportation police," who as far as I'm concerned, serve little purpose in Moldova except to keep the inflation ball rolling. These coppers stop intrastate traffic at all hours of the day, find something wrong with a driver's paperwork, and settle the "problem" on the spot by accepting a donation into their individual "policeman's fund." Subsequently, drivers/owners of buses end up charging more from passengers, and since there is now more legal money at hand, the cops can charge a higher "document correction" fee. And so the bullshit circle of corruption continues. I mentioned earlier that when I first started traveling to Cahul from Chisinau (a two-and-a-half to three-hour journey one way), the price was 30 Lei each way. Two years later, the cost is now 48 Lei—

almost a 60 percent increase. At the end of my service, I finally asked Alex, the PC safety and security officer, what the deal with the transportation police was. He told me exactly what I knew, or thought I knew: "They stop drivers and find something wrong with their paperwork, easily correctable on the spot with a small payment. Otherwise, they must pull over to the side of the road and all of the passengers must exit the vehicle and make their way to the final destination by some other means." And that's the worst of it. The people, whose livelihood depends on public transportation, are at the mercy of a corrupt system that claims to be a democratic republic. It's comical on one hand. In a country no bigger than the smallest of states of the American Union, the transportation coppers see the same damn drivers day after day as they make their way to and from Chisinau to some podunk little village. Yet the police officers question these drivers as if they've never seen them before. The whole thing is one big circus act. On one trip from Cahul to Chisinau, our bus was stopped five times! The keystone coppers have walkie-talkies. Why the hell couldn't they radio ahead to their buddies, literally down the road, and say, "I just checked bus so and so. Let it through?"

Although I cannot openly encourage students to boycott the public transportation system, I can and did explain what a boycott is, why one might boycott, and how it has effectively been used in American history—oppressed and segregated black Americans in 1950s Alabama forced the public bus system to overturn its segregation policies. On a trip that Julia was on within Moldova, the patrons were so inconvenienced by the frequent police stops that they decided to write and sign a disgruntled letter to the government—one giant leap for Moldovan-kind.

Even the Peace Corps Moldova administrative policy has its own elements of Big Brotherness. I pointed out earlier how the training staff took notes on each trainee's happenings, right down to whether or not a trainee took notes during instructional sessions. Granted, part of this unnerving (for some) behavior on behalf of PC administrators was designed to see if we have what it takes to be in the "Corps" for a whole two years. But then again, the prying eyes didn't stop after we were sworn in as volunteers. For reportedly safety and security reasons, each volunteer is required to speak with his or her Moldovan program manager—TEFL, health, etc.—no later than twenty-four hours before the volunteer plans on staying overnight away from the primary site. When my group first swore in, one could just shoot off an e-mail about his or her whereabouts for the upcoming weekend. And it was "suggested" that for the first three months after swearing in volunteers stay at their sites without visiting other volunteers. This was supposed to encourage (force) volunteers to integrate into the local community better.

After my first week at site (the booming metropolis of Chisinau—not a lot of cross-cultural integration to be had there), I sent an e-mail to the program manager telling, not asking, her that I was heading to Cahul for the upcoming weekend, and of course I would be staying at Julia's. The assistant program manager, a very sweet Moldovan lady named Lucia, stated the "suggested policy" about staying at site for the first three months, "Well, you know, Robert, Chisinau is a community too . . . I think you should seriously [re]consider your plans for the weekend." I told her, "I will consider them," while thinking: *I will consider them still in effect as planned.* Julia and I knew that three months of not seeing each other at the beginning of our relationship would not be the best for the future, if we really wanted to give it a go. Apparently, other volunteers with significant others expressed the same concerns to the admin personnel. So Lucia called me that night and told me what I already knew: I *could* go to *Cahul* for the weekend, but I shouldn't abuse this privilege by going too often. Usually Julia and I alternate between Chisinau and Cahul. It was after our group swore in that PC Moldova wrote an official policy stating that volunteers could not leave site during the first three months of service, unless there was a work-related excuse. And because some knuckleheads from the next group of volunteers got caught taking advantage of the "notification via e-mail" option by notifying the day of or the day after leaving site, all volunteers were then obliged to receive *concurrence* from the program manager before leaving site for the night.

Whether you are a twenty-three-year-old right out of college or a sixty-something-year-old pensioner, it's like asking your mommy or daddy for permission to spend the night at a friend's house. *Concurrence* then changed to an *agreement* between the volunteer and the manager. And if a volunteer was suspected of abusing the "out-of-site policy," he or she would have a counseling session with the program manager. Many volunteers simply ignored these constricting policies, risking being expelled from the dormitory (Peace Corps) by leaving site without "properly" notifying the headmaster (program manager). The first thing said by a few out-of-town volunteers staying at my place in Chisinau was: "Don't tell Nina (TEFL program manager) that I'm here." Some of my Moldovan colleagues, not understanding a "twenty-four-hour notification policy," used to ask me, "You mean you can't go somewhere today because you didn't call [PC] yesterday?" But there were times when our managers were lenient, some more than others, when giving volunteers permission to leave site the day of notification. Nina might get mad that you were asking the day of, but if you were a good volunteer and didn't usually give her trouble (or because of the trouble you've given her—Cheryl's whiny "It's all about me" sniveling attitude and Dr. Marie's nonexistent work ethic come to mind), she would give in. She wants volunteers to be happy. A happy volunteer is one who stays around for two years.

Expatriates

I realized early in my service, after talking with my Romanian language tutor, that we (Peace Corps volunteers) were not the only Americans in town, just as I was not her only student. She worked with some of these other Americans. In fact, she once had to cancel a couple of sessions with me in order to teach for a longer period of time at some sort of missionary retreat, and of course be paid accordingly (whenever a Moldovan canceled on me because of an opportunity to make a few extra bucks on the side, I always thought, *Good for them*). And so the missionary knife, like the Peace Corps and other elements of the U.S. government, along with various private enterprises, has cut its way into the ex-Soviet world of Eastern Europe. We volunteers, for good or bad, have run into a few of these zealots, mostly in Chisinau. I don't really see many of them roughing it in a small village or town for a lengthy duration of godly service.

On one occasion, Patrick and I were eating kebabs in front of the Kebab House in Chisinau when we encountered two missionaries, dressed in white shirts with ties and everything. Wearing greeting smiles, they asked us what we were doing in Moldova. In typical Patrick fashion, he unwelcomingly responded, "*We do God's work.*" Sensing the tone that they were not on the same team as us, they slinked out of our presence. As the British writer Tony Hawks stated, the jury is still out as to whether or not the Peace Corps is a benevolent organization or a tool of U.S. political and business interests; the same issues can be raised about the missionaries—are they serving themselves, Moldovans, or both? Of course, they would tell you that they are serving God, and there are a few religiously inclined volunteers who would give them the benefit of the doubt. As long as they are not preaching "believe or burn," they are probably doing some good work. I haven't followed them that closely.

And of course there is the diplomatic community, comprised of U.S. Embassy personnel—fifty-thousand-dollar-a-year-plus salaried government employees living like royalty in a developing country while receiving additional pay because of the "hardships" of living in Chisinau. And as a Chisinau volunteer, I've had more opportunities than the average volunteer to schmooze with diplomats at various embassy functions, not that I go in for that sort of thing usually. I often felt uncomfortable being a "measly" Peace Corps volunteer around what should have been the best and the brightest, at least the most diplomatic, of what American society has to offer. But as a volunteer living on a fixed stipend (not counting the few bucks in my bank account back home), it has been nice consuming quality foods and beverages at U.S. taxpayer expense. Many of the Moldovan guests at these functions do it up right, filling their pockets and/or purses with leftover cookies, candies, pastries, and half-drunk bottles of champagne before heading out the door.

There are plenty of U.S. Foreign Service personnel who fit the typical image of a diplomat—charismatic and likeable individuals working to establish friendly relations with Host Country Nationals (HCNs) and other Americans (Peace Corps volunteers) in-country. The public affairs representative of the U.S. Embassy—Alison—unfortunately was anything but the typical diplomat. Alison, a Mormon zealot, was a cross between a diplomat, a missionary, and a politician. On the diplomatic side, she was a condescendingly smug woman with more than an air of superficiality about her. Her unpleasantly grinning paper-thin mask of superficial niceties gave way to a patronizing demeanor that left those in her presence feeling very awkward at the least and disdainfully annoyed at the most. And when she publicly spoke at official gatherings (English teachers' conferences, the opening of this or that teaching resource center, academic Olympiads for Moldovan students), she often left the volunteers in attendance highly irritated and the Moldovan attendees highly confused by some of her brainless comments. Yet the sad irony is that she was the official public affairs representative—one step below the ambassador—of the United States of America! A few of us volunteers commented that we could do a much better job than she in projecting a more positive image of the U.S. and U.S. citizens in general. Basically, it wouldn't have taken much effort to be more diplomatic than she was.

One of our tasks as volunteers, some would say our primary task, is to serve in an unofficial diplomatic capacity, strengthening U.S.-Moldova relations in the process. And for some volunteers, PC service is a precursor to a career in diplomacy with the U.S. State Department or some other international organization. I took the Department of State's Foreign Service Written exam, offered once a year, during my first year of PC service, along with a few other volunteers. I did not pass it, so I was told, unlike a few other volunteers. My "cone" of preferred work in the foreign service was listed as *consular affairs*: issuing visas and things of that sort. I opted not to take the exam during my second year in the Peace Corps. But I did vow for the next time around, after witnessing how Alison operates, to go for her "cone": *public affairs*.

I attended a two-day international conference, entitled "Language Development and Teaching," in the northern Moldovan city of Balti (pronounced Belts). At the conference, I presented the topic, "Britain in the World and the United Kingdom's Multiculturalism" for a group of Moldovan educators. Plus I had a write-up on the topic published in the conference proceedings, along with the write-ups of others who presented. I was a bit offended the day before I held my "workshop" when an American Embassy representative [Alison] presented a topic on the American electoral system [This is where the political side of her came out. She looked more as if she were running for office in the American elec-toral system than presenting on it at an academic forum], stating something to the effect, "Well, I'm not British so I can't present something on Britain." I started out my seminar with "Well, I'm not British but I'm presenting something on Britain." With her reasoning, perhaps she was only trying to be funny (it didn't work), then women can only teach subjects that pertain to women. Some of the most presti-gious American professors specialize in Asian or European studies. Because they have done the time/work in a field, they are given the benefit of the doubt. It all comes down to not what you are but who you are. That's how we become "experts" at something. We continuously build on what we already know. Before I arrived at my university here, some of my colleagues were obliged to teach American Studies. As I teach it, I'm learning a few things myself.

At the opening of the English Resource Centre (note the British spelling of *cen-ter*) in Cahul, where Julia worked in conjunction with her colleagues and support-ive funding from the British Embassy, Alison made a guest appearance, speaking on behalf of the U.S. Embassy. She was all too "happy to help with the opening of another one of these English centers," as if this were some small nickel-and-dime achievement that exists everywhere in Moldova (imagine small-town U.S.A. ten times smaller and three hours away from the big city, with no local library and no amazon.com), and as if Alison herself had something to do with it. The day of the opening, the embassy personnel dropped off a couple of last-minute boxes of donated books, adding to the fabulously British-furnished—resources and furni-ture—Centre for English teachers and students. At least Alison could have acknowl-edged that fact. At a later date, a friend and fellow volunteer—Glendon—presented a speech, in Romanian, at an academic Olympiad gathering of Moldovan students. This was followed by a round of applause for his diplomacy. Apparently, Alison got up and said, "I would speak in Romanian but I am lazy." Once again, there was irri-tation among the volunteer(s) and confusion among the Moldovans assembled. Then she went on to tell the young Moldovans that learning foreign languages is their key to a better life, as if they needed to hear this from her.

On the missionary side, neighbors of hers mentioned hearing Alison holding a "Soup for Scriptures" gathering at her U.S. citizen-paid-for Moldovan house, where locals from around the area would supposedly compete to find scriptures from the Book of Mormon, followed by the consumption of some type of soup dish. I'm personally not sure what happened, but the whole thing sounds bizarre. What happened to that whole "separation of Church and State" thing? Was that a similar pipe dream imagined by the Founding Fathers, much like a few of the Communist ideals envisioned by Marx and then fanatically twisted by Lenin and Stalin into evil opposites of their original selves? There was speculation among a few of us that perhaps she was sent to Moldova as a "punishment" for having used her government position to proselytize (convert others to Mormonism). Maybe that's why her personality left a lot to be desired. She was a disgruntled diplomat and a righteous Mormon to boot. And there is a federal law on the books that makes it nearly impossible to fire a "tenured" government employee, no matter how incompetent or non-likable the person is. It is one thing to show up some-where because a group of Moldovan Mormons invited you to their temple (there is one down the street from where she lived), and it's another thing to have a Mormon proselytising function at your government-paid-for house.

Educational Endeavors

Seeing as how my primary job in the Peace Corps, and my most recent employment in general, was that of a university-level teacher in Moldova, it is only fitting that I conclude my story, before the concluding chapter of course, with a closer look at *what it means* to teach in the Moldovan post-secondary educational system.

I am teaching a course [during my first semester, fall 2003], English for Information, which basically means English for Computer Usage. I don't really know what the hell to teach, so I just improvise, using articles from Newsweek *(every volunteer has a free subscription) about computer technology. So I often use such articles for in-class assignments and teach different vocabulary words/expressions related to computers—"cut," "paste," "select all," "gigabyte," things of that sort. Anyway, for the most recent class (this class meets only once on Mondays for eighty minutes), I assigned homework where they [the students] were required to send me an e-mail. Here is one [unedited] from a student of mine who is in both my Information and Civilization classes.*

Hi, Robert! How are you?

I [Victoria] have the task to write you, so I have decided to write the letter right now. We are lucky to have you as our English teacher this year. What a pitty that it's the last one. I had the occasion to meet with people from the U.S.A You are great. Wnen you feel bad, you don't show it, you are behaving as usual. I like this. You encourage students even if they don't know English very well. It's a great stimulus for them. But what I appreciate at you is that you say how a certain word shall be pronounced if it hasn't been spelt correctly. This improves student's pronunciation.

Robert, your English lessons are something special. I enjoy each of them and I am waiting impatiently the next class. I wonder why other students ignore them. But I can't impose them to come. It is their right to do

how they want. I think you are a special man. You can catch people's attention in a specific way. Your career as teacher waits for you. It seems to me
that these are all ideas and thoughts at this moment. So I say you good-bye.
See you on Mondey.

Besides this student's obvious, according to my girlfriend, crush on the teacher,
such sentiments of appreciation are bits of reflective evidence regarding the
teacher's performance in the classroom. As Peace Corps teachers of English, and
as teachers in general, there were more days than not when we doubted the effectiveness of our (attempted) contributions to Moldovan society. Part of this comes
from the inability or unwillingness to look at the big picture of focusing on the students who want to learn, while encouraging others who are "on the fence." As a
university-level volunteer, though my students were obligated to be in class to some
extent, I had no qualms about telling them to leave if they weren't interested in
learning or at least staying quiet. Another part of this self-doubt about effective
teaching comes from the person's realization that educating pupils is not for him
or her. And for a teaching volunteer in Moldova, the final part of self-doubt officially comes from the Moldovan educational system's total lack of academic standards, where "everybody passes" and the volunteer becomes frustrated, if not infu-
riated, with the system that he or she is trying to work within.

*Today I finished my courses for the [first] semester, and I don't go back until
January 20, I think. But I feel a bit overwhelmed with the planning and paperwork
needed to be done for next semester. Next week are final exams, but I already gave
that one exam I had to give. My other classes were graded pass-fail, so if they did a
final presentation, they received a pass (admiss). One boy, out of the two for my
entire class load, would not say anything during his pair-presentation.
Coincidentally, today was his third time being in class all semester. So I asked him,
in Romanian, if he knew English. He said, in Romanian, that he did. I said,
"Poftim" (go ahead). Then he just stood there. I asked him if he prepared any notes
for his presentation. He said no. So I told him to take a seat, not intending to pass
him. Then he came up to me at the end of class and asked when the final test would
be. I said it was today, between 8:00 and 9:20; "You weren't prepared." Then he
asked if he could make up the test later on in the day. I said no, come back next
semester. Two weeks ago, he was informed about the final exam, and I even gave
him a handout that would help him for his presentation. What can you do?*

It's ridiculous how less-than-ideal students drift through the university system
grouped with their peers, lumped together with more advanced students, yet officially remaining at the same level. The Moldovan Ministry of Education literally
means what it says, "Nobody fails." In typical Moldovan fashion, this is more of
an order than a sentiment of wishful thinking. As educators, as noted above in my
interactions with this particular student, it is the teacher's fault if the student fails
the course. But since no one fails, the teacher must use his or her spare time to
meet with the student and ensure that a passing grade is achieved. I'm talking
university, not some exclusive college-prep high school. A colleague of mine one
day came into our department office crying, claiming that her pay—already at an

appallingly low level—had been cut because too many of her students were "failing." So she is basically held responsible because her students, the ones who are failing, do not come to class. If teacher unions existed in Moldova, she could have gone to see her union rep. If a union did form, the government would probably fire all of its members and hire recent college graduates to take their places. At Julia's university in Cahul, the workforce of faculty members is made up of young twenty-something-year-olds who were recent college students themselves only months ago, now teaching the same students they once called peers.

Part of our official "evaluation" as Peace Corps teachers, actually the only one we really undergo, is a "site visit," where our Moldovan Peace Corps boss—the program manager—comes to one or two of our classes and observes what it is we are doing.

One of my Peace Corps bosses, a Moldovan, came to observe one of my classes. It's a requirement for all volunteers. It was supposed to happen last semester [fall 2003] for me, but it kept getting put off for this reason or that. The class she came to observe is definitely my most advanced group of English speakers. They are great to work with. Some of them won't shut up in English! But a normal problem is that most of them are late to class (at eight o'clock in the morning, I have a problem myself getting there on time). They usually come straggling in at 8:00, 8:15, 8:30. I thought: "This will not be a good scene for my boss." So the day before, I happened to run into one student [Christina], who is definitely one of the more advanced students [if not the most advanced]. I told her my boss was coming and that I would appreciate it if she and the other students would be there around eight o'clock. Sure enough, all of them were there at eight o'clock sharp. We had a good class about the U.S. Constitution and the Articles of Confederation that preceded it.

We had the perfect class: all paying attention and asking pertinent questions, though Tatiana, also an exceptional student, made a comment that Virginia is "the land of the Virgins." I chuckled a bit, commenting that it *was* named after "the Virgin Queen." But seeing as how my boss—Nina—was administering her facial paint using a portable mirror, the day's content was oblivious to her. But she wasn't there for a history and geography lesson, only to see that I was engaging as a teacher. After the class, she and I met up with the rector of the university, where we promptly had a bit of cognac and coffee in his office at 9:30 A.M. She was right: I didn't have any more classes that day. Then she proceeded to tell me, "Remember Robert, you're teaching English, not history." Yet in my official job description, I'm to teach content-based information, in English. After all, it was a Civilization class with advanced learners, not beginning grammar constructs with non-speakers. Regardless, getting my all-female students to put on such a "show" tells you of the kind of rapport that I had with them, as well as the type of indoctrination they've had growing up in Moldova. Other English-teaching volunteers around the country, at the primary and secondary school levels, have witnessed "open-lessons," where a Moldovan educator will be observed by peers, administrators, and other students, in all of his or her splendor in front of a classroom. What takes place weeks beforehand are the constant dress-rehearsals between the teacher and students leading up to the orchestrated circus act, where neither the students nor the teacher deviate from the scripted performance.

One of my biggest fears as a first-year Peace Corps teacher, which I can only imagine to be the case for "normal" teachers in general, was whether or not I would be able to tell if my students were actually progressing in the English language, i.e., learning something. At the end of my first year of teaching, this fear was somewhat laid to rest, while others came to the fore.

Well, I finished my first year of teaching here in Moldova, accompanied with some all-time highs and lows as a teacher. A week ago, Monday, May 24, I gave an oral exam to three different groups of Conversation students from this spring semester. Within one of the groups, students range from non-English speakers to fairly advanced. The other two groups combined range from intermediate to highly advanced/fluent. As is often the case in Moldova, and the United States as well, students show up for the first time on the day of the final exam, expecting to receive a passing mark. For my Conversation courses, students are supposed to receive either an admiss (pass) or respins (fail), but teachers are not allowed to write respins in a student's official grade book, which would be the very rough equivalent of an unofficial college transcript. A student with a temporary mark of respins must set a time with the teacher in the future to retake the exam, doing this until the mark of admiss is obtained. Bottom line—nobody fails. Some colleagues and students expressed shock upon hearing that in the United States, if a university student earns a non-passing grade, that student will be required to take the entire course the next time it is offered, either the next quarter/semester or the next year, in an attempt to pass the course.

Regardless, I passed students who clearly were not at a "conversational" level of English—students who should not have been in my class in the first place. I felt a bit disgusted with myself about that. But then again, these students didn't sign up for my course, as they would do at an American university. The school administration tells them what courses they will take within the student-chosen "major." Upon seeing a few new faces on exam day, I said to them, "Hi, my name is Robert!" I was surprised to hear how well two of them spoke in English [maybe that's one reason they never bothered coming to class]. For these students, part of their oral exam included the question from me, "So where have you been all semester?" The answer was either, "I was ill" or "I have a job." Regarding the second answer, from what I have noticed and have heard, this is a highly nepotistic society where a job at McDonald's is considered a valued job, not a temporary part-time job merely for extra weekend cash. I have some great students who often miss class because of their valued and much-sought-after jobs. For the "illness" answer, you'd be amazed to hear how many students spend the semester in the hospital for whatever sickness—real or imagined.

After dealing with the admiss/respins system of grading, I have concluded that I much prefer the Moldovan 1-10 grading system, which I had to use for my Civilization courses. A mark of 1-4 is a negative mark/grade, the difference between a 1 and 4 being the same difference between an "F-" and an "F+"—NO DIFFERENCE, the student fails! But as I said before, nobody fails. A mark of 5 equates to a "D-," 6 is a "D," 7 a "C," 8 a "B," 9 an "A-/A," and a 10 is an "A/A+". Last semester over half of the students in my English for Computer Information course initially received a 4 on the final exam. When I handed back their written exams, I asked the class if anyone knew what the word CORRELATION meant. One student [Victoria, who wrote that initial e-mail of praise to me, and who was the only one to get a 10 (A+) in this course, took an unsuccessful stab at it.] Then I explained, "Over half of you never come to class and over half of you failed the exam. There is a CORRELATION between the number of students who never come to class and the number who failed the exam." So in order for these mark 4 receiving students to receive an "official" passing grade, I had them write a paper over the winter holidays about computer technology. For the ones who clearly copied information off of the internet or each other, I gave them a 5; for papers with some originality a 6; and if they were truly exceptional a 7. One good student, who coincidentally has a job, was not happy with the 7 she received on her exam and wrote a paper to get bumped up to an 8. This semester I decided to forgo the assigning of any extra task. [My grading and testing policies changed each semester.] Solution: no student who shows up for the exam or consults with me prior to the exam, will receive less than a "D-." I mean a 5.

The students from my Conversation courses on Monday are also in my Civilization courses either on Tuesday or Wednesday. On Monday, one very advanced English speaker, whom I've seen in my class once (he has a job), told me that he would be unable to take the written exam on Tuesday for Civilization. He was flying to Italy or somewhere for supposed work-related reasons and would be out of the country for a while. I told him I could give him a 5 then and there and that was it. He said okay, a "5 or 6" would be good. So I wrote 5 in his grade book. Then he presented me with a wrapped bottled (I could not see what it actually was) of "the best Transdniestrian cognac" (pronounced CONE-YACK). Looking a bit dumbfounded, I said something to the effect, "Thanks. . . have a nice trip."

Needless to say, I felt a bit conflicted. Was he saying "thanks for the passing grade (wink, wink)" or "this is a token gift to a foreign/American teacher at my university?" On the one hand, I felt that I had perhaps done something unprofessional/unethical and on the other, I felt/hoped that I was showing cross-cultural sensitivity—something reiterated by the Peace Corps time and time again—by accepting such a gift. I prefer wine, beer, or champagne anyway. We often walk a thin line between adapting to and/or embracing the local culture and championing our American/Western customs above all else. Regarding this gift-giving incident, I talked with a married friend of mine—he and his wife are also volunteers in Moldova—who taught high school in New York City for a few years. He basically said, "Yeah, I would NOT have accepted it. But you live and learn." So I really felt like garbage. As he was leaving my apartment, I jokingly said, "So would you like a bottle of Cognac to take back to your site [the town of Soroca is in the northern part of Moldova, on the western side of the Nistru River that separates part of Moldova from the Ukraine]?" He said, "Sure, my wife drinks cognac. Do you want any money for it?" Laughing, I gave it to him, for free, and said thanks for the lesson in professionalism.

After speaking with fellow volunteers who also teach at universities, as well as my tutor of Romanian, I have come to the conclusion that I committed no impropriety. My tutor teaches at the pre-university level and explained to me that it is common for students to bring flowers or champagne for teachers on exam day! But she says these gifts don't influence her decision about what grade to give a student. Regardless, it is common knowledge that here in Moldova, corruption at all levels of education [and society, as pointed out in the chapter "The Police Republic"] is the standard. Some teachers have a set scale, in hard Moldovan currency, or dollars or euros, for the price of grades. I can honestly say that under the value sys- tem that I was brought up in, I would never accept money in lieu of a student's work performance in my course. But I try to look at it from a Moldovan professor's point of view. If I earned 75-100 dollars a month on an inconsistent basis (salaries are much lower in villages), would I offer students a chance to bump their grade up with a donation to my wallet? Would I still uphold some sort of semblance of fairness? "The maximum grade you can buy is an 8, but those who do their work can receive a 9 or 10." Yes, these are questions I have pondered.

So the Civilization exam that I gave, Civilization meaning American Studies, was basically what I would consider to be the equivalent of a high school history exam. It was a mixture of multiple choice, true/false, fill in the blank, short answer, essay, and even an extra-credit "artistic" section—please draw a diagram of the "Triangle Trade" system that flourished in the 1600's and 1700's, and label it appropriately— worth up to five points. If they drew a triangle, they received a point. Before the test began, I had one of my top students translate my test guidelines into Russian for the less than advanced English speakers. I would have stated them in Romanian, but many of them don't speak a word of Romanian either [refer to the chapter "A Tower of Babel" for clarification]. During this Civilization course, we covered some political, economic, social, literary, and historical topics that occurred in the United States from colonial times through the immediate post-Civil War period. One multiple choice question:

8. What happened as a result of the Missouri Compromise of 1820-21?
    a. Maine and Missouri came into the Union as slave states.
    b. Maine came into the Union as a free state and Missouri came into the Union as a slave state.
    c. Maine and Missouri came into the Union as free states.
    d. Maine and Missouri declared war on New York.

At least one person picked "d."

One of the high points for me was watching my intermediate students, who come to class every week, take the exam. I could see their wheels spinning, searching, and finding the appropriate/correct answers. As a whole, their test scores shredded those of my highly advanced students, whose knowledge of English is much better but who often miss class or zone out in class. The desire of the intermediates to learn and excel was apparent during the exam, if not before, and while I graded their tests. As a teacher, I felt proud to have taught them.

The other high point, possibly the highest point, occurred on Tuesday afternoon, when I gave my Russian/English speakers their conversational exam. It's actually less than an exam and more of an opportunity for each of them to speak one on one with a native speaker. I have two groups of these students, one group being beginner/intermediate and the other being intermediate/advanced. And both have been with me since I began last September. When speaking with the first group, I could literally hear the improvement of spoken English coming from some of them. Remarkable, I thought, seeing as how some of them could barely get out a couple of basic phrases last semester. As a teacher, I felt elated. But even though I am their only native teacher of English, they do have other English courses with teachers of English. If nothing else, I hoped that at least by serving as their teacher, I was a motivating factor in their desire to better their knowledge and understanding of the English language. While conversing with a couple of students, I felt a bit choked up. I began one exam, "So, how was your weekend?" After answering, she turned the question on me, "So, how was YOUR weekend?" Fair enough, I thought, and told her that I did some paperwork for Peace Corps and wrote an exam for my Civilization students. She said, "We [the students] know that you work so hard, because your lessons are always so inter-esting." I smiled and said to myself, "I fooled them all!"

I feel much more prepared this time around [during the second year], and more creative as well. For my Civilization classes, I created a course entitled Mass Media and Religion in the United States. My students seem to be into it. We are looking at various forms of media in the United States, and other places, including Moldova—Internet, radio, television, newspapers, film (Hollywood)—with a special emphasis on religious issues (religious diversity, evolution versus creation, and religious portrayals in the media). I even showed an episode from "The Simpsons," where the oldest daughter, Lisa, converts to Buddhism and is temporarily ostracized from her family and community.[xxiv] Who said that "The Simpsons" have no educational value? Today (Monday), I am showing the film "Inherit the Wind" with Spencer Tracy, which is a fictionalized account of the famous 1925 Scopes "Monkey" Trial that pitted Creation against Evolution. Before the showing of the film, we looked at headlines and pictorials from the actual trial. After the film, we will read real excerpts from the trial itself. Part of what we have discussed in class deals with the question: What is the main goal of Hollywood?—to sell tickets of course. Another part of what I am doing is showing Moldovan students how university courses are conducted in the United States.

Regarding this last point, I decided to forgo a "high school style" test and give them essay exam questions, what one would call a bluebook exam at UC Santa Barbara and probably every other university in the United States. This absolutely blew their minds, since most of them had never done anything quite like this. A few of them could barely write their names in English, and here they now were being expected to think critically in an unscripted essay format. In a universal reflection of academic standards across the globe, at least in the United States, a few students did brilliantly, a few more did well, more than that did so-so, and a small percentage (though probably a larger one than at most U.S. universities) did appalling work, if any work was done at all. But I graded rather leniently—points being awarded for recognizable English words, regardless if they came together to form a coherent sentence. Forget an argument!

For the students who benefited from, and even appreciated, my service as a Peace Corps volunteer, I am interested in seeing where they will be in a few years' time. Despite the superstructural considerations confronting each one of them, or because of them, this will be a gauge of the effectiveness I've had as a teacher. Thus the journey continues . . . I wish them well in the meantime.

Continuing Service?

As I sit here at a Starbucks in Cambridge, Massachusetts, the question arises, "Okay, what next?" I've been pondering this question long before my Peace Corps service ended two months ago (July 2005). And of course, the prospect of continuing federal service is a strong possibility, should one of the governmental agencies I recently submitted resumes to get back to me about the positions I've applied for. Besides the excellent benefits, including the over six years of public service I've accumulated while working for Uncle Sam, it might be difficult to find something more exciting and fulfilling, and yes, more worthwhile, than working for the United States of America as a federal employee; a *community college instructor* would possibly be an approximate equivalent, educating young minds as to what exists outside of their nation's borders, while finding other worthy things to write about. And the thought of doctoral studies has crossed my mind. For the moment, I am enjoying finishing this work, a book I began a year ago in my concrete Soviet apartment high-rise, in the Moldovan capital of Chisinau.

In this work, I tried to paint a literal picture of *what it means to serve* in two seemingly opposing federal governmental organizations—the Army and Peace Corps—through my own experiences and perceptions. By no means does the journey I took through federal service represent a typical, or even abnormal, one for other governmental employees. I merely tried to show what did happen to me (and what I made happen), what can happen to others, and what others can avoid if wishing to do so. If nothing else, I wanted to share my story with persons interested in reading about it. What good is a memoir if it's not made available to the reading masses? So thanks for reading!

References

Bowden, Mark and Ken Nolan. *Black Hawk Down.* Directed by Ridley Scott. Columbia Pictures Corporation, Revolution Studios, Jerry Bruckheimer Films, and Scott Free Productions, 2001.

Keane, David. *The True Story of Black Hawk Down.*

Notes

i   Groening, Matt. *The Simpsons.* 20th Century Fox.

ii   Spade, David, and Fred Wolf. *Joe Dirt.* Directed by Dennie Gordon. Columbia Pictures Corporation and Happy Madison Productions, 2001.

iii   *Time Life* Books (Time Warner, Inc.).

iv   Kubrik, Stanley, Michael Herr, and Gustav Hasford. *Full Metal Jacket.* Directed by Stanley Kubrik. Natant and Warner Brothers, 1987.

v   Devlich, Dean, and Roland Emmerich. *Independence Day.* Directed by Roland Emmerich. 20th Century Fox and Centropolis Entertainment, 1996.

vi   Rodat, Robert. *Saving Private Ryan.* Directed by Steven Spielberg. Amblin Entertainment, Dream Works SKG, Mark Gordon Productions, Mutual Film Company, and Paramount Pictures, 1998.

vii   Kubrik, Herr, and Hasford.

viii   *Looney Tunes,* Warner Brothers.

ix   Groening, Matt. "Homer at the Bat." *The Simpsons.* Original air date: 20 February 1992. 20th Century Fox.

x   Lucas, George, Leigh Brackett, and Lawrence Kasdan. *Star Wars: Episode V- The Empire Strikes Back.* Directed by Irvin Kershner. Lucasfilm Ltd., 1980.

xi   Hedges, Chris. *War Is a Force That Gives Us Meaning.* 2nd ed. New York: Anchor Books, 2003.

xii   *Stars and Stripes,* Summer 1995.

xiii   *Stars and Stripes,* Summer 1995.

xiv   Hobsbawm, Eric. *The Age of Extremes: A History of the World, 1914-1999.* 3rd ed. New York: Vintage Books, 1996.

xv King, Charles. *The Moldovans: Romania, Russia, and the Politics of Culture.* Stanford: Hoover Institution Press, 2000.

xvi King, 183.

xvii International Crisis Group. *Moldova: No Quick Fix.* ICG Europe Report #147: Chisinau/Brussels, 12 August 2003.

xviii King, 112.

xix King, 185-186.

xx Groening, Matt. "Lost our Lisa." *The Simpsons.* Original air date: 10 May 1998. 20th Century Fox.

xxi Popa, Adela. "The Moldavian Immigration to Milan." *The Romanian Journal of Society and Politics,* 4:1. May 2004.

xxii "Country Profile: Moldova." *BBC* [news source on-line] (updated 14 September 2005, accessed 3 October 2005). <http://news.bbc.co.uk/2/hi/europe/country_profiles/3038982.stm>.

xxiii "Ex-premier Says Moldova Is Becoming a Police State; Susarenco Calling on Candidates to Cease Electioneering." *INFOTAG* [news source on-line] (Chisinau, Moldova: 19 July 2005, accessed 28 September 2005). <http:// www.azi.md/news?ID=35142>.

xxiv Groening, Matt. "She of Little Faith." *The Simpsons.* Original air date: 16 December 2001. 20th Century Fox.